Revenue Statistics in Asia and the Pacific 2021

EMERGING CHALLENGES FOR THE ASIA-PACIFIC REGION IN THE COVID-19 ERA

1990-2019

OECD
dev
DEVELOPMENT CENTRE

This work is published under the responsibility of the Secretary-General of the OECD. The opinions expressed and arguments employed herein do not necessarily reflect the official views of OECD member countries.

This document, as well as any data and map included herein, are without prejudice to the status of or sovereignty over any territory, to the delimitation of international frontiers and boundaries and to the name of any territory, city or area.

Please cite this publication as:
OECD (2021), *Revenue Statistics in Asia and the Pacific 2021: Emerging Challenges for the Asia-Pacific Region in the COVID-19 Era*, OECD Publishing, Paris, *https://doi.org/10.1787/ed374457-en*.

ISBN 978-92-64-91134-5 (print)
ISBN 978-92-64-86544-0 (pdf)

Revenue Statistics in Asia and the Pacific
ISSN 2788-9351 (print)
ISSN 2788-936X (online)

Photo credits: Cover © some of the graphic elements in the main cover illustration were adapted from Freepik.com.

Corrigenda to publications may be found on line at: *www.oecd.org/about/publishing/corrigenda.htm*.

Foreword

Revenue Statistics in Asia and the Pacific is a joint publication by the OECD Centre for Tax Policy and Administration and the OECD Development Centre with the co-operation of the Asian Development Bank (ADB), the Pacific Island Tax Administrators Association (PITAA), and the Pacific Community (SPC) and the financial support from the governments of Ireland, Japan, Luxembourg, Norway, Sweden, Switzerland and the United Kingdom. It presents detailed, internationally comparable data on tax revenues for 24 Asian and Pacific economies: Australia, Bhutan, People's Republic of China, the Cook Islands, Fiji, Indonesia, Japan, Kazakhstan, Korea, Lao People's Democratic Republic, Malaysia, the Maldives, Mongolia, Nauru, New Zealand, Papua New Guinea, the Philippines, Samoa, Singapore, the Solomon Islands, Thailand, Tokelau, Vanuatu and Viet Nam. It also provides information on non-tax revenues for Bhutan, the Cook Islands, Fiji, Kazakhstan, Lao People's Democratic Republic, the Maldives, Mongolia, Nauru, Papua New Guinea, the Philippines, Samoa, Singapore, Thailand, Tokelau, Vanuatu and Viet Nam. Four of these economies are OECD members (Australia, Korea, Japan and New Zealand). The approach used in Revenue Statistics in Asia and the Pacific is based on the well-established methodology of the OECD Revenue Statistics (OECD, 2020), which has become an essential reference source for OECD member countries. Comparisons are also made with the averages for OECD economies, Latin American and Caribbean (LAC) countries and 30 African countries.

In this publication, the term "taxes" is confined to compulsory, unrequited payments to general government. As outlined in the Interpretative Guide to the Revenue Statistics, taxes are "unrequited" in the sense that benefits provided by government to taxpayers are not normally in proportion to their payments. The OECD methodology classifies a tax according to its base: income, profits and capital gains (classified under heading 1000), payroll (heading 3000), property (heading 4000), goods and services (heading 5000) and other taxes (heading 6000). Compulsory social security contributions paid to general government are treated as taxes, and are classified under heading 2000. Greater detail on the tax concept, the classification of taxes and the accrual basis of reporting is set out in the Interpretative Guide in Annex A.

Information is also presented on non-tax revenues in 16 economies. The term "non-tax revenue" includes all general government revenue that does not meet the OECD definition of tax revenues. Non-tax revenues include grants (e.g. foreign aid), returns on government market investments, rents on the extraction of resources from public lands, sales of government-produced goods and services, and the collection of fines and forfeits. More details on the definition of these revenues are available in Annex B.

Chapter 1 of this report provides an overview of the main tax revenue trends in the 24 economies and non-tax revenue trends in the 16 relevant economies from 2010 to 2019. A special feature on the emerging challenges for the Asia-Pacific region in the COVID-19 era is found in Chapter 2, while Chapter 3 contains comparative tables on the level and structure of taxation in the 24 economies since 1990. Chapter 4 contains detailed information on tax revenues on a country-by-country basis. Chapter 5 includes information on the level and structure of non-tax revenues in selected economies.

Acknowledgements

Revenue Statistics in Asia and the Pacific is jointly produced by the Organisation for Economic Co-operation and Development (OECD)'s Centre for Tax Policy and Administration (CTP) and the OECD Development Centre (DEV) with the co-operation of the Asian Development Bank (ADB), the Pacific Island Tax Administrators Association (PITAA), and the Pacific Community (SPC), with financial support from the governments of Ireland, Japan, Luxembourg, Norway, Sweden, Switzerland and the United Kingdom. The authors would like to thank the ADB, PITAA and SPC for co-organising with the OECD a technical webinar held on 8 April 2021, which informed the analysis in this year's edition.[1]

The staff with responsibility for producing the publication were: Michelle Harding, Head, Tax Data and Statistical Analysis, Emmanuelle Modica, Statistician/Analyst, Leonie Cedano, Statistician/Junior Analyst, Talita Yamashiro Fordelone, Advisor and Koji Ono, Senior Advisor, Global Relations of the OECD Centre for Tax Policy and Administration under the supervision of the Director Pascal Saint-Amans, Deputy Director Grace Perez-Navarro and the Head of the Tax Policy and Tax Statistics Division David Bradbury; Jingjing Xia of the OECD Development Centre under the supervision of the Director and Special Advisor to the OECD Secretary-General on Development, Mario Pezzini, Deputy Director Federico Bonaglia, Kensuke Tanaka, Head of the Asia Unit, and Alexander Pick, Coordinator of Revenue Statistics for the Development Centre. The special feature was written by Daisuke Miura, Public Management Specialist (Taxation), SDCC, and Go Nagata, Public Management Specialist (Taxation), SDCC, at the ADB.Elizabeth Nash and Delphine Grandrieux at DEV and Marie-Aurélie Elkurd, Karena Garnier and Natalie Lagorce at CTP assisted with the production and publication of this report.

The authors would like to thank other officials for their invaluable help in completing this publication. Advice and support were provided by Nilima Lal, Economic Statistics Advisor at the SPC; Koni Ravono, Head of Secretariat, and Petero Maivucevuce, Training Coordinator at PITAA; by Piera Tortora, Economist/Policy Analyst at the OECD Development Co-operation Directorate; by Bert Brys, Dimitra Koulouri, Hakim Hamadi, Joseph Stead, Koji Ono, Oliver Petzold, Peter Green, Pierce O'Reilly, Piet Battiau, Rex Arendsen, Sarah Perret and Stéphane Buydens at the OECD Centre for Tax Policy and Administration. The authors would like to thank colleagues working in national administrations with whom they have consulted regularly. These institutions include finance ministries, national tax agencies and national statistical institutes of the participating countries. The authors are also very grateful to all participants at the technical webinar on 8 April 2021.

This document was produced with financial support from the governments of Ireland, Japan, Luxembourg, Norway, Sweden, Switzerland and the United Kingdom. The views expressed herein can in no way be taken to reflect the official opinion or policies of the governments of Ireland, Japan, Luxembourg, Norway, Sweden, Switzerland and the United Kingdom.

Table of contents

FIGURES

TABLES

Follow OECD Publications on:

http://twitter.com/OECD_Pubs

http://www.facebook.com/OECDPublications

http://www.linkedin.com/groups/OECD-Publications-4645871

http://www.youtube.com/oecdilibrary

http://www.oecd.org/oecddirect/

This book has... StatLinks

A service that delivers Excel® files from the printed page!

Look for the *StatLinks* at the bottom of the tables or graphs in this book. To download the matching Excel® spreadsheet, just type the link into your Internet browser, starting with the *https://doi.org* prefix, or click on the link from the e-book edition.

Executive summary

Achieving the Sustainable Development Goals (SDGs) of the United Nations' 2030 Agenda for Sustainable Development will require the mobilisation of increasing levels of public revenue. *Revenue Statistics in Asia and the Pacific* presents key indicators to track progress on domestic resource mobilisation and to inform tax policy and reform that could help fill the financing gap to fund the SDGs.

Revenue Statistics in Asia and the Pacific 2021 presents detailed, internationally comparable data on tax revenues for 24 Asian and Pacific economies: Australia, Bhutan, People's Republic of China, the Cook Islands, Fiji, Indonesia, Japan, Kazakhstan, Korea, Lao People's Democratic Republic, Malaysia, the Maldives, Mongolia, Nauru, New Zealand, Papua New Guinea, the Philippines, Samoa, Singapore, the Solomon Islands, Thailand, Tokelau, Vanuatu and Viet Nam.

Tax-to-GDP ratios in Asia and the Pacific

In 2019, the Asia-Pacific (24) average tax-to-GDP ratio was 21.0%, below the OECD and LAC averages, (33.8% and 22.9%, respectively) and higher than the Africa (30) average (16.6%, 2018 figure). Tax-to-GDP ratios in the 24 Asian and Pacific economies ranged from 10.3% in Bhutan to 48.2% in Nauru. Most Asian countries in this report had a tax-to-GDP ratio below the Asia-Pacific (24) average, except for Japan (32.0%, 2018 figure), Korea (27.4%), Mongolia (24.2%) and China (22.1%). By contrast, only four of the ten Pacific economies had a tax-to-GDP ratio below the Asia-Pacific (24) average, including Papua New Guinea (12.4%), Vanuatu (17.1%), Tokelau (19.2%) and the Solomon Islands (20.4%).

Between 2018 and 2019, tax-to-GDP ratios decreased in over two-thirds (15) of the 22 economies for which 2019 data are available. They decreased by more than one percentage point (p.p.) in six economies: Bhutan, China (exclusive of social security contributions), the Cook Islands, Fiji, Samoa, and the Solomon Islands. Two of the three largest decreases, in the Cook Islands and Bhutan, were influenced by the inclusion of part of the 2020 calendar year in the 2019 fiscal year: the decrease of 3.0 p.p. in the Cook Islands was driven by lower income tax revenue due to the collapse in tourism as a result of COVID-19 travel restrictions; and in Bhutan a decline in revenue from taxes on goods and services during the COVID-19 pandemic contributed to the 2.3 p.p. decrease. The largest decrease, of 3.6 p.p. in the Solomon Islands, was due to lower economic activity during the national elections and a decline in logging exports.

Of the seven economies where tax-to-GDP ratios increased in 2019, the largest increases were in Nauru and Tokelau (12.9 p.p. and 1.2 p.p., respectively). In Nauru, tax-to-GDP ratios increased following increases in income tax rates for employees and service providers of the Regional Processing Centre. The increase in the tax-to-GDP ratio in Tokelau was driven by higher income taxes following general increases in salaries. Increases in the remaining five economies were smaller than one percentage point.

Over a longer timeframe, fourteen of the 24 Asian and Pacific economies have increased their tax-to-GDP ratios. The highest increases over the last decade were observed in Korea (5.0 p.p.), Japan (5.5 p.p., 2010 to 2018), Samoa (6.2 p.p.), the Maldives (9.6 p.p.) and Nauru (39.8 p.p., since 2014). Across the same period, Viet Nam, Papua New Guinea and Kazakhstan experienced the largest decreases in their tax-to-

GDP ratios (4.1 p.p., 4.5 p.p. and 7.1 p.p., respectively), driven in all three countries by decreases in corporate income tax (CIT) revenues, which were negatively affected by lower resource prices in Papua New Guinea and Kazakhstan and by several decreases of the standard CIT rate in Viet Nam.

Tax structures in Asia and the Pacific

On average, taxes on goods and services were the main source of tax revenues in the Asia-Pacific region in 2019, accounting on average for 49.8% of total tax revenues, similar to the Africa (30) and the LAC averages (51.9%, 2018 figure and 50.3%, respectively) and higher than the OECD (32.7%, 2018 figure). However, within this category, the average share of value-added taxes in total revenues was lower in Asia-Pacific (24) (22.8%) than in Africa (30) and LAC (29.7%, 2018 figure and 28.0%, respectively) and similar to the OECD average (20.4%, 2018 figure).

Revenues from personal income taxes (PIT) accounted for an average of 17.0% of total tax revenues in Asia-Pacific, similar to the Africa (30) average of 17.5% (2018 figure), above the LAC average (9.1%) and below the OECD average (23.5%, 2018 figure). Corporate income tax revenues accounted for a larger share of total tax revenues in the Asian-Pacific region, on average, at 20.1%, similar to the Africa (30) average (19.2%, 2018 figure) and above the shares in LAC (15.5%) and the OECD (10.0%, 2018 figure). In Pacific economies, PIT accounted for a larger share of total taxation than CIT (with the exception of Fiji); whereas the CIT share was higher than the PIT share in Asian countries, except in Korea and Japan.

Social security contributions (SSCs) played a small role in revenues for most Asian and Pacific economies, at 6.6% of total revenues. None of the Pacific economies levy SSCs and most of the Asian countries in the publication have very low SSCs. However, four Asian countries derive more than 15% of total tax revenues from SSCs: Japan (40.2%, 2018 figure); China (27.5%), Korea (26.7%) and Mongolia (19.8%).

Non-tax revenues in selected economies

This publication also includes data on non-tax revenues for sixteen economies (Bhutan, the Cook Islands, Fiji, Kazakhstan, Lao PDR, the Maldives, Mongolia, Nauru, Papua New Guinea, the Philippines, Samoa, Singapore, Thailand, Tokelau, Vanuatu and Viet Nam).

In 2019, non-tax revenues were greater than 10% of GDP in Samoa (11.0%), the Cook Islands (15.3%), Bhutan (19.2%), Vanuatu (24.2%), Nauru (85.2%) and Tokelau (220.1%). Grants were an important source of revenue in 2019 in seven economies (Bhutan, the Cook Islands, Lao PDR, Papua New Guinea, Samoa, Tokelau, and Vanuatu), exceeding 30% of total non-tax revenues. Property-related income accounted for the largest share of non-tax revenues in Singapore (85.7%), Kazakhstan (78.1%), Nauru (53.8%), Thailand (52.6%) and Tokelau (51.2%), and also contributed more than 40% in the Philippines, Fiji and Mongolia.

Special feature: Emerging challenges for the region in the COVID-19 era

A special feature sheds light on potential challenges that Asian and Pacific economies could face during the recovery from COVID-19, particularly in managing government finances in a sustainable way. The chapter explores strategies to address these challenges and to enhance domestic resource mobilisation, such as the creation of medium term revenue strategies, digitalisation of tax administrations and active participation in international tax initiatives. The recently launched ADB Asia-Pacific Tax Hub could serve as a support mechanism for countries to develop and sustain healthy government finances.

Notes

[1] https://www.oecd.org/tax/tax-policy/revenue-statistics-asia-pacific-technical-webinar-2021.htm.

1 Tax revenue trends in Asian and Pacific economies

Chapter 1 provides information on trends in tax and non-tax revenues in 24 Asian and Pacific economies, including changes in tax-to-GDP ratios, tax structures, taxes by level of government and non-tax revenue levels and structures.

Achieving the Sustainable Development Goals in the 2030 Agenda for Sustainable Development requires mobilising additional resources – in particular government revenues – to fund public goods and services in developing countries. Taxation provides the largest share of government revenues in almost all countries and is relatively predictable and sustainable, in contrast with non-tax revenue sources such as official development assistance and royalties.

Revenue Statistics in Asia and the Pacific 2021 is published at a time when the COVID-19 pandemic continues to pose severe challenges to health systems and economies across the Asia and Pacific region, as well as to citizens themselves. Data on fiscal revenues discussed in Chapter 1 demonstrate the strength of the region's tax systems going into the crisis and are thus a valuable tool not only for understanding how the crisis will affect different countries but also for supporting countries to build more resilient fiscal systems in its aftermath. Chapter 2 of this report discusses the emerging challenges for the Asia-Pacific region in the COVID-19 era and ways to address them.

This report presents detailed and internationally comparable data on tax revenues in 24 Asian and Pacific economies: Australia, Bhutan, People's Republic of China (hereafter "China"), the Cook Islands, Fiji, Indonesia, Japan, Kazakhstan, Korea, Lao People's Democratic Republic (hereafter Lao PDR), Malaysia, the Maldives, Mongolia, Nauru, New Zealand, Papua New Guinea, the Philippines, Samoa, Singapore, the Solomon Islands, Thailand, Tokelau, Vanuatu and Viet Nam. It also provides information on non-tax revenues for Bhutan, the Cook Islands, Fiji, Kazakhstan, Lao PDR, the Maldives, Mongolia, Nauru, Papua New Guinea, the Philippines, Samoa, Singapore, Thailand, Tokelau, Vanuatu and Viet Nam. This chapter discusses key tax indicators for these 24 economies: the tax-to-GDP ratio; the tax structure and the share of tax revenue by level of government; and non-tax revenue for selected economies. The discussion is supplemented by the comparative tables in Chapter 3 and detailed information for each economy in Chapters 4 and 5.

Tax ratios

Tax-to-GDP ratios in 2019

In 2019, tax-to-GDP ratios in Asia and the Pacific ranged from 10.3% in Bhutan to 48.2% in Nauru (Figure 1.1). Ten of the 24 economies had tax-to-GDP ratios above the Asia-Pacific (24) average of 21.0% in 2019, and all economies in the publication had lower ratios than the OECD average of 33.8%, with the exception of Nauru. Most of the Asian countries covered in this report had a tax-to-GDP ratio below the average of 21.0%, with the exceptions of Japan (32.0%, 2018 figure), Korea (27.4%), Mongolia (24.2%) and China (22.1%). By contrast, six of the ten Pacific economies in this publication had a tax-to-GDP ratio above 21.0%, with the exception of Papua New Guinea (12.4%), Vanuatu (17.1%), Tokelau (19.2%) and the Solomon Islands (20.4%).

The tax-to-GDP ratio measures tax revenues as a proportion of gross domestic product (GDP). Taxes are defined as compulsory, unrequited payments to general government. In the OECD classification, taxes are classified by the base of the tax and include taxes on incomes and profits, compulsory social security contributions (SSCs) paid to the general government, taxes on payroll and workforce, taxes on property, taxes on goods and services and other taxes.

Tax-to-GDP ratios in Asian and Pacific economies, inclusive and exclusive of SSCs, are shown in Figure 1.1. In countries that levy SSCs, tax-to-GDP ratios exclusive of SSCs range from 11.1% of GDP in Indonesia to 20.1% of GDP in Korea in 2019 (Lao PDR and Viet Nam are not included as data are not available). For all countries with SSC data, seven countries in Asia had tax-to-GDP ratios exclusive of SSCs between 15% and 20% of GDP: the Philippines (15.5%), China (16.0%), Kazakhstan (16.1%), Thailand (16.2%), Maldives (18.6%), Japan (19.2%) and Mongolia (19.4%), while four countries had tax-to-GDP ratios exclusive of SSCs below 15%: Bhutan (10.3%), Indonesia (11.1%), Malaysia (12.1%) and

Singapore (13.3%). While excluding revenues from social security contributions does not impact the tax-to-GDP ratios in Pacific economies, where social protection is funded predominantly from general revenues and not through SSCs, it plays a more significant role in the ratios of all Asian economies except Bhutan, Maldives and Singapore which also do not levy SSCs.

Figure 1.1. Tax-to-GDP ratios in Asian and Pacific economies, including and excluding social security contributions (2019)

Percentage of GDP

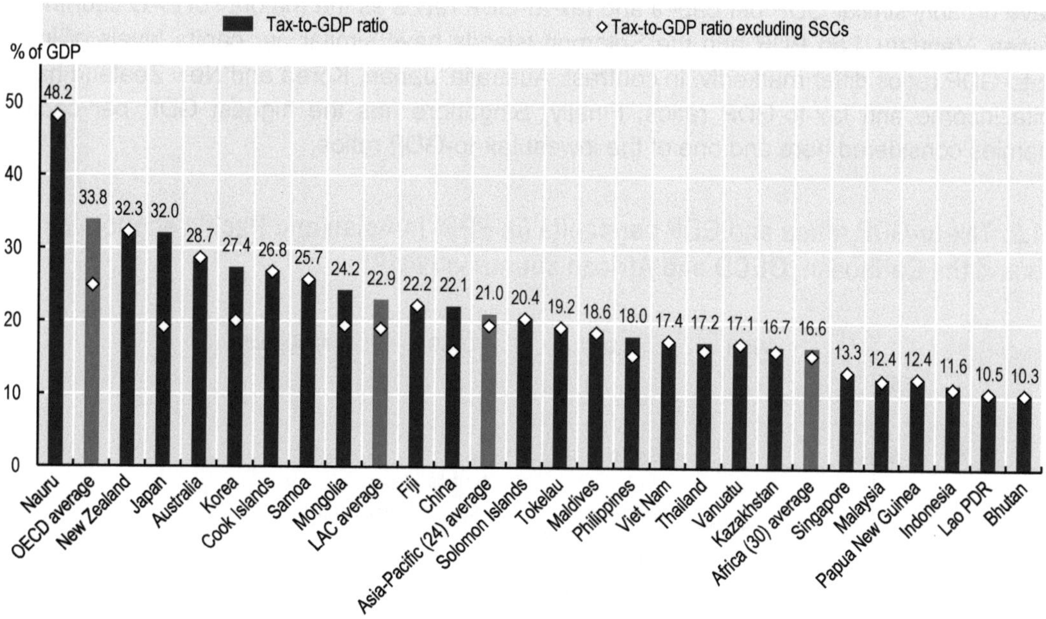

Notes: The figures do not include sub-national tax revenue for the Cook Islands, Fiji, Lao PDR, Malaysia, the Maldives, Papua New Guinea, Samoa, the Solomon Islands and Viet Nam as the data are not available.

The averages for Africa (30 countries), for Asia-Pacific (24 economies), for LAC (26 Latin American and Caribbean countries) and the OECD (37 countries) are unweighted.

Australia, Japan, Korea and New Zealand are part of the OECD (37) group. Data for Australia, Japan, Korea, New Zealand and the OECD average are taken from *Revenue Statistics 2020* (OECD, 2020[1])

2018 data are used for the Africa (30) average, Australia and Japan, as 2019 data are not available.

Source: Authors' calculations based on Table 3.1 in Chapter 3.

StatLink https://stat.link/49g12z

Structural factors are a key determinant of tax-to-GDP ratios across economies. These include the importance of agriculture in the economy, openness to trade and the size of the informal economy. Agriculture, for example, is a challenging sector to tax: most people in the agriculture sector in developing economies are on low incomes and many are not registered for tax purposes (PEAKS, 2013[2]). In addition, agriculture benefits from numerous tax exemptions. For example, Malaysia allows an agriculture allowance to be deducted from profits of eligible businesses (Inland Revenue Board of Malaysia, 2016[3]), and goods and services related to the agriculture sector are exempt from import duty and excise duty (Ministry of International Trade and Industry of Malaysia, 2016[4]) The common challenges that small island developing states (SIDS) confront, such as remoteness, exposure to natural disasters and low economic diversification, also influence tax-to-GDP ratios and tax structures in these islands. These factors are discussed in more detail in Box 1.1.

In addition to structural factors, tax policy and tax administration settings also strongly influence the level of tax revenues. These include tax rules and statutory rates, the power of tax administrations, the levels of corruption within these administrations and tax morale (i.e. willingness of people to pay taxes) (OECD, 2014[5]). For example, Aizenman (2015[6]) found that tax-to-GDP ratios in Asia are positively correlated with government effectiveness and institutional quality. Finally, tax-to-GDP ratios tend to be higher in high-income economies, although the relationship is not direct and is less pronounced at lower levels of income due to the influence of other factors. (Figure 1.2).

The relationship between GDP per capita and tax levels across the Asian and Pacific economies in this publication is less direct than that observed across LAC or OECD countries. Nine Asian and Pacific economies (China, Fiji, Kazakhstan, the Maldives, Mongolia, the Philippines, Samoa, Thailand and Viet Nam) have broadly similar GDP per capita and tax-to-GDP ratios as the majority of LAC countries. Papua New Guinea, Vanuatu, Lao PDR and the Solomon Islands have similar per capita levels of income but their tax-to-GDP ratios differ markedly. In contrast, Australia, Japan, Korea and New Zealand have higher per capita income and tax-to-GDP ratios. Finally, Singapore has the highest GDP per capita of the 24 economies considered here and one of the lowest tax-to-GDP ratios.

Figure 1.2. Tax-to-GDP ratios and GDP per capita (in PPP) in Asian and Pacific economies, Latin America and the Caribbean, OECD and African countries (2019)

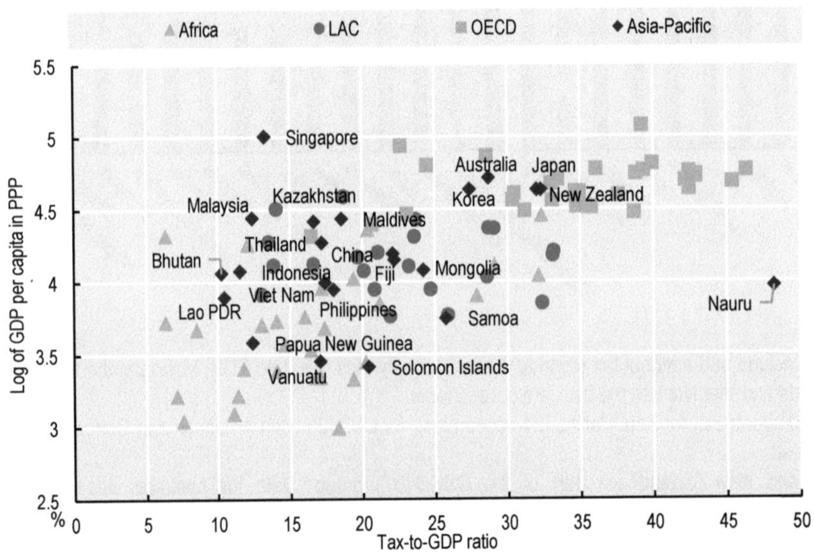

Notes: The y-axis is on a logarithmic scale.
2018 data used for Australia, Japan and all African countries.
The Cook Islands and Tokelau are excluded as GDP per capita data was unavailable for these countries.
The purchasing power parity (PPP) between two countries is the rate at which the currency of one country needs to be converted into that of a second country to ensure that a given amount of the first country's currency will purchase the same volume of goods and services in the second country as it does in the first. The implied PPP conversion rate is expressed as national currency per current international dollar. An international dollar has the same purchasing power as the US dollar has in the United States. An international dollar is a hypothetical currency that is used as a means of translating and comparing costs from one country to the other using a common reference point, the US dollar (definitions derived from (IMF, 2019[10]) and (WHO, 2015[11])).
Source: GDP per capita from *World Economic Outlook, April 2021* (IMF, 2021[12])

StatLink https://stat.link/z0onyi

The high GDP per capita in Singapore results from significant inward flows of foreign direct investment (FDI) (UNCTAD, 2012[7]), whereas the tax-to-GDP ratio is explained by lower income tax rates (particularly on corporate income) and value added tax (VAT) rates compared to other Asian and Pacific economies (UNESCAP, 2014[8]). Nauru, on the other hand, has a similar GDP per capita level to Lao PDR, Viet Nam and the Philippines but reports the highest tax-to-GDP ratio of the 24 economies in this publication, as a result of high revenues generated in connection with the Refugee Processing Centre (RPC) (Government of Nauru, 2020[9]).

Box 1.1. Enhancing domestic resource mobilisation in Small Island Developing States through revenue statistics

Small Island Developing States (SIDS) comprise a diverse group of the smallest and most remote economies in the world located across Africa, Asia and the Pacific, and Latin America and the Caribbean. They share a common and unique set of development challenges owing to their small populations and landmasses, spatial dispersion and remoteness from major markets, and exposure to severe climate-related events and natural disasters. With small and undiversified economies, SIDS are highly vulnerable to external shocks, as they rely strongly on the global economy for financial services, tourism, remittances and concessional finance.

Two common challenges faced by SIDS are the achievement of adequate domestic resource mobilisation and debt sustainability. Domestic revenues are often erratic due to narrow economic productive bases, often concentrated in sectors that are exposed to external fluctuations, such as natural resources or tourism. At the same time, SIDS typically have large current expenditures, as the high unit costs of providing services to small and scattered populations increase public sector expenditures above the average levels of other developing countries (31.7% of GDP in SIDS, compared to 21.3% in other developing countries) (World Bank, 2020[13]). Severe climate events and natural disasters also tend to have heavy fiscal and economic impacts. These factors lead to high levels of public debt for many SIDS [59.5% of GDP, compared to 44.6% for other developing countries (World Bank, 2020[14])] and reduce the fiscal space to invest in development.

Taxes are an important and relatively more stable source of revenues in many SIDS, although economies' ability to raise domestic revenues varies significantly. The *Global Revenue Statistics* publications and database (OECD, 2021[15]) show that Pacific Islands had the biggest variation of tax-to-GDP ratios among SIDS, from 12.4% in Papua New Guinea to 48.2% in Nauru in 2019. Among African SIDS, Cabo Verde had a tax-to-GDP ratio of 21.2%, Mauritius of 20.4% and Seychelles of 32.4% in 2018 (OECD/AUC/ATAF, 2020[16]). Finally, for SIDS in Latin America and the Caribbean, ratios varied from 13.5% in the Dominican Republic to 42.0% in Cuba in 2019 (OECD et al., 2021[17]).

The COVID-19 pandemic is hampering SIDS' ability to mobilise and improve the stability of domestic revenues. Public revenues in SIDS have been affected by the crisis via a variety of channels, most notably the sharp fall of tourism activity, the decline in overall economic activity, and fluctuations in commodity and natural resource prices. To recover from the COVID-19 crisis, enhanced management of key sectors, including fisheries, tourism and natural resource extraction, may provide opportunities to enhance domestic revenue mobilisation in SIDS. Policies to reduce "leakages" from these sectors – especially tourism – and to support backward and forward linkages with other domestic sectors (e.g. food and agriculture, consumer goods and construction) could expand the taxable production base.

Improving the efficiency of revenue collection, enlarging the tax base and employing efficient tax policies are also essential to increase the resources required to sustain development. The *Global Revenue Statistics* project supports 21 SIDS in these efforts by providing accurate, comparable and detailed data on their tax revenues. This information is essential for tax policymaking and administrative reforms, and forms a common evidence base for mutual learning across SIDS on how to scale up domestic resource mobilisation.

Source: Piera Tortora and Talita Yamashiro Fordelone, based on OECD (2018[18]), (World Bank, 2020[14]), (World Bank, 2020[13]) and on the *Global Revenue Statistics* database (OECD, 2021[15]).

Changes in tax-to-GDP ratios in 2019

Since 2018, over two-thirds of the economies in this publication for which 2019 data are available have experienced decreases in their tax-to-GDP ratios (Figure 1.3). Fifteen economies had lower tax-to-GDP ratios in 2019 relative to 2018, whereas seven had higher ratios than in 2018 (Australia and Japan do not have 2019 data). The largest increases were seen in Nauru and Tokelau at 12.9 percentage points (p.p.) and 1.2 p.p, respectively. The increases in the remaining economies were smaller than 1 percentage point. By contrast, six economies experienced decreases in their tax-to-GDP ratios larger than 1 percentage point: China (1.0 p.p., exclusive of SSCs), Fiji (1.3 p.p.), Samoa (1.4 p.p.), Bhutan (2.3 p.p.), the Cook Islands (3.0 p.p.) and the Solomon Islands (3.6 p.p.). The 2019 fiscal year in some of these economies includes part of the 2020 calendar year, and their tax-to-GDP ratios were therefore impacted by the COVID-19 crisis (indicated by an asterisk in Figure 1.3). In the remaining nine countries with decreases, the difference was less than 1 percentage point.

Figure 1.3. Annual changes in tax-to-GDP ratios (2018-19)

Percentage point (p.p.) change

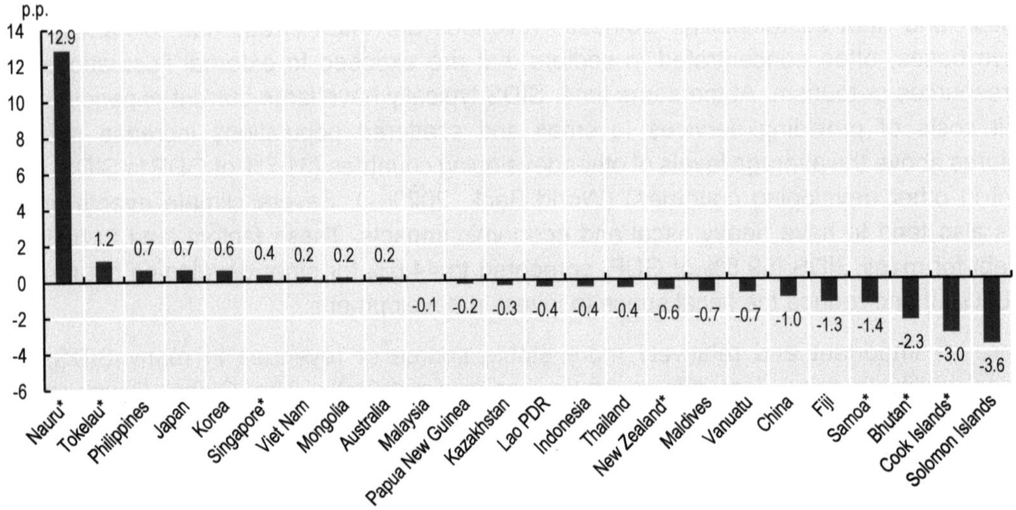

Notes: Countries with an asterisk report data on a fiscal year basis which includes part of 2020 in this publication. Please see the notes to the country tables in Chapter 4 for further information.
Australia, Japan, Korea and New Zealand are part of the OECD (37) group. Data for Australia, Japan, Korea and New Zealand are taken from *Revenue Statistics 2020* (OECD, 2020[1])
Data for the change between 2017 and 2018 are used for Australia and Japan.
The tax-to-GDP ratios for China are shown exclusive of SSCs which are only available for 2019.
Source: Authors' calculations based on Table 3.1 in Chapter 3.

StatLink https://stat.link/hl8vb7

Higher revenues from taxes on income were the main reason for the largest increases in the tax-to-GDP ratios in the region between 2018 and 2019 (Figure 1.4).

In Nauru, income taxes increased by 13.1 p.p. in 2019. This increase was due to higher tax rates for employees and service providers of the Regional Processing Centre (RPC) and higher than expected revenue from the Centre ((Republic of Nauru, 2019[19]), (2020[20])). The government of Nauru is committed to a positive fiscal budget (IMF, 2020[21]) and is aware of the uncertainty of revenues from the RPC after the contract with the Australian government expires in 2021 ((Republic of Nauru, 2021[22]), (2020[23])). The increase in income tax revenue was slightly offset by a decrease in revenues from other taxes on goods and services (-0.2 p.p.), leading to an overall increase in tax-to-GDP ratio of 12.9 p.p. between 2018 and 2019. In Tokelau, where the 2019 fiscal year includes the first six months of 2020, an increase in income tax revenues of 1.8 p.p. of GDP was primarily the result of general increases in salaries. [1] This increase was partially offset by a decrease in revenues from other taxes on goods on services, reflecting lower imports in 2020 due to the COVID-19 pandemic, leading to a total increase in tax-to-GDP ratios of 1.2 p.p. in the 2019 fiscal year.

Figure 1.4. Net changes in tax-to-GDP ratios between 2018 and 2019 by main type of tax

Percentage point (p.p.) change

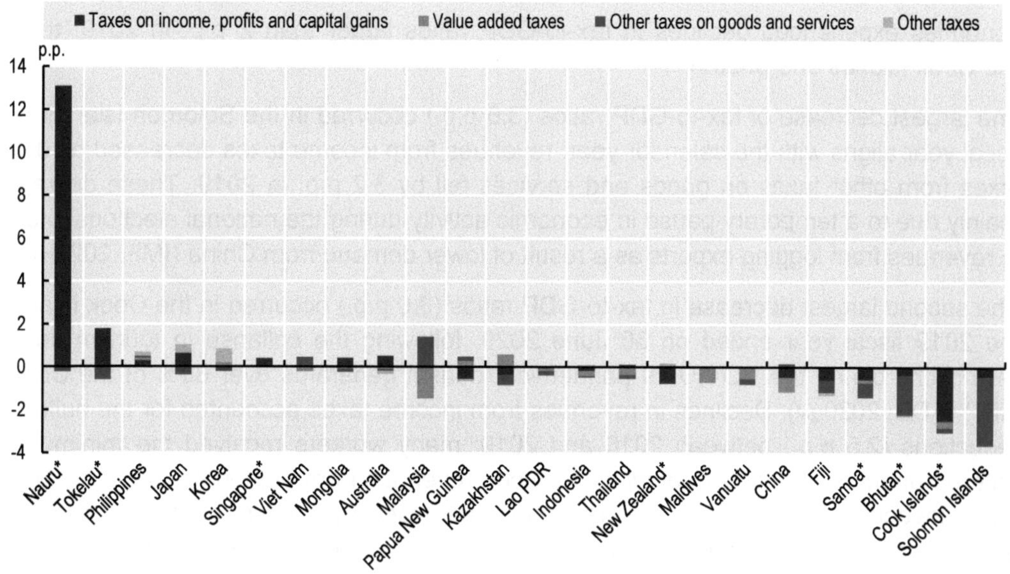

Notes*:*
Countries with an asterisk: Part of 2020 is included in the fiscal year 2019.
Australia, Japan, Korea and New Zealand are part of the OECD (37) group. Data for Australia, Japan, Korea and New Zealand are taken from *Revenue Statistics 2020* (OECD, 2020[1])
Data for the change between 2017 and 2018 are used for Australia and Japan.
The tax-to-GDP ratios for China are shown exclusive of SSCs.
Source*:* Authors' calculations based on (OECD, 2021[24]), "Revenue Statistics - Asian and Pacific Economies: Comparative tables", *OECD Tax Statistics* (database).

StatLink https://stat.link/d25efc

A variety of factors drove the decreases in tax-to-GDP ratios observed in the region in 2019, and as noted, six countries saw decreases of over 1 percentage point (China, Fiji, Samoa, Bhutan, the Cook Islands and the Solomon Islands) between 2018 and 2019:

- The decrease of 1.0 p.p. in China's tax-to-GDP ratio, exclusive of SSCs, was the result of lower revenues from VAT (0.7 p.p.), especially on imports, and from PIT (0.5 p.p.), due to a reform of individual income taxes[2], which was partially offset by an increase of 0.2 p.p. in revenues from other taxes on goods and services.
- Fiji's tax-to-GDP ratio decreased by 1.3 p.p. due to a general economic downturn (IMF, 2020[25]), which led to decreases in revenues from corporate income taxes and from other taxes on goods and services via lower import revenue. Both categories declined by 0.6 p.p. in 2019. Revenues from other taxes also decreased by 0.1 p.p. in 2019.

- The tax-to-GDP ratio in Samoa, where the 2019 fiscal year ends on 30 June 2020, declined by 1.4 p.p. because of a downturn in economic activity related to a measles outbreak in late 2019 and due to the COVID-19 pandemic in the first months of 2020 (Central Bank of Samoa, 2020[26]). GDP contracted by 3.5% in the fiscal year 2019. The economic downturn particularly impacted commerce, business services, electricity and water, and food and beverage manufacturing (Central Bank of Samoa, 2020[26]). The revenue from VAT declined by 0.2 p.p. between 2018 and 2019, while income taxes and other taxes on good and services both declined by 0.6 p.p.. Declines in corporate tax revenue and in custom duty revenues were the main driver of the falls in these last tax categories, respectively, which both decreased sharply in the second quarter of 2020.

Three economies experienced declines in tax-to-GDP ratios larger than 2 p.p. in 2019: the Solomon Islands, the Cook Islands and Bhutan.

- The largest decrease of tax-to-GDP ratios (3.6 p.p.) occurred in the Solomon Islands, where the fiscal year aligns with the calendar year: revenues from income taxes decreased by 0.4 p.p. and taxes from other taxes on goods and services fell by 3.2 p.p. in 2019. These decreases were mainly due to a temporary pause in economic activity during the national elections and a decline in revenues from logging exports as a result of lower demand from China (IMF, 2020[27]).
- The second largest decrease in tax-to-GDP ratios (3.0 p.p.) occurred in the Cook Islands, where the 2019 fiscal year ended on 30 June 2020, following the collapse in tourism due to travel restrictions during the COVID-19 pandemic. Tourism generates over 60% of the Cook Islands' GDP (ADB, 2020[28]). Declines in revenues from income taxes accounted for the bulk of revenue reductions (2.5 p.p.) between 2018 and 2019: many workers received the minimum wage or entered unemployment, both of which reduced revenues from personal income tax (PIT) by 1.3 p.p. between 2018 and 2019.[3] CIT revenues decreased by 1.2 p.p. during the same period. In addition, government measures such as tax payment deferrals or reductions in instalment payments and increasing the provisional tax threshold also contributed to the overall decrease (Ministry of Finance of the Cook Islands, 2020[29]).
- Revenues in Bhutan, whose 2019 fiscal year ended on 30 June 2020, decreased by 2.3 p.p. between 2018 and 2019 due to lower revenues from income taxes (0.4 p.p.) and other taxes on goods and services (1.8 p.p.). Income tax revenue decreased due to tax deferrals for businesses to the next fiscal year, introduced in response to the COVID-19 pandemic (ADB, 2021[30]). The decrease in other taxes on goods and services was due to the cessation of the excise duty refund from India, which accounted for 11.5% of total taxes in 2018, following the introduction of a goods and services tax in India, which subsumed excise duty [4] (IMF, 2018[31]).

Box 1.2. Calculation of the Asia-Pacific (24) average

This edition of *Revenue Statistics in Asia and the Pacific* features a regional average of the 24 Asian and Pacific economies for the tax indicators presented in this publication for the first time.

Country coverage in this publication has been expanding continuously since its first edition: the number of participating economies has increased from four in 2014 to 24 economies in 2021, which together account for 77% of GDP in the Asia-Pacific region. The publication now covers 14 Asian and 10 Pacific economies, accounting for 76% and 99% of regional GDP respectively[5].

The Asia-Pacific (24) average is an unweighted average of the 24 economies, calculated for the years 2010 to 2019, for tax revenue as percentage of GDP and tax revenue by tax type as percentage of total taxation. The average includes all 24 economies between 2014 and 2019, but excludes Nauru between 2010 and 2013 due to lack of data. For individual tax types, data is not yet available for some economies. For example, SSC data are not yet available for Lao PDR and Viet Nam, while they are partially reported for China (available only for 2019). The regional average should therefore be interpreted with caution, particularly when compared across time.

In addition, it should be noted that ten of the 24 economies report their data on a fiscal year instead of a calendar year. Japan and Singapore have a fiscal year from April to March; the fiscal year in Australia, Bhutan, Cook Islands, Nauru, New Zealand, Samoa and Tokelau runs from July to June; and Thailand's fiscal year is from October to September. The use of fiscal years can raise difficulties for some countries to provide revenue data for the latest period and this is especially true for data for the 2019 fiscal year due to the COVID-19 pandemic. As a result, regional averages for the latest year may be subject to change as more information arrives. For example, revenue data for the fiscal year 2019 were not available for Australia and Japan (in both countries, this would include at least three months of 2020) in *Revenue Statistics 2020*. As a result, 2018 data are used for the calculation of 2019 regional average, which is likely to change once the revenue data of Australia and Japan are available.

In comparison with the other regional averages that are part of the *Global Revenue Statistics Initiative,* the OECD average, the Latin American and Caribbean (LAC) average and the Africa (30) average, variation across the 24 economies included in the Asia-Pacific average is relatively small, reflected by lower standard deviations for tax-to-GDP ratios (around 5-6%) than those of Africa (above 6%), LAC (around 7%) and OECD (around 7-8%) between 2010 and 2017. However, the recent hike in tax revenues of Nauru has contributed to rising standard deviations in 2018 and 2019.

Additionally, the following observations can be made about the Asia-Pacific (24) average:

- The tax-to-GDP ratio for the Asia-Pacific (24) average (21.0%) is higher than the Africa (30) average (16.6%, 2018 figure) and below the LAC average (22.9%) in 2019 while all three regions have significantly lower tax-to-GDP ratios than the OECD average (33.8%).
- In terms of tax structure, the Asia-Pacific average is similar to the Africa average, with a heavy reliance on taxes on goods and services as well as income taxes but a minor contribution from SSCs. However, tax structures may vary among sub-regions within the group. For example, ASEAN member states receive higher revenues from CIT than PIT, while the reverse is the case for Pacific Island economies (see Box 1.1).

Evolution of tax-to-GDP ratios since 2010

Across a longer time horizon, 14 of the 24 economies in the publication have increased their tax-to-GDP ratios since 2010 (Figure 1.5).[6] Across the period, the largest decreases in tax-to-GDP ratios were observed in Viet Nam, Papua New Guinea and Kazakhstan (by 4.1 p.p., 4.5 p.p. and 7.1 p.p., respectively), which were affected by the fall in mineral resource prices between 2010 and 2019. By contrast, the tax-to-GDP ratios of Korea, Japan, Samoa, the Maldives and Nauru (since 2014) grew by over 5 p.p. during the same period. For Korea and Japan, the tax-to-GDP ratios were particularly low in 2010 as a result of the global financial crisis and increased again in the following years. The change in the tax-to-GDP ratios for the remaining economies ranged from a decrease of 3.8 p.p. in Bhutanto an increase of 3.9 p.p. in the Philippines.

Across the Asian countries in the publication, the change in tax-to-GDP ratios ranged from -7.1 p.p. in Kazakhstan to 9.6 p.p. in the Maldives, with ratios increasing in six of the 14 Asian economies considered and decreasing in eight. Across the Pacific economies in this publication, tax-to-GDP ratio changes ranged from -4.5 p.p. in Papua New Guinea to 6.2 p.p. in Samoa. The majority of Pacific economies increased their tax-to-GDP ratios since 2010 (Nauru since 2014), while only two (the Cook Islands and Papua New Guinea) had lower tax-to-GDP ratios in 2019 than in 2010.

In eight Asian and Pacific economies, changes in tax-to-GDP ratios over the last decade did not reflect the more recent trend in tax-to-GDP ratios in the last five years. While tax-to-GDP ratios in the Cook Islands, Mongolia, Viet Nam and Kazakhstan decreased between 2010 and 2019, tax-to-GDP ratios in these economies showed either no change (in the Cook Islands) or an increase between 2015 and 2019. The opposite can be observed in Indonesia, Fiji, the Solomon Islands and the Maldives: while tax-to-GDP ratios increased in these economies over the last decade, they decreased between 0.5 p.p. in the Indonesia and 2.7 p.p. in the Solomon Islands during the last five years (2015 to 2019).

Figure 1.5. Changes in tax-to-GDP ratios (2010-19 and 2015-19)

Percentage point (p.p.) change

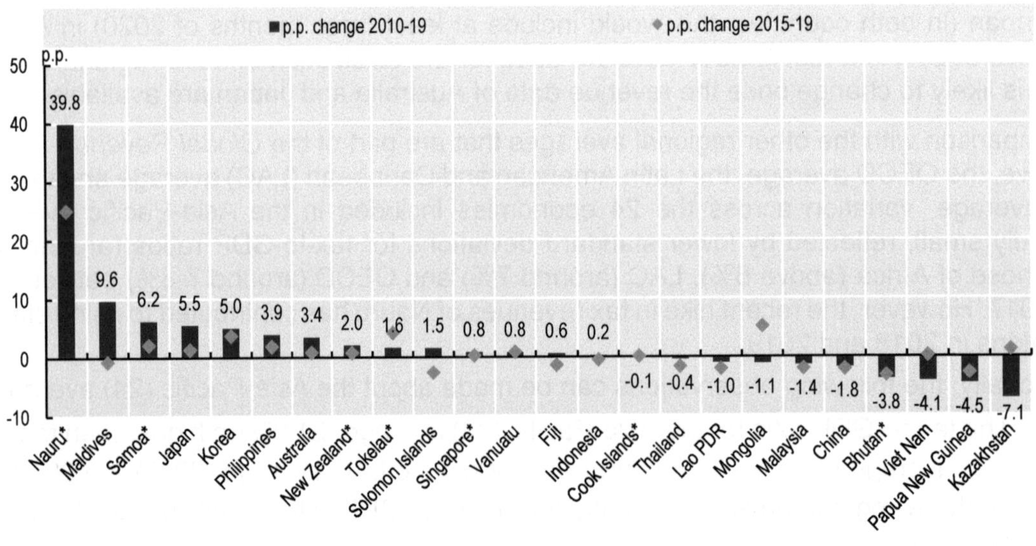

Notes: Countries with an asterisk: Part of 2020 is included in the fiscal year 2019.
Australia, Japan, Korea and New Zealand are part of the OECD (37) group. Data for Australia, Japan, Korea and New Zealand are taken from *Revenue Statistics 2020* (OECD, 2020[1]).
2018 data are used for Australia and Japan.
The tax-to-GDP ratios for China are shown exclusive of SSCs.
Data for Nauru are only available from 2014 onwards.
Source: Authors' calculations based on Table 3.1 in Chapter 3.

StatLink https://stat.link/7hyqbi

Changes in tax-to-GDP ratios between 2010 and 2019 by tax category

Between 2010 and 2019, corporate income tax (CIT) revenues were the major driver of decreases observed in tax-to-GDP ratios in many economies, whereas different tax types drove the increases (Figure 1.6). These changes reflect the diverse range of policy measures and economic developments in the 24 Asian and Pacific economies over this period.

Of the ten economies where tax-to-GDP ratios declined between 2010 and 2019, lower CIT revenues contributed to the declines in eight. The largest declines in the tax-to-GDP ratios were in Bhutan (3.8 p.p.), Viet Nam (4.1 p.p.), Papua New Guinea (4.5 p.p.) and Kazakhstan (7.1 p.p.) and resulted primarily from declines in CIT revenues:

- The decrease in Bhutan (3.8 p.p.) was mainly driven by decreases in revenue from CIT (3.2 p.p.) and excises (1.6 p.p.), due to lower revenues from the business income tax and a generally lower economic activity (World Bank, 2021[32]). Additionally, as described in the previous section, the removal of the excise duty refund from India due to the introduction of Goods and Service Tax caused a decrease in revenues from excises in 2019. The use of a fiscal year which includes the first six months of 2020 also means the 2019 figures were affected by the COVID-19 pandemic.
- The decrease in tax-to-GDP ratio between 2010 and 2019 in Viet Nam was the result of lower revenues from CIT (2.4 p.p.), VAT (1.2 p.p.) and excises (1.2 p.p.). Over the last decade, Viet Nam lowered the CIT rate from 25% to 22% in 2013, and to 20% in 2016, introduced preferential tax rates for SMEs in 2018 and reduced several excises (OECD, 2015[33]) (PwC, 2021[34]).
- Papua New Guinea and Kazakhstan were affected by declines in natural resource prices:
  - Between 2010 and 2019, CIT revenues in Papua New Guinea decreased by 4.4 p.p. due to lower revenues from the mining and petroleum tax, which accounted for half as much tax revenue in nominal terms in 2019 as it did in 2010. Other factors such as slower economic growth and an earthquake in 2018 also contributed to the decline in the tax-to-GDP ratio in Papua New Guinea (IMF, 2020[35]).
  - The decline in tax-to-GDP ratio for Kazakhstan was mainly driven by decreases in CIT (3.3 p.p.), decreases in customs and import duties (1.1 p.p.) and decrease in taxes on the production of useful minerals (3.1 p.p.). Kazakhstan was particularly affected during the commodity price shock in 2014, as more than one-third of budgetary revenues are generated through the oil sector (OECD, 2019[36]).

Fourteen economies recorded increases in their tax-to-GDP ratios between 2010 and 2019. The highest increases were seen in the Maldives, Nauru (since 2014), and Samoa, which all recorded increases larger than 6 percentage points.

- In Samoa, the increase in the tax-to-GDP ratio of 6.2 p.p. was due to VAT increasing by 3.9 p.p., other taxes on goods and services by 1.5 p.p. and income taxes by 0.8 p.p.. Samoa has implemented a variety of reforms to broaden the tax base and remove exemptions, and to improve tax administration efficiency and tax compliance (IMF, 2018[37]; Cullen, 2017[38]).
- Both the Maldives and Nauru have introduced a variety of taxes over the last decade to increase government revenues:
  - Since 2014, Nauru has introduced an employment and services tax and a business tax, and improved revenue collection (IMF, 2020[21]).
  - The Maldives have undertaken a large tax policy reform since 2011 to increase tax revenue. Key policy changes included the introduction of a goods and services tax in 2011, a business tax, a corporate profit tax and a personal income tax (ADB, 2017[39]). For example, the tax-to-GDP ratio increased by 3.2 p.p. between 2010 and 2011, mainly due

to the introduction of VAT. Subsequent rate increases in these three taxes have also contributed to the increase in tax revenues (ADB, 2017[39]).

Figure 1.6. Net changes in tax-to-GDP ratios between 2010 and 2019, by main type of taxes

Percentage point (p.p.) change

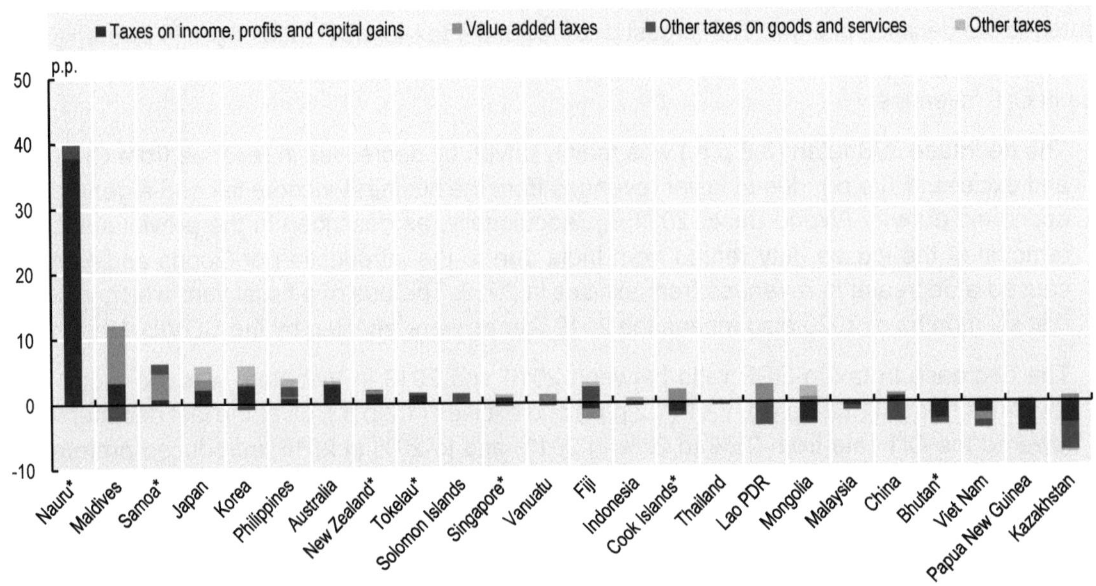

Notes: Countries with an asterisk: Part of 2020 is included in the fiscal year 2019.
Australia, Japan, Korea and New Zealand are part of the OECD (37) group. Data for Australia, Japan, Korea and New Zealand are taken from *Revenue Statistics 2020* (OECD, 2020[1])
2018 data are used for Australia and Japan.
Data for Nauru are only available from 2014 onwards The tax-to-GDP ratios for China are shown exclusive of SSCs.
Source: Authors' calculations based on (OECD, 2021[24]), "Revenue Statistics - Asian and Pacific Economies: Comparative tables", *OECD Tax Statistics* (database).

StatLink https://stat.link/w3pmy4

Levels of revenues from tax categories in 2019 (as a percentage of GDP)

Australia, New Zealand and Tokelau had the highest levels of personal income tax (PIT) revenues as a percentage of GDP in 2019 (Figure 1.7). Revenue from PIT equated 12.8% of GDP in New Zealand, 11.8% of GDP in Australia (2018 figure) and to 10.3% of GDP in Tokelau. In the other Pacific economies covered in this publication, revenue from PIT was above 3.0% of GDP and closer to the Asia-Pacific (24) average of 3.6%, except in Fiji (1.7%) and Vanuatu (which does not have a PIT). For Nauru, it is not possible to distinguish between revenues from PIT and CIT. However, Nauru has the highest level of revenue from income taxes of all economies included in the publication, at 37.9% of GDP. In the Asian countries in this publication (excluding the Maldives, which do not levy PIT, and Japan and Korea), revenue from PIT in 2019 ranged from 1.0% of GDP in Lao PDR to 2.6% of GDP in Malaysia and the Philippines. Japan and Korea both had higher revenues from PIT than the rest of the Asian countries included in this publication, at 6.1% (2018 figure) and 4.8% respectively.

Figure 1.7. Tax structures as a percentage of GDP (2019)

Percentage of GDP

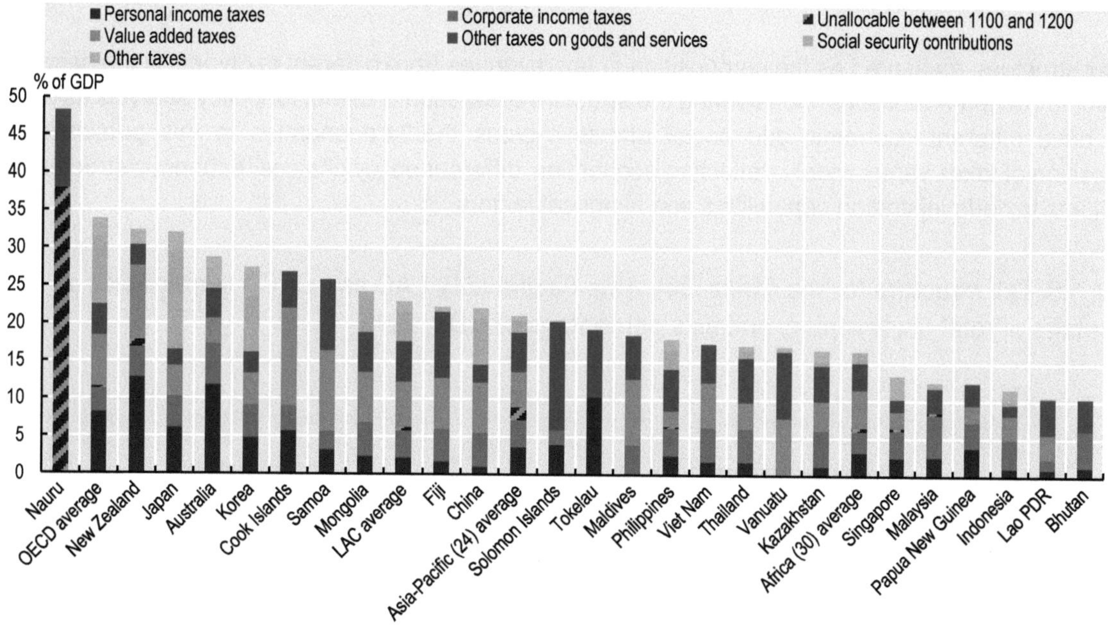

Notes: The averages for Africa (30 countries), for Asia-Pacific (24 economies), for LAC (26 Latin American and Caribbean countries) and the OECD (37 countries) are unweighted.
Australia, Japan, Korea and New Zealand are part of the OECD (37) group. Data for Australia, Japan, Korea, New Zealand and the OECD average are taken from *Revenue Statistics 2020* (OECD, 2020[1]).
2018 data are used for the Africa (30) average, Australia, Japan and the OECD average.
Source: (OECD, 2021[40]), "Revenue Statistics - Asian and Pacific Economies: Comparative tables", *OECD Tax Statistics* (database).

StatLink https://stat.link/fm0zgv

Revenues from corporate income tax (CIT) accounted on average for 3.6% of GDP across the Asia-Pacific region. They were higher than revenues from PIT in 13 of the 21 economies considered here (excluding Tokelau and Vanuatu, which do not have a corporate tax, and Nauru, for which a distinction between PIT and CIT revenues is not possible). Revenues from CIT ranged from 1.3% of GDP in the Lao PDR, to 5.6% in Malaysia. CIT revenue exceeded 5% of GDP in two countries, Australia and Malaysia, at 5.5% of GDP (2018 figure) and 5.6% of GDP respectively.

SSCs play a small role in the tax revenues of Asian and Pacific economies. Thirteen economies in this publication, including all Pacific economies, do not levy SSCs. In most of the other economies, revenues from SSCs were relatively low in 2019, including in Malaysia (0.3% of GDP), Indonesia and Kazakhstan (0.5% of GDP), Thailand (1.0% of GDP) and the Philippines (2.6% of GDP). These levels are significantly below the LAC average (3.9% of GDP) and the OECD average (9.0% of GDP in 2018). Four Asian countries reported relatively high revenues from SSCs: Mongolia (4.8% of GDP), China (6.1%), Korea (7.3%) and Japan (12.9%, 2018 figure).[7] Data on SSC were not available for Viet Nam and Lao PDR.

Revenues from taxes on goods and services amounted to 9.9% of GDP on average across the 24 Asian and Pacific economies. In most of the Asian economies in this publication, revenues from taxes on goods and services as a percentage of GDP were below 10%, with the exception of Viet Nam (11.1%), Mongolia (12.0%) and the Maldives (14.6%) in 2019. In contrast, the majority of the Pacific economies in this publication generated revenues from taxes on goods and services above 10% of GDP, ranging from 10.3%

of GDP in Nauru to 20.1% in Samoa in 2019. The exceptions in the Pacific were Papua New Guinea (5.2% of GDP), Australia (7.3% of GDP, 2018 figure) and Tokelau (8.9% of GDP).

Tax structures

The tax structure, measured as the composition of tax revenues from different tax types, is the second key indicator in *Revenue Statistics*. Considering the structure of taxation is useful for policy analysis as different taxes have different economic and social effects. Across the 24 economies in this publication, the composition of taxes varies widely, reflecting economies' different policy choices, economic structures and conditions, tax administration capabilities and historical factors.

Figure 1.8. Tax structure for the Africa (30), Asia-Pacific (24), LAC and OECD averages as a percentage of total tax revenues and as a percentage of GDP, 2019

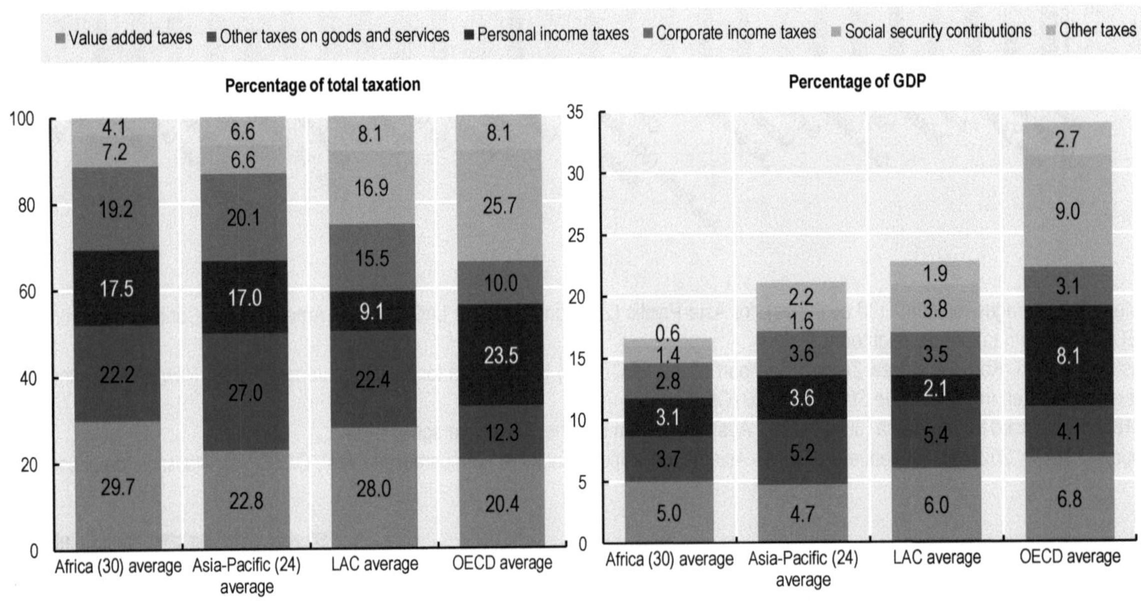

Note: 2018 data are used for the Africa (30) average and the OECD average.
Source: (OECD, 2021[40]), "Revenue Statistics in Asia and the Pacific: Comparative tables", *OECD Tax Statistics* (database).

StatLink https://stat.link/h1zbl8

Tax structures in 2019 and evolution since 2010

Average tax structures across the Asian-Pacific region, Africa, Latin America and the Caribbean and the OECD, shared some similarities in 2019. Revenues from goods and services contributed a similar share to total tax revenues across the Africa, Asia-Pacific and LAC regions, with 51.9% (2018 figure), 49.8% and 50.3% respectively and were higher than the OECD average of 32.7% (2018 figure). Taxes from other goods and services generated the largest share of total tax revenue (27.0%) in the Asia-Pacific region (Figure 1.8), which is significantly higher than the share in Africa (22.2%, 2018 figure) and the LAC average (22.4%), and is more than twice the level of the OECD average (12.3%, 2018 figure). Revenues from VAT were equivalent to 4.7% of GDP in Asia-Pacific, which had the smallest average share. At 22.8% of total taxation, they were closer to the OECD average of 20.4% (2018 figure), which was lower than the average share of VAT in Africa (29.7%, 2018 figure) or LAC (28.0%).

On average, income tax revenues in the Asian-Pacific region accounted for a similar share of total taxation as in Africa (39.2% and 38.7% (2018), respectively). In the Asian-Pacific region, revenues from PIT accounted for 17.0% of total taxes, similar to the Africa (30) average of 17.5% (2018 figure), above the LAC average (9.1%) and below the OECD average (23.5%, 2018 figure). CIT revenues accounted for a larger share of total tax revenues in the Asian-Pacific region, on average, at 20.1%, similar to the Africa (30) average (19.2%, 2018 figure) and above the shares in LAC (15.5%) and the OECD (10.0%, 2018 figure). The Asian-Pacific region had the lowest share of SSCs of the four averages: they contributed 6.6% of total taxes in Asia-Pacific, 7.2% in Africa (2018 figure), 16.9% in LAC and 25.7% of total taxes in OECD countries (2018 figure).

Within the Asia-Pacific region, tax structures also varied greatly in 2019. In 13 economies, the main source of tax revenue was taxes on goods and services, while ten economies obtained the primary share of tax revenues from income taxes. Japan is the only country in which the greatest share of revenues was derived from SSCs. There were also notable differences between the ASEAN countries in the publication and the Pacific Islands, discussed further in Box 1.3.

In 2019, income taxes were the largest source of revenue for Australia (2018 figure), Bhutan, Indonesia, Korea, Malaysia, Nauru, New Zealand, Papua New Guinea, Singapore and Tokelau. Among these economies, the share of income tax revenue in total tax revenue varied from 33.2% in Korea to 78.6% in Nauru. CIT revenues were higher than PIT revenues in four Asian countries (Bhutan, Indonesia, Malaysia and Singapore), while all Pacific economies in this group (Australia, New Zealand, Papua New Guinea and Tokelau), as well as Korea, raised higher shares of revenue from PIT.[8]

Taxes on goods and services were the main source of tax revenue in China, the Cook Islands, Fiji, Kazakhstan, Lao PDR, the Maldives, Mongolia, Philippines, Samoa, the Solomon Islands, Thailand, Vanuatu and Viet Nam in 2019, contributing between 41.3% (China) and 96.4% (Vanuatu) of total tax revenue. In seven of these economies, taxes on goods and services other than VAT, such as excises and import duties, typically contributed a larger share than VAT revenues to total tax revenues. Revenues from other taxes on goods and services in these economies ranged from 28.5% of total tax revenues in Kazakhstan to 70.6% in the Solomon Islands, while six economies received a larger share of revenue from VAT, ranging from 27.5% in Mongolia to 48.5% in the Cook Islands.

Box 1.3. Tax revenue developments in the ASEAN (7) and in Pacific Island economies since 2010

Among the 24 economies included in this publication, two distinct subgroups can be identified: a group of eight Pacific Island economies and a group of seven members of the Association of Southeast Asian Nations (ASEAN). The Pacific Island economies share, despite their diversity, common characteristics, such as remoteness, small populations, limited economic diversification, particular exposure to natural disasters and climate change (ADB, 2016[41]). The eight Pacific Island economies included in this publication are the Cook Islands, Fiji, Nauru, Papua New Guinea, Samoa, the Solomon Islands, Tokelau and Vanuatu, and form the Pacific Islands (8) average. The second sub-regional group includes the seven ASEAN member states in this publication. ASEAN is a regional organisation, founded in 1967, that promotes economic, political and social collaboration amongst its member states and within the region (ASEAN, 2021[42]). Seven of the ten ASEAN members are included in this publication: Indonesia, Lao PDR, Malaysia, the Philippines, Singapore, Thailand and Viet Nam, grouped into the ASEAN (7) average.[9]

The Pacific Island economies generally had higher tax-to-GDP ratios than the ASEAN (7) countries (Figure 1.9). Tax-to-GDP ratios ranged from 12.4% of GDP in Papua New Guinea to 48.2% in Nauru in 2019 across the Pacific Island economies, with an average of 24.0%. Across the ASEAN (7) economies, tax-to-GDP ratios ranged from 10.5% in Lao PDR to 18.0% in the Philippines in the same year, with an average of 14.4%.

Since 2010, tax-to-GDP ratios in the Pacific Island economies increased, while they decreased on average in the ASEAN (7) economies. Most Pacific Island economies increased their tax-to-GDP ratios between 2010 and 2019, with the exception of the Cook Islands (declined by 0.1 p.p.) and Papua New Guinea (declined by 4.5 p.p.). The increases varied between 0.6 p.p. in Fiji to 39.8 p.p. in Nauru (since 2014), while the average tax-to-GDP ratio in Pacific Island economies, excluding Nauru, increased by 0.9 p.p. between 2010 and 2019. Tax-to-GDP ratios decreased in four of the seven ASEAN countries, and increased in Indonesia (0.2 p.p.), Singapore (0.8 p.p.) and the Philippines (3.9 p.p.).

Figure 1.9. Tax-to-GDP ratios in ASEAN and Pacific Island economies, 2010-19

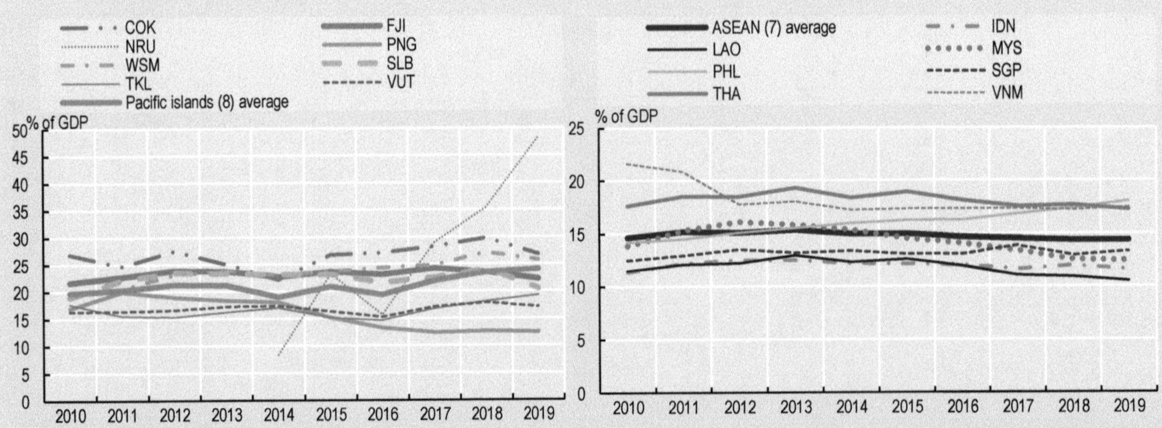

Note: Data for Nauru are only available from 2014 onwards

Source: Author's calculation based on (OECD, 2021[40]), "Revenue Statistics - Asian and Pacific Economies: Comparative tables", *OECD Tax Statistics* (database).

StatLink https://stat.link/34dirg

Regional differences are also reflected in the average tax structures, as displayed in Figure 1.10. While revenues from taxes on goods and services play an important role in both regions (47.6% of total taxes in the ASEAN (7) countries and 61.4% in the Pacific Island economies), the composition of the taxes on goods and services differs. Revenues from VAT contributed on average 20.4% of total taxation in the ASEAN (7) economies in 2019, which is lower than the Asia-Pacific (24) average (22.8%) and the Pacific Islands (8) average (23.0%). Revenues from other taxes on goods and services accounted for the largest share of total taxes in both the ASEAN (7) and the Pacific Island economies. However, the share of these taxes was 38.4% in the Pacific Island economies, 10 p.p. larger than the average share of 27.2% in the ASEAN (7) countries in 2019.

Another difference in structure between the averages is seen in the balance of personal and corporate income tax revenues. CIT revenues played a relatively small role in the tax structures of Pacific Island economies and contributed only 9.7% on average to total tax revenue in 2019, whereas revenues from CIT accounted for 27.0% on average in the ASEAN (7) countries and 20.1% of total taxes of the Asia-Pacific (24) average. Revenues from PIT accounted for an average of 13.3% of total taxes in the ASEAN (7) countries, 17.0% in the Asia-Pacific region and 18.1% in Pacific Island economies in 2019.

Figure 1.10. Tax structure in Asia-Pacific, ASEAN (7) and Pacific Island economies in 2019

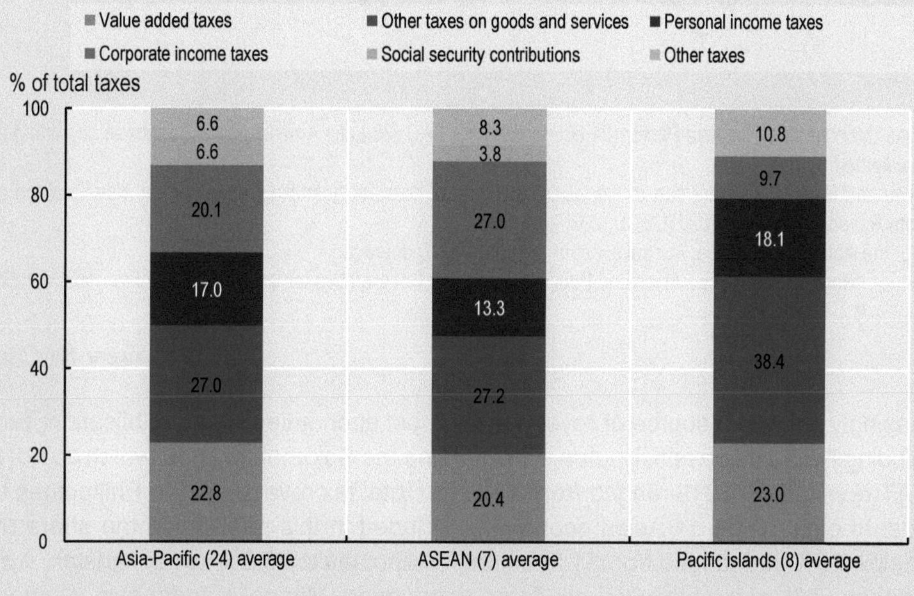

Note: Asia-Pacific (24) average: Unweighted average of the 24 Asian and Pacific economies included in this publication.

ASEAN (7) average: Unweighted average of the 7 ASEAN economies (Indonesia, Lao PDR, Malaysia, the Philippines, Singapore, Thailand, and Viet Nam) included in this publication.

Pacific islands (8) average: Unweighted average of the 8 Pacific island economies (the Cook Islands, Fiji, Nauru, Papua New Guinea, Samoa, the Solomon Islands, Tokelau and Vanuatu) included in this publication.

Source: Author's calculation based on (OECD, 2021[40]), "Revenue Statistics - Asian and Pacific Economies: Comparative tables", *OECD Tax Statistics* (database).

StatLink https://stat.link/nyw8ft

As discussed earlier, SSCs played a small role in revenues for most Asian and Pacific economies, with a few exceptions in Asian countries. Japan derived the largest share of total tax revenues from SSCs (40.2% in 2018) while these also played a significant role in revenues in Mongolia (19.8%), Korea (26.7%) and China (27.5%).

Figure 1.11. Tax structures as a percentage of total taxation in 2019

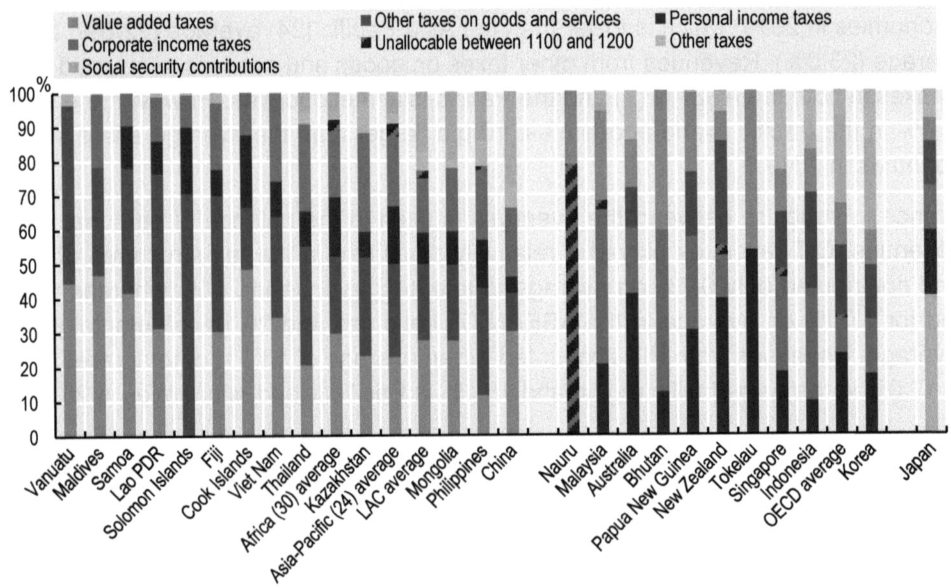

Notes:

The averages for Africa (30 countries), for Asia-Pacific (24 economies), for LAC (26 Latin American and Caribbean countries) and the OECD (37 countries) are unweighted.

Australia, Japan, Korea and New Zealand are part of the OECD (37) group. Data for Australia, Japan, Korea, New Zealand and the OECD average are taken from *Revenue Statistics 2020* (OECD, 2020[1]).

2018 data are used for the Africa (30) average, Australia, Japan and the OECD average.

Source: (OECD, 2021[40]), "Revenue Statistics - Asian and Pacific Economies: Comparative tables", *OECD Tax Statistics* (database).

StatLink https://stat.link/um39gs

VAT is an increasingly important source of revenues for most economies in this publication, particularly in the Pacific. Excluding Nauru, Malaysia, Bhutan, Tokelau and the Solomon Islands, which do not have value added taxes, VAT revenues in 2019 ranged from 11.5% of total tax revenue in the Philippines to 48.5% in the Cook Islands. In eight of the 14 Asian economies included in this publication the share of revenues from VAT was below 25% and ranged from11.5% in the Philippines to 23.2% in Kazakhstan, whereas VAT generated more than 25% of total taxes in six Asian economies (Mongolia, Indonesia, China, Lao PDR, Viet Nam and the Maldives). The share of revenues from VAT in total taxes was generally higher across Pacific economies, with only two economies (Australia at 11.7% and Papua New Guinea at 18.8% of total taxes) reporting shares below 30%, while the share in the rest of the economies ranged from 30.4% in New Zealand to 48.5% in the Cook Islands in 2019. On average, the share of VAT in total tax revenue in Asia-Pacific (24) in 2019 (22.8%) was similar to the OECD average of 20.4% (2018 figure) and lower than the LAC (27.7%) and Africa (30) averages (29.7%, 2018 figure).

In 2019, revenues from other goods and services contributed between 6.7% of total tax revenue in Japan (2018 figure) and 70.6% in the Solomon Islands (Figure 1.11). The high share in the Solomon Islands was derived from general taxes on goods and services, such as the goods tax and the sales tax and export duties on various products, particularly logging (the Solomon Islands do not apply a VAT). Shares of other taxes on goods and services in total revenue are also comparatively high in Bhutan, Fiji, Samoa, Tokelau, Lao PDR and Vanuatu, where they are larger than 35% of total tax revenues.

In 2019, revenue from other taxes on goods and services played a more prominent role in the Pacific economies than in the Asian countries covered in this publication. Seven of the ten Pacific economies generated more revenue from other taxes on goods and services than from VAT, whereas eight of the 14 Asian countries received more revenue from VAT. For the Africa, LAC and OECD averages, revenue from VAT contributed a larger share to total tax revenue than other goods and services while the opposite was true for the Asia-Pacific (24) average.

Between 2010 and 2019, the share of revenue from VAT increased most in the Maldives (by 46.9 p.p.), Lao PDR (25.8 p.p.) and Kazakhstan (10.2 p.p.). Both the Maldives and Lao PDR introduced VAT within this timeframe (in 2011 and 2010, respectively). While Lao PDR replaced the earlier turnover tax with a VAT, (Keomixay, 2010[43]) the Maldives introduced a VAT (also known as the goods and sales tax) for the first time to raise revenue (ADB, 2017[39]). Increases in the share of VAT in total taxation in Kazakhstan were mainly the result of improved VAT administration (IMF, 2020[44]).

Seven economies experienced a decline in the share of VAT revenues over this period: Australia, Fiji, Korea, New Zealand, the Philippines, Singapore and Thailand. In Fiji, the share of VAT revenue declined by 7.5p.p. in 2019 to 30.5% of total tax revenue, following a decrease of the VAT rate from 15% to 9% in 2016. Decreases in Australia (2010 to 2018), Korea and the Philippines were less than 2 p.p., while the share decreased by 3.1 p.p. in Singapore over the same period. The share of VAT revenues decreased the least in New Zealand (-0.3 p.p.) and Thailand (-0.2 p.p.).

Figure 1.12. Revenues from VAT and other taxes on goods and services and revenues from PIT and CIT, as percentage of total taxation, 2019

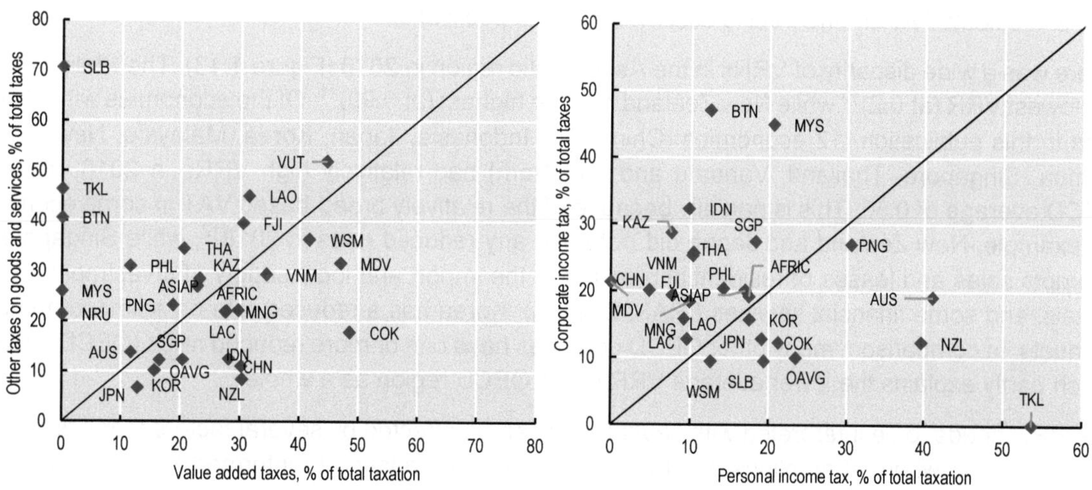

Source: (OECD, 2021[24]), "Revenue Statistics - Asian and Pacific Economies: Comparative tables", *OECD Tax Statistics* (database).

StatLink https://stat.link/hx0veg

The composition of revenues from income taxes between CIT and PIT also varied in Asian and Pacific economies (Figure 1.12). In most Asian economies included in this publication, the share of revenues from CIT as percentage of total taxation was higher than the share of revenues from PIT in 2019, except for Japan and Korea. In contrast, all Pacific economies, with the exception of Fiji, reported higher shares of revenues from PIT than CIT (see Box 1.3).

In 2019, revenues from CIT contributed between 9.4% of total tax revenue in Samoa and 47.0% of total tax revenue in Bhutan. In eight economies, the share of CIT revenues in total tax revenue exceed 25% and many of these economies receive a significant share of CIT from companies in the oil and mining sector (Mongolia, Malaysia, Kazakhstan, Indonesia and Bhutan). By contrast, revenue from PIT as a percentage of total tax ranged from 4.8% in China to 53.7% in Tokelau (the latter does not have a CIT).

Between 2010 and 2019, revenues from CIT and PIT were relatively variable as a share of total tax revenues in all economies covered in this publication, while the magnitude of the change was greater for CIT than PIT revenues. The share of CIT revenues was lower in 2019 than in 2010 in twelve economies, by between 0.5 p.p. of total tax revenues in the Solomon Islands and 18.7 p.p. in Papua New Guinea.

The share of revenues from PIT decreased for four Asian and Pacific economies between 2010 and 2019, and decreased by 1.0 p.p. in Samoa and the Solomon Islands and by 6.5 p.p. and 7.6 p.p., respectively, in Fiji and the Cook Islands. Revenue from PIT increased as a share of total taxation for 17 economies (excluding China, Nauru and Vanuatu) over this period, from 0.3 p.p. in Thailand to 6.9 p.p. in Papua New Guinea.

Box 1.4. VAT revenue ratios in selected Asian and Pacific economies

The VAT revenue ratio (VRR) measures the difference between the VAT revenue collected and what would theoretically be raised if VAT was applied at the standard rate to the entire potential tax base in a "pure" VAT regime and all revenue was collected. A VRR of 1 suggests no loss of VAT revenue as a consequence of exemptions, reduced rates, fraud, evasion or tax planning. This box describes the VRR levels in selected Asian and Pacific economies in this publication.

There was a wide disparity of VRRs in the Asia-Pacific region in 2018 (Figure 1.13). The Philippines had the lowest VRR (at 0.2)[10] while New Zealand had the highest (at 0.99)[11]. Of the economies with available data in this publication, 12 economies (China, Fiji, Indonesia, Japan, Korea, Malaysia, New Zealand, Samoa, Singapore, Thailand, Vanuatu and Viet Nam) had relatively high VRRs in 2018, above the OECD average of 0.56. This is partially because of the relatively broad-based VAT in some economies: for example, New Zealand and Japan did not have any reduced rates in 2018[12], while Singapore only exempts sales and leases of residential properties, the import and local supply of investment precious metals, and some financial services (IRAS, 2021[45]). Korea has a reduced rate on a limited number of products. In comparison, many other OECD countries have one or more reduced rates (OECD, 2020[46]), which partly explains the lower average VRR in the OECD region as a whole.

The VRR needs to be interpreted with caution and can be affected by several factors that inflate it. One reason can be where exemptions on products and services relating to intermediate consumption can lead to a cascading effect that increases VAT revenue (IMF, 2017[47]). For example, in Thailand, a large number of exemptions on a variety of products may cause "cascading", which artificially increases the VRR. Another reason the VRR may be inflated is if refund processes do not work correctly, which may discourage taxpayers from claiming their VAT refunds, resulting in artificially higher VAT revenue and VRR.

In addition, the interpretation of the VRR is also more difficult for economies relying significantly on tourism, such as many Pacific Island economies. These economies may record a high VRR due to methodological reasons: purchases by non-residents may not be included in final consumption expenditure (the denominator) whereas the VAT on these purchases is included in the overall VAT revenues (the numerator) (Keen, 2013[48]).

On the other hand, the VRR can be deflated by the absence of rules and mechanisms for the collection of VAT on inbound business-to-consumer (B2C) supplies of services resulting from the ever-growing digital trade. To date, over 60 countries in the world have adopted rules for the application of VAT to such supplies and 40 of them have implemented simplified registration and collection regimes for the actual collection of VAT according to the OECD standards. Japan and Korea collect VAT on these supplies since 2015; Indonesia and Singapore implemented similar measures in July 2020 and January 2021 respectively.

Figure 1.13. VAT revenue ratios (VRRs) in selected Asian and Pacific economies, 2018

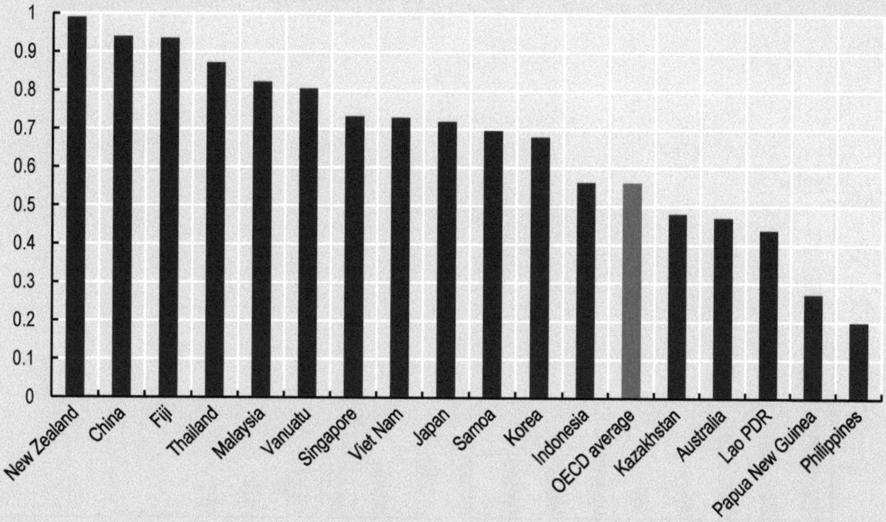

Notes: Data for OECD members (Australia, Japan, Korea and New Zealand) and the OECD average are taken from (OECD, 2020[46]).
Philippines: The VRR measure is currently underestimated as the VAT revenue collected at customs is not accounted for in total VAT revenue in this publication (this revenue could not be distinguished from revenue from other import duties and is currently classified under heading 5120 (taxes on specific goods and services).
Sources: Countries, Trading Economics and KPMG websites and OECD (OECD, 2020[46]) for VAT rates; *World Economic Outlook April 2021* (IMF, 2021[49]) and *OECD Annual National Accounts* (OECD, 2020[50]) for final expenditure consumption figures; and country tables in Chapter 4 for VAT revenues.

StatLink https://stat.link/tjfkgu

Environmental taxes in Asia and the Pacific

Environmentally related taxes,[13] and price-based policy instruments more generally, play an increasingly significant role in many countries to support a transition to a sustainable and low-carbon economic growth. By incorporating a price signal into consumer and producer decisions, these taxes give effect to the polluter-pays principle and encourage businesses and households to consider the environmental costs of their behaviour. Although environmentally related tax revenues[14] are not separately identified in the standard OECD tax classification, they can be identified through the detailed list of specific taxes included for most countries within this overarching classification. It is on this basis that they are included in the *OECD Policy Instruments for the Environment* (PINE) database.[15]

A detailed examination of country-specific taxes for the Asian and Pacific economies for which information is available demonstrates that revenue from environmentally related taxes in 2019 ranged from no (or very close to zero) environmentally related taxes in Tokelau, Viet Nam and Papua New Guinea, to 5.4% of GDP in the Solomon Islands.[16] The case of the Solomon Islands is notable as their environmentally related tax revenue is particularly high compared to other Asian and Pacific economies or the OECD average, due in large part to higher export duties, particularly on timber. The next highest revenues from environmentally related taxes in the region in 2019 were found in Mongolia, Japan, New Zealand and Fiji, amounting to 1.7% of GDP in Mongolia and 1.3% in the other three countries. On average, environmentally related taxes amounted to 1.1% of GDP in the Asia-Pacific region.

Figure 1.14. Environmentally related tax revenue in Asian and Pacific economies, by main tax base, 2019

Percentage of GDP

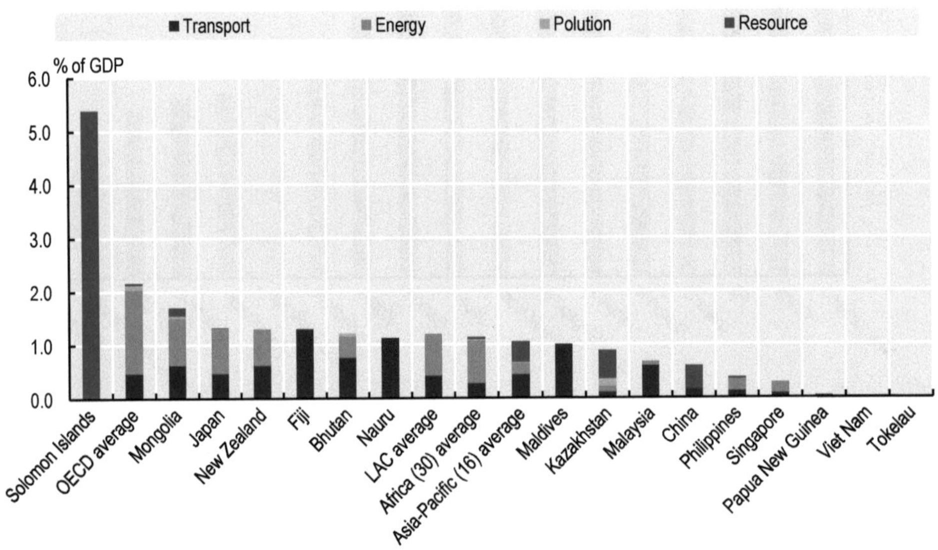

Notes: It has not been possible to identify environmentally related tax revenue for Australia, Indonesia, Korea, Lao PDR, Samoa, Thailand and Vanuatu due to data availability issues. 2018 data are used for Africa (30) average.
Sources: Restricted ERTR database based on PINE database for Japan and New Zealand; (OECD, 2020[51]) and (OECD, 2021[40]), "Revenue Statistics - Asian and Pacific Economies: Comparative tables", *OECD Tax Statistics* (database) for the remaining countries.

StatLink https://stat.link/nxdtv2

Asian and Pacific economies rely on different environmentally related tax revenue (ERTR) bases:

- In the Solomon Islands and Kazakhstan, the majority of ERTRs comes from resource taxes (excise taxes on timber in the Solomon Islands, and excise taxes on minerals in Kazakhstan). They represent the totality for the Solomon Islands and 69.6% of total environmentally related tax revenue in China.
- In other Asian and Pacific economies, ERTRs are principally raised via taxes on energy (five countries, most commonly from diesel and petrol excises) and from transport taxes (six countries, registration or road use of motor vehicles or departure taxes). In almost all of these countries, a combination of these two types of taxes is used; Nauru and Maldives are the exception as they resort entirely to transport taxes, sourcing most of the ERTRs from departure taxes and passenger taxes.

- The composition of environmentally related tax revenues is markedly different in Asian and Pacific economies than in African, LAC and OECD countries. In 2019, revenues from transport taxes and resources taxes generated the highest share of total environmentally related tax revenue in the Asia-Pacific region (0.4% of GDP for both), whereas energy taxes amounted to 0.2% of GDP on average (19.6% of total environmentally related tax revenue in Asia-Pacific). In contrast energy taxes were the principal share of environmentally related tax revenue in the other regions (69.8% in Africa [2018 figure], 69.9% in the OECD [2018 figure] and 62.9% in LAC).

In general, the use of taxation to address environmental issues is low in the region and there is scope to increase use of such instruments, as recently shown by Singapore. In 2019, Singapore became the only country in Southeast Asia to impose a carbon tax. Its payment was first levied in 2020, based on emissions in 2019. The tax is applied on the total direct emissions of facilities that emit 25 000 tCO_2e or more annually, and covers six greenhouse gases (NCCS, 2020[52]). This tax complements the carbon emissions-based vehicle scheme (CEVS) introduced in January 2013, which levies a tax on all new cars, taxis and newly-imported used cars, based on their CO_2/km performance.

The under-utilisation of environmental taxes in the Asia-Pacific region needs also to be understood in the context of the extensive use of fossil fuels subsidies. Reforming energy subsidies is considered by ADB (2016[53]) as "one of the most important policy challenges for developing Asian economies". UN ESCAP (2016[54]) recommends that governments gradually phase out energy subsidies while implementing measures to compensate vulnerable groups and to ensure international competitiveness in a sustainable way. Reforming energy subsidies while at the same time implementing environmental taxation has the potential to mobilise significant government revenues and help to meet the Sustainable Development Goals (SDGs).

Taxes by level of government

This section discusses the relative share of tax revenues attributed to different levels of government in 2019: central government, regional or provincial government (including state government, where relevant), and local government as well as social security funds.

In many economies included in this publication, sub-national taxes generated a small share of total tax revenues in 2019 (Table 1.1). Shares of sub-national government tax revenue in the Asian countries ranged from 0.1% of total revenues in Bhutan to 35.3% in China. In Indonesia, revenues attributed to sub-national governments rose to over 11% in 2019, following the shift of property taxation to the local level in 2014. Revenue collected by sub-national governments accounted for 14.5% of total taxes in 2019 in Mongolia. In New Zealand, sub-national government revenues were 7.0% and in Australia, subnational revenues (including both state and local tax revenues) amounted to 18.8% of total tax revenues (2018 figure).

The types of taxes levied by local governments vary between countries. Local governments in the Philippines have a narrow range of taxes under their jurisdiction, relying on property taxes and taxes on income and profits. Sub-national governments in Japan and Korea raised revenue from taxes on income and profits, property taxes, taxes on goods and services, payroll (Korea only) and other taxes. The share of sub-national government revenue also depends on the range of services that local governments are expected to provide: for example, local revenues are higher in Japan, where local governments finance a wide range of goods and services including public welfare and are responsible for financing some education and debt servicing (Beshho, 2016[55]).

Between 2000 and 2019, the share of revenues collected by sub-national governments was stable, with the exception of Indonesia and Kazakhstan. In Indonesia, the share of revenues attributed to sub-national governments increased by 8.2 p.p., whereas in Kazakhstan it decreased by 29.6 p.p.

With SSCs generating a smaller proportion of total revenues in Asia and the Pacific than in other regions, the share of revenues attributed to social security funds was also low. Australia, Bhutan, New Zealand and Singapore do not have social security funds and the proportion of total tax revenues collected by social security funds therefore was zero in 2019, and was under 6% of total revenues in Indonesia, Kazakhstan, Malaysia and Thailand. By contrast, countries that source a greater share of their revenues from SSCs also had higher shares of revenues attributed to social security funds: at 40.2% of tax revenues in Japan in 2018, 27.5% in China, 26.7% in Korea,19.8% in Mongolia in 2019. The share of tax revenues attributed to social security funds has increased in Japan (by 5.0 p.p.) and Korea (by 10.0 p.p.) since 2000, and in Mongolia since 2006 (by 9.6 p.p.).

Table 1.1. Attribution of tax revenues to sub-sectors of general government

Percentage of total tax revenue (2000-19)	Federal or Central government				Sub-national government				Social Security Funds			
	2000	2010	2015	2019	2000	2010	2015	2019	2000	2010	2015	2019
Australia	81.8	80.2	79.3	81.2	18.2	19.8	20.7	18.8	0.0	0.0	0.0	0.0
Bhutan	99.7	99.9	99.6	99.9	..	0.1	0.4	0.1	..	0.0	0.0	0.0
China	..	..	..	37.2	..	..	..	35.3	..	..	..	27.5
Indonesia	96.8	92.8	88.9	84.3	..	7.2	10.6	11.4	..	..	0.6	4.3
Japan	38.7	33.0	36.7	36.6	26.1	25.9	23.9	23.2	35.2	41.1	39.4	40.2
Kazakhstan	50.3	81.3	72.2	76.7	49.7	16.2	24.0	20.2	..	2.5	3.8	3.2
Korea	68.2	60.0	55.4	56.0	15.1	16.6	18.0	17.3	16.7	23.3	26.6	26.7
Mongolia	..	75.5	61.5	65.7	..	11.4	16.5	14.5	..	13.1	22.0	19.8
Malaysia	98.0	98.2	98.3	97.6	..	..	..	..	2.0	1.8	1.7	2.4
New Zealand	94.3	92.8	93.2	93.0	5.7	7.2	6.8	7.0	0.0	0.0	0.0	0.0
Philippines	81.5	82.2	80.5	80.6	5.3	5.2	5.4	5.2	13.1	12.7	14.1	14.2
Singapore	100.0	100.0	100.0	100.0	..	..	..	..	0.0	0.0	0.0	0.0
Thailand	88.9	86.3	86.4	85.4	7.5	6.6	8.0	8.6	3.7	7.1	5.6	5.9

Notes: Australia, Japan, Korea and New Zealand are part of the OECD (37) group. Data for Australia, Japan, Korea and New Zealand are taken from (OECD, 2020[1])
2018 data are used for Australia and Japan.
Australia: Sub-national figures include data of state and local government.
Data for China are included for 2019. Detailed data on revenue from social security contributions were not available in previous years.
Source: (OECD, 2021[24]), "Revenue Statistics - Asian and Pacific Economies: Comparative tables", *OECD Tax Statistics* (database).

StatLink https://stat.link/lhf450

Non-tax revenues in selected economies

This publication also includes information on non-tax revenues for selected economies for which data are available. Non-tax revenues are defined as all revenues received by general government that do not meet the OECD definition of taxes, as set out in the Interpretative Guide (Annex A). They are further divided into five categories according to the definitions set out in Annex B: grants; property income; sales of goods and services; fines, penalties and forfeits; and miscellaneous and unidentified revenues.

Non-tax revenues as a percentage of GDP

Non-tax revenues were equivalent to a significant share of GDP in 2019 for six economies for which data are available. Non-tax revenues amounted to 11.0% of GDP in 2019 in Samoa, 15.3% in the Cook Islands, 19.2% in Bhutan and 24.4% of GDP in Vanuatu, whereas they amounted to 85.2% of GDP for Nauru and to 220.1% of GDP for Tokelau. The very high level of non-tax revenues in Tokelau, measured as a share of GDP, is due to the fact that non-tax revenues are derived primarily from payments by foreign vessels for access to Tokelau's fishing waters. In the 2008 System of National Accounts, these revenues are recorded as part of GNI but they do not add to GDP. By contrast, non-tax revenues are below 8.5% of GDP in the remaining economies.

Table 1.2. Non-tax revenue of main headings as a percentage of GDP in selected Pacific economies, 2010-19

	2010	2011	2012	2013	2014	2015	2016	2017	2018	2019
Bhutan	22.1	21.5	16.6	20.6	14.8	17.7	15.0	16.4	13.2	19.2
Cook Islands	13.5	8.2	8.4	14.3	16.2	13.9	16.4	14.3	12.9	15.3
Fiji	2.9	3.6	3.0	2.9	2.9	2.9	3.2	3.5	3.6	3.4
Kazakhstan	1.0	1.4	1.8	1.0	1.5	1.3	1.2	1.1	1.7	1.5
Lao PDR	9.5	6.7	10.2	7.3	9.6	7.7	4.5	5.1	5.4	4.8
Maldives	10.2	9.0	6.3	5.1	7.0	6.7	7.2	6.8	6.8	6.2
Mongolia	6.5	7.4	6.9	7.2	7.8	6.3	5.1	4.3	4.6	4.4
Nauru	..	..	..	..	28.7	65.4	64.0	71.0	92.7	85.2
Papua New Guinea	4.7	3.3	3.1	2.4	3.1	3.2	3.2	3.3	3.7	2.8
Philippines	..	..	..	..	1.8	2.1	1.8	1.7	1.9	2.0
Samoa	9.0	6.0	4.8	7.0	4.8	4.7	4.7	5.7	6.4	11.0
Singapore	3.5	3.5	3.4	3.5	3.9	4.4	4.4	5.3	4.3	7.2
Thailand	3.3	2.7	2.9	2.9	3.1	3.6	3.7	3.6	3.8	3.8
Tokelau	154.6	196.4	192.6	246.6	173.4	230.4	236.5	210.0	236.4	220.1
Vanuatu	8.3	5.9	5.2	4.2	5.8	14.8	9.6	14.2	19.8	24.4
Viet Nam	5.7	5.1	4.9	5.1	5.1	6.5	7.2	8.4	8.6	8.2

Note: Tokelau receives significant revenues from foreign vessels for access to Tokelau fishing waters. In the 2008 SNA, these revenues are recorded as part of GNI, but they do not add to GDP.
Source: (OECD, 2021[24]), "Revenue Statistics in Asia and the Pacific: Comparative tables", *OECD Tax Statistics* (database).

StatLink https://stat.link/ndou7q

Non-tax revenues have been increasing since 2010 (or earliest available year) as a share of GDP in the majority of the economies but declining for Bhutan, Lao PDR, Maldives, Mongolia and Papua New Guinea. The largest increases occured in Tokelau (65.5 p.p.), Nauru (56.4 p.p., since 2014) and Vanuatu (16.1 p.p.). The upward trend for Tokelau has been driven by higher revenues from property income, which is entirely sourced from fishery income. Tokelau receives support from New Zealand to strengthen the management of its Exclusive Economic Zone to maximise Tokelau's revenue collection from its international fisheries (New Zealand Foreign Affairs & Trade, 2018[56]). Fisheries income also increased after Tokelau became a partner to the Nauru Agreement, which administers the fishing vessel-day scheme (VSD). The VSD is the system to sustainably manage the world's largest tuna fishery in the Western and Central Pacific Ocean, and has increased revenue to participating islands by over 500% in the past six years (Parties to the Nauru Agreement, 2016[57]). The increase in non-tax revenue for Vanuatu is mainly due to the government citizenship programme (Department of Finance and Treasury of Vanuatu, 2018[58]).

Structure of non-tax revenues

Non-tax revenues are divided into different categories: grants; property income; sales of goods and services; fines, penalties and forfeits; and miscellaneous and unidentified revenues.

In 2019, the shares of each of these categories in total non-tax revenues varied across the 16 economies for which data are available (Figure 1.15). Notable trends include:

- Grants were an important source of revenues for half of the economies in 2019, exceeding 30% of total non-tax revenues in seven economies: Lao PDR (33.2%), Vanuatu (42.6%), Tokelau (44.7%), Bhutan (48.1%), the Cook Islands (65.4%), Samoa (68.6%) and Papua New Guinea (75.8%). In 2019, they were the main source of non-tax revenues for the Cook Islands, Samoa, Papua New Guinea and Bhutan.
- Property income accounted for over 40% of total non-tax revenue in more than half of the economies for which non-tax revenue data are available. There were only four economies in which property income accounted for less than 20% of total non-tax revenue: Vanuatu, which does not generate revenues from property income, Samoa (4.9%), Viet Nam (7.4%) and the Maldives (18.9%). Property income accounted for more than half of the total non-tax revenues in five economies in 2019: Tokelau (51.2%), Thailand (52.6%), Nauru (53.8%), Kazakhstan (78.1%) and Singapore (85.7%). Property income in Tokelau and Nauru was derived predominantly from fisheries (i.e. fishing rents, fishing days, support vessels, etc.), which represented more than 80% of total property income in both economies. Rents and royalties accounted for 70.2% of total non-tax revenue in Kazakhstan in 2019, mainly from oil revenues. Interests and dividends represented the majority of non-tax revenues for Thailand (39.3%) and Singapore (81.9%).

Figure 1.15. Structure of non-tax revenues, 2019

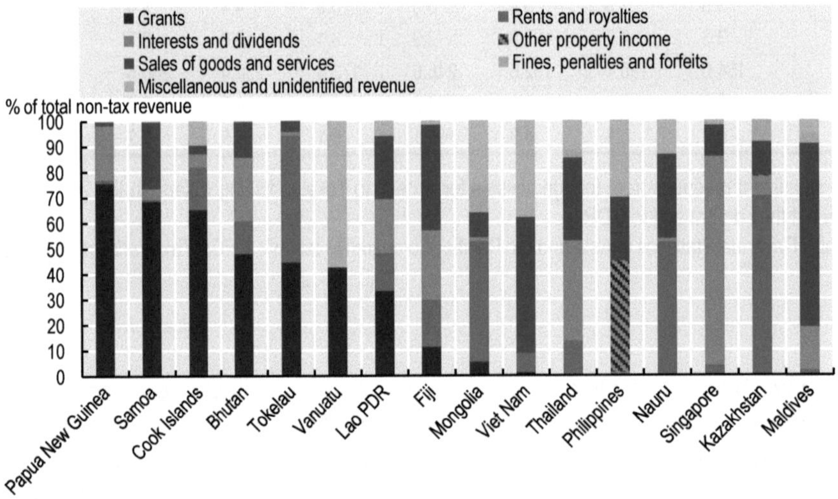

Source: (OECD, 2021[24]), "Revenue Statistics - Asian and Pacific Economies: Comparative tables", *OECD Tax Statistics* (database).

StatLink https://stat.link/sgpq5f

References

ADB (2021), *Bhutan | ADB COVID-19 Policy Database*, https://covid19policy.adb.org/policy-measures/BHU. [30]

ADB (2020), *COVID-19 Active Response and Economic Support Program: Report and Recommendation of the President.* [28]

ADB (2017), "Fast-Track Tax Reform Lessons from Maldives", http://dx.doi.org/10.22617/TIM178673-2. [39]

ADB (2016), *Fossil Fuel Subsidies in Asia: Trends, Impacts, and Reforms*, https://www.adb.org/sites/default/files/publication/182255/fossil-fuel-subsidies-asia.pdf. [53]

ADB (2016), *Pacific Approach 2016-2020*, https://www.adb.org/documents/pacific-approach-2016-2020 (accessed on 4 June 2021). [41]

Aizenman, E. (2015), "Tax revenue trends in Asia and Latin America: A comparative analysis", *NBER Working Paper* No.217555, Cambridge, http://www.nber.org/papers/w21755. [6]

ASEAN (2021), *History - ASEAN | ONE VISION ONE IDENTITY ONE COMMUNITY*, https://asean.org/asean/about-asean/history/ (accessed on 4 June 2021). [42]

Beshho, S. (2016), "Case Study of Central and Local Government Finance in Japan", *ADBI Working Paper No.599*, https://www.adb.org /publications/case-study-centraland-centraland-and-local-government-finance-japan/. [55]

Central Bank of Samoa (2020), *CBS maintains easing monetary policy stance for FY2020/21*, https://www.cbs.gov.ws/index.php/media/press-releases/ (accessed on 6 May 2021). [26]

Cullen, R. (2017), *E-government in Pacific Island countries*, Springer, http://dx.doi.org/10.1007/978-3-319-50972-3_1. [38]

Department of Finance and Treasury of Vanuatu (2018), *Treasury Monthly Budget Report-November 2018*, https://doft.gov.vu/images/2019/November_Monthly_Report_FINAL.pdf (accessed on 10 June 2020). [58]

Government of Nauru (2020), *GON 2019-20 Final Budget Outcome*, https://naurufinance.info/wp-content/uploads/2020/10/GON-Final-Budget-Outcome-2019-20-20201018.pdf (accessed on 3 June 2021). [9]

IMF (2021), *World Economic Outlook, April 2021: Managing Divergent Recoveries*, https://www.imf.org/en/Publications/WEO/Issues/2021/03/23/world-economic-outlook-april-2021 (accessed on 11 May 2021). [12]

IMF (2021), *World Economic Outlook, April 2021: Managing Divergent Recoveries*, International Monetary Fund, Washington, DC, https://www.imf.org/en/Publications/WEO/Issues/2021/03/23/world-economic-outlook-april-2021 (accessed on 15 June 2020). [49]

IMF (2020), *Papua New Guinea : 2019 Article IV Consultation and Request for Staff Monitored Program-Press Release; Staff Report; and Statement by the Executive Director for Papua New Guinea*, https://www.imf.org/en/Publications/CR/Issues/2020/04/06/Papua-New-Guinea-2019-Article-IV-Consultation-and-Request-for-Staff-Monitored-Program-Press-49307 (accessed on 17 May 2021). [35]

IMF (2020), *Republic of Fiji : 2019 Article IV*, https://www.imf.org/en/Publications/CR/Issues/2020/03/19/Republic-of-Fiji-2019-Article-IV-Consultation-Press-Release-Staff-Report-and-Statement-by-49279 (accessed on 6 May 2021). [25]

IMF (2020), *Republic of Kazakhstan : 2019 Article IV Consultation-Press Release; and Staff Report*, https://www.imf.org/en/Publications/CR/Issues/2020/01/29/Republic-of-Kazakhstan-2019-Article-IV-Consultation-Press-Release-and-Staff-Report-49002 (accessed on 10 May 2021). [44]

IMF (2020), *Republic of Nauru : 2019 Article IV Consultation*, https://www.imf.org/en/Publications/CR/Issues/2020/01/29/Republic-of-Nauru-2019-Article-IV-Consultation-Press-Release-Staff-Report-and-Statement-by-49001 (accessed on 30 June 2020). [21]

IMF (2020), *Solomon Islands : 2019 Article IV Consultation*, https://www.imf.org/en/Publications/CR/Issues/2020/02/18/Solomon-Islands-2019-Article-IV-Consultation-Press-Release-Staff-Report-and-Statement-by-the-49060. (accessed on 28 May 2020). [27]

IMF (2019), *World Economic Outlook - Frequently Asked Questions*, https://www.imf.org/external/pubs/ft/weo/faq.htm#q4d (accessed on 6 September 2019). [10]

IMF (2018), *Bhutan : 2018 Article IV Consultation*, https://www.imf.org/en/Publications/CR/Issues/2018/10/30/Bhutan-2018-Article-IV-Consultation-Press-Release-Staff-Report-and-Statement-by-the-46319 (accessed on 6 May 2021). [31]

IMF (2018), *Samoa : 2018 Article IV Consultation-Press Release; Staff Report; Staff Statement; and Statement by the Executive Director for Samoa*, https://www.imf.org/en/Publications/CR/Issues/2018/06/04/Samoa-2018-Article-IV-Consultation-Press-Release-Staff-Report-Staff-Statement-and-Statement-45934 (accessed on 24 June 2020). [37]

IMF (2017), *Indonesia : Selected Issues*, https://www.imf.org/en/Publications/CR/Issues/2017/02/11/Indonesia-Selected-Issues-44654 (accessed on 24 June 2020). [47]

Inland Revenue Board of Malaysia (2016), "Agriculture allowances public ruling no. 1/2016", http://www.hasil.gov.my/pdf/pdfam/PR_01_2016.pdf. [3]

IRAS (2021), *Supplies Exempt from GST*, Inland Revenue Authority of Singapore, https://www.iras.gov.sg/irashome/GST/GST-registered-businesses/Working-out-your-taxes/When-is-GST-not-charged/Supplies-Exempt-from-GST/. [45]

Keen, M. (2013), *The anatomy of VAT, WP/13/111*, International Monetary Fund, https://www.imf.org/en/Publications/WP/Issues/2016/12/31/The-Anatomy-of-the-VAT-40543. [48]

Keomixay, D. (2010), *Value Added Tax in Lao PDR: Agenda for the Future*. [43]

Ministry of Finance of the Cook Islands (2020), *COVID-19 Tax Updates - Cook Islands - Ministry of Finance and Economic Management*, http://www.mfem.gov.ck/rmd-tax/covid-19-tax-updates (accessed on 6 May 2021). [29]

Ministry of International Trade and Industry of Malaysia (2016), *http://www.miti.gov.my/index.php/pages/view/content5235.html*. [4]

NCCS (2020), *Carbon Tax*, https://www.nccs.gov.sg/faqs/carbon-tax/ (accessed on 22 June 2020). [52]

New Zealand Foreign Affairs & Trade (2018), "Aid partnership with Tokelau", https://www.mfat.govt.nz/en/aid-and-development/our-work-in-the-pacific/tokelau/. [56]

OECD (2021), *"Revenue Statistics in Asia and the Pacific: Comparative tables", OECD Tax statistics (database).* [24]

OECD (2021), *ERTR restricted database.* [60]

OECD (2021), *Global Revenue Statistics Database*, OECD Publishing, http://www.oecd.org/tax/tax-policy/global-revenue-statistics-database.htm. [15]

OECD (2021), *Revenue Statistics - Asian and Pacific Economies: Country tables, OECD Tax statistics (database).* [40]

OECD (2020), *Annual national accounts (database)*, https://stats.oecd.org/Index.aspx?DataSetCode=SNA_TABLE1. [50]

OECD (2020), *Consumption Tax Trends 2020: VAT/GST and excise rates, trends and policy issues*, OECD Publishing, Paris, https://doi.org/10.1787/152def2d-en. [46]

OECD (2020), *Database on Policy Instruments for the Environment*, https://pinedatabase.oecd.org/ (accessed on 15 June 2020). [51]

OECD (2020), *Revenue Statistics 2020*, OECD Publishing, Paris, https://dx.doi.org/10.1787/8625f8e5-en. [1]

OECD (2019), *Application of the Going for Growth Framework to Kazakhstan.* [36]

OECD (2018), *Making Development Co-operation Work for Small Island Developing States*, OECD Publishing, Paris, https://dx.doi.org/10.1787/9789264287648-en. [18]

OECD (2017), *Policy INstruments Environment*, http://oe.cd/pine (accessed on 15 June 2020). [59]

OECD (2014), *Development Co-operation Report 2014 : Mobilising Resources for Sustainable Development.*, OECD Publishing, Paris. [5]

OECD/AUC/ATAF (2020), *Revenue Statistics in Africa 2020: 1990-2018*, OECD Publishing, Paris, https://dx.doi.org/10.1787/14e1edb1-en-fr. [16]

OECD et al. (2021), *Revenue Statistics in Latin America and the Caribbean 2021*, OECD, http://dx.doi.org/10.1787/96ce5287-en-es. [17]

OECD, I. (2015), *Examples of Successful DRM Reforms and the Role of International Co-operation*, https://www.oecd.org/ctp/tax-global/examples-of-successful-DRM-reforms-and-the-role-of-international-co-operation.pdf (accessed on 17 May 2021). [33]

Parties to the Nauru Agreement (2016), "PNA members confirm: Vessel Day Scheme is here to stay", https://www.pnatuna.com/node/340. [57]

PEAKS, E. (2013), *Taxation and Developing Countries*, Overseas Development Institute training notes. [2]

PwC (2021), *Vietnam - Corporate - Taxes on corporate income*, https://taxsummaries.pwc.com/vietnam/corporate/taxes-on-corporate-income (accessed on 17 May 2021). [34]

Republic of Nauru (2021), *2021-22 Fiscal Strategy*, https://naurufinance.info/wp-content/uploads/2021/06/Nauru-Fiscal-Strategy-2021-22.pdf (accessed on 4 June 2021). [22]

Republic of Nauru (2020), *Quarterly budget performance report Quarter 4 2019-20*, https://naurufinance.info/wp-content/uploads/2020/08/GON-Quarterly-report-Q4-2019-20-20200812.pdf (accessed on 12 May 2021). [20]

Republic of Nauru (2020), *Republic of Nauru Government Gazette*, http://www.naurugov.nr/media/136527/gazette_234-20.pdf (accessed on 8 June 2021). [23]

Republic of Nauru (2019), *Employment and Service Tax Act.* [19]

UNCTAD (2012), *World Investment Report 2012, Towards a new Generation of Investment Policies, New York*, http://unctad.org/en/PublicationsLibrary/wir2012_embargoed_en.pdf. [7]

UNESCAP (2016), *Environmental Tax Reform in Asia and the Pacific*, https://www.unescap.org/sites/default/files/S2_Environmental-Tax-Reform.pdf (accessed on 25 June 2020). [54]

UNESCAP (2014), *Economic and Social Survey of Asia and the Pacific 2014, Regional Connectivity for Shared Prosperity*, UN, https://www.unescap.org/sites/default/files/Economic20and%20Social%20Survey%20of%20Asia%20and%20the%20Pacific%202014.pdf. [8]

WHO (2015), *Purchasing Power Parity 2005*, http://www.who.int/choice/costs/ppp/en/. [11]

World Bank (2021), *GDP growth (annual %) - Bhutan, World Development Indicators*, https://data.worldbank.org/indicator/NY.GDP.MKTP.KD.ZG?locations=BT. [32]

World Bank (2020), *"Central government debt, total (% of GDP)", World Development Indicators (database)*, https://data.worldbank.org/indicator/GC.DOD.TOTL.GD.ZS. [14]

World Bank (2020), *"Expense (% of GDP)", World Development Indicators (database)*, https://data.worldbank.org/indicator/GC.XPN.TOTL.GD.ZS. [13]

Notes

[1] This information was provided by the Tokelau Statistical Office during exchanges with the OECD Secretariat in preparation of this publication.

[2] This information was provided by the Ministry of Finance of China during exchanges with the OECD Secretariat in preparation of this publication.

[3] This information was provided by the Ministry of Finance of the Cook Islands during exchanges with the OECD Secretariat during the technical webinar held on April 8 2021.

[4] This information was provided by the Ministry of Finance of Bhutan during exchanges with the OECD Secretariat in preparation of this publication.

[5] Calculation based on data from WEO 2021 (IMF).

[6] Data for Bhutan and Fiji are only available from 2008, so the data used for both economies in this section are from 2008-18. Data for the Africa (26) average cover 2008 to 2017. In addition, 2018 data for Australia,

Japan and the OECD average are not available in (OECD, 2021[60]), so 2017 data are used instead. Nauru is excluded from this analysis as data are only available from 2014 onwards.

[7] Detailed data on SSCs for China were not available, but the OECD Secretariat estimates SSCs to be approximately 4.0% of GDP in 2018 based on publicly available data from China's Ministry of Human Resources and Social Security.

[8] For Nauru, it is not possible to distinguish between revenues from PIT and CIT.

[9] The ASEAN members not included are Cambodia, Myanmar and Brunei Darussalam.

[10] The low VRR observed in the Philippines is partly due to missing VAT revenue collected at customs as this revenue could not be distinguished from import duties.

[11] The constant very high VRR in New Zealand is caused by three factors. First, New Zealand operates a very broad GST tax base with limited exemptions and a limited use of zero rates. Second, New Zealand treats public services as GST taxable. Although this does not generate actual additional revenue, this increases the share of revenues from GST in total tax revenues, which has an upward effect on the VRR. Third, the potential GST base determined on the basis of the national accounts does not include the value added by the government (OECD, 2020[46]).

[12] Japan introduced a reduced rate on 1 October 2019.

[13] An environmentally related tax is a tax whose base is a physical unit (or a proxy of a physical unit) of something that has a proven, specific harmful impact on the environment regardless of whether the tax is intended to change behaviours or is levied for another purpose (OECD, 2005[33]).

[14] The figures in this report do not include revenues (that may be significant) from other policies addressing environmental issues such as fees and charges or revenues from emissions trading schemes. However the PINE database provides additional data on fees and charges, subsidies, voluntary approaches, tradable permits, deposit-refund systems for more than 80 countries (OECD, 2017[59]).

[15] Data on environmentally related tax revenue are presented for four tax-base categories: energy (including all CO_2 related taxes); transport (mostly motor vehicle taxes); pollution (e.g. discharges of waste or pollutants, taxes on waste or packaging); and resources (e.g. water extraction, hunting and fishing, mining) (OECD, 2017[59]).

[16] These figures need to be treated with caution as some environmentally related taxes may not be captured if the data are not sufficiently disaggregated.

2 Emerging Challenges for the Asia-Pacific Region in the COVID-19 Era

Chapter 2 is a special chapter summarising emerging challenges for the Asia-Pacific region in the COVID-19 era as well as key approaches and tools to achieve effective tax policy and administration reforms that support domestic resource mobilisation in the Asia-Pacific region.

Why does domestic resource mobilisation (DRM) matter for Asia and the Pacific?

The coronavirus (COVID-19) pandemic has caused a multidimensional health and economic crisis, and adversely affected businesses and households everywhere. To support businesses and households, fiscal policy has played a big role in the immediate response to the crisis and will continue to play an important role in the economic recovery from COVID-19. In Asia and the Pacific, developing countries' governments committed close to USD 3.7 trillion (ADB, 2021[1]) to respond to the pandemic as of March 2021 but even with this eye-wateringly large sum, economic losses for the region are estimated by the Asian Development Bank (ADB) at between USD 1.4 trillion to USD 2.2 trillion for 2020 alone (ADB, 2020[2]). ADB also estimates the region will lose up to 167 million jobs with 78 million more people falling into extreme poverty, undoing several years of progress in poverty reduction (ADB, 2021[3]). Income inequality, already a significant problem in the region, has become even more marked as the vulnerable, including women and informal workers, have suffered job losses and slumping incomes at a faster rate than other groups (ADB, 2021[4]). Policies have varied depending on the challenges each country faces, with measures ranging from increased public spending on health to enhanced unemployment benefits, business investment incentives, and direct cash transfers to the most vulnerable. Tax administration measures have also been widespread across the world, including Asia.

Figure 2.1 GDP growth ratios in the Asia and Pacific region, 2020-22

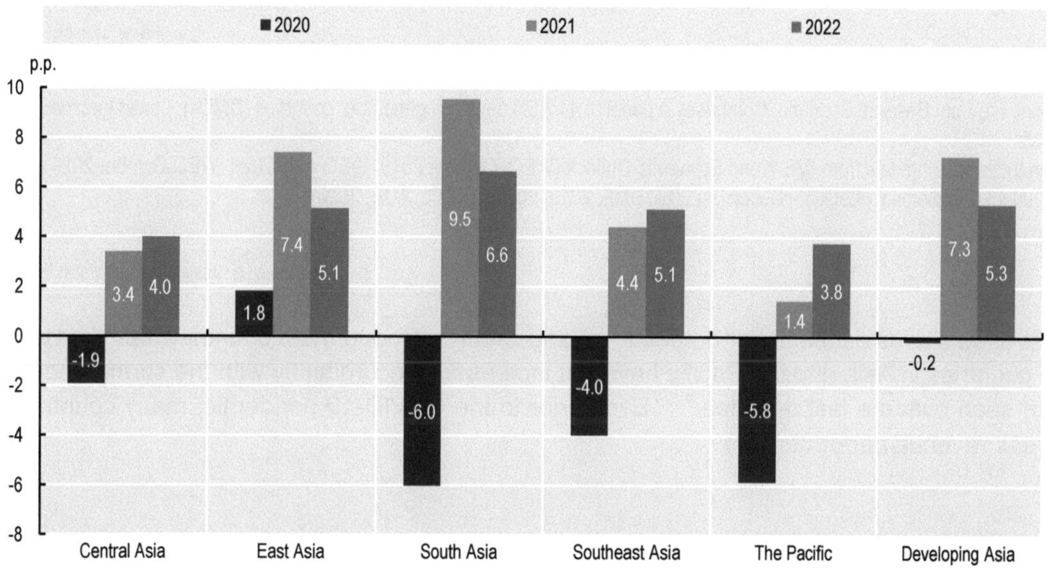

Source: ADB (2021), Asian Development Outlook (April 2021).

StatLink https://stat.link/e4ilnk

The COVID-19 crisis has adversely impacted tax revenue collections in countries in the Asia and Pacific region because of the economic slowdown and fiscal stimulus packages that included tax stimulus measures (ADB, 2021[4]). Growth of Asia-Pacific developing countries' gross domestic product (GDP) is projected to rebound to 7.3% in 2021 (ADB, 2021[5]), and to an extent, economic growth will recover revenue collection (Figure 2.1). However, the pandemic has exacerbated existing structural challenges in public finance. Unanticipated increases in public debt as a result of large fiscal measures to mitigate the impact of COVID-19, and shrinking tax revenues during the pandemic have worsened fiscal balances and created debt sustainability challenges in many developing countries in Asia and the Pacific (Figure 2.2).

These facts imply that there is little room left for these countries to further increase external borrowing and vividly remind us of the importance of enhancing domestic resources to address debt sustainability.

Figure 2.2. Public debt and fiscal balance in Asia-Pacific developing countries, 2019 and 2021

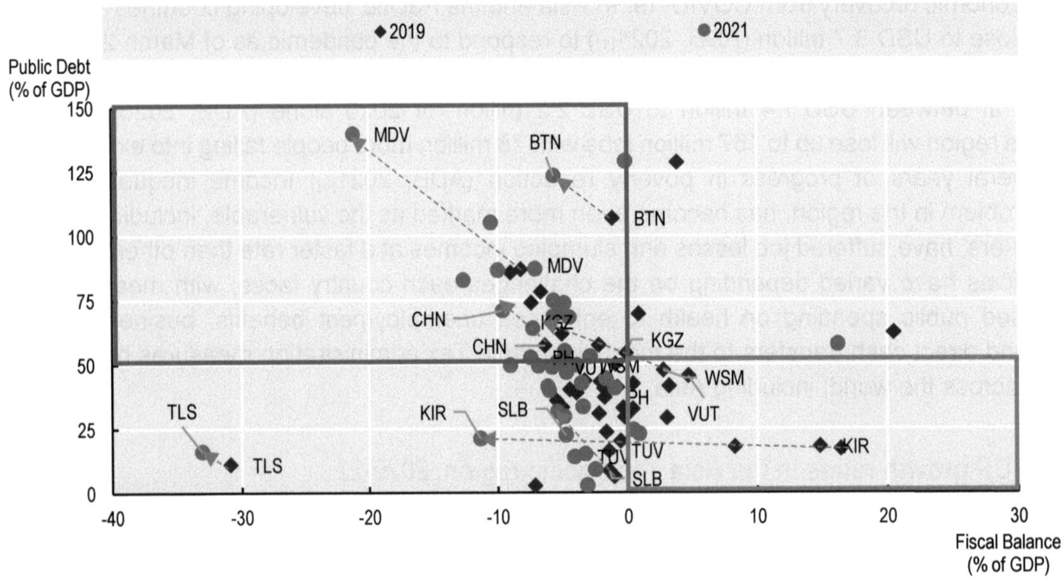

Notes: Projections are from Baseline Scenario. Comprises a panel of 44 ADB developing member countries (DMCs). Lower-income DMCs are shown with labels.

Source: ADB projections using data from IMF World Economic Outlook (WEO) October 2019, WEO April 2020, WEO October 2020 and Asian Development Outlook Supplement (ADOS) – December 2020 (IMF, 2019; 2020a; 2020b; ADB, 2020).

StatLink https://stat.link/40wiuv

While tax revenue serves as the major domestic revenue source among most countries, tax yields across developing countries in Asia and the Pacific have not increased concomitantly with the strong and steady GDP growth seen over the last decades.[1] Even prior to the COVID-19 pandemic, many countries had recorded weak revenue performance.

Figure 2.3. Comparisons of tax-to-GDP ratios, excluding social security contributions, in the Asia-Pacific region and the OECD, 2018

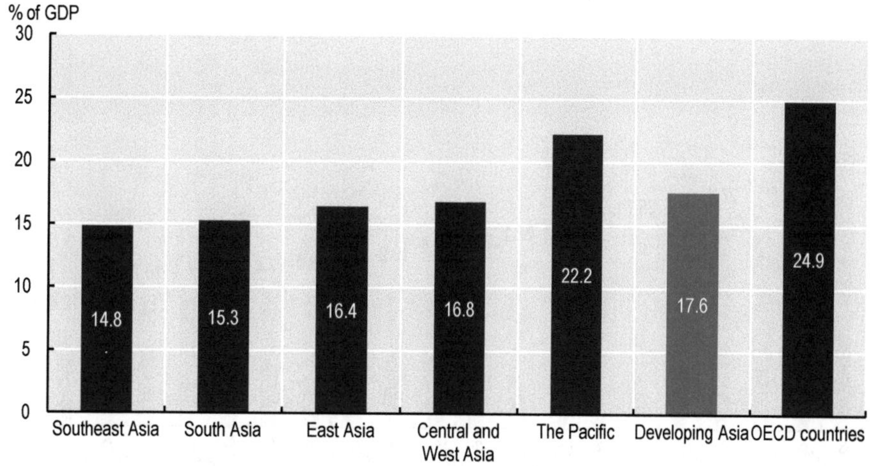

Note: Data do not include social security contributions.
Source: (ADB, 2021[6]) Key indicator database, (OECD, 2020[7]) Revenue Statistics, World Bank Open Data, and IMF Article IV Report

StatLink https://stat.link/e2ylq5

Tax yields across Asia-Pacific developing countries are still on average substantially lower than in OECD countries, and have also been comparatively volatile in recent years. (Figure 2.3). The tax-to-GDP ratio in several developing Asia-Pacific countries remains below 15% (Bhutan, Indonesia, Lao PDR, Malaysia, Papua New Guinea) (Figure 2.4), undermining governments' ability to provide a minimum level of public services to their citizens and to achieve development goals.

Overall, weaknesses are found in most tax types including personal income tax (PIT), corporate income tax (CIT) and tax on goods and services (Figure 2.4). In terms of PIT, many jurisdictions have numerous tax exemptions and concessions with overall low statutory tax rates on salary, wages and personal business income. Tax revenues from PIT in developing economies in Asia are lower than in advanced economies. Taxes on goods and services (e.g. value-added tax and excise tax) tend to dominate in some developing economies.

Aging populations will increase pressure on social security systems. However, financing for social security systems could be improved, as social security contributions are yet to be introduced in many countries or, even when in place, are often underutilised across the region. Similarly, the comparatively low use of recurrent taxes on immovable property may result in significant gaps in the revenue of subnational governments.

Figure 2.4. Comparison of tax revenue composition in the Asian and Pacific economies in 2019

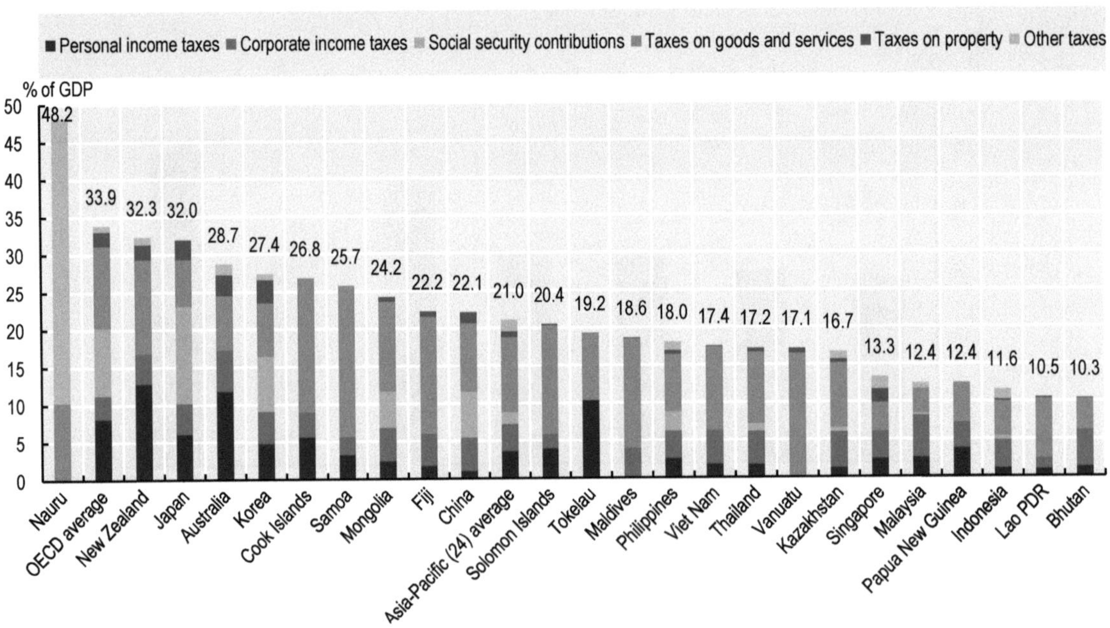

Source: OECD (2021), *Revenue Statistics in Asia and the Pacific 2021.*

StatLink https://stat.link/kyz5q7

These examples demonstrate the importance of careful revenue management and attention to underlying vulnerabilities. These issues require strong attention now because governments need to secure sufficient financial resources to contain the spread of COVID-19, procure safe and effective vaccines and healthcare, and get the economy back on a sustainable recovery track without losing market confidence.

Achieving the Sustainable Development Goals (SDGs) is also important for Asia and the Pacific as the region is falling short on all of them (Figure 2.5). The Economic and Social Survey of the United Nations Economic and Social Commission for Asia and the Pacific found that developing countries in Asia and the Pacific would need USD 1.5 trillion annually to end extreme poverty and ambitiously move toward universal health coverage, quality education, and infrastructure, while staying on track to limit climate change (UNESCAP, 2019[8]). However, this amount will likely increase because of the impact of COVID-19. In this regard, while the role of external finance is crucial in filling fiscal gaps, domestic resource mobilisation (DRM) will be a crucial pillar as SDG 17, which includes targets to strengthen DRM, is the foundation for achieving all of the other SDGs. Raising domestic resources is not only pivotal in providing a source of direct financing to contain the spread of COVID-19, procure safe and effective vaccines, and get the economy back to a sustainable recovery track without losing market confidence, but tax policy also offers governments the tools to achieve other specific goals under the SDGs.

Figure 2.5. Progress of 17 SDGs in Asia and the Pacific

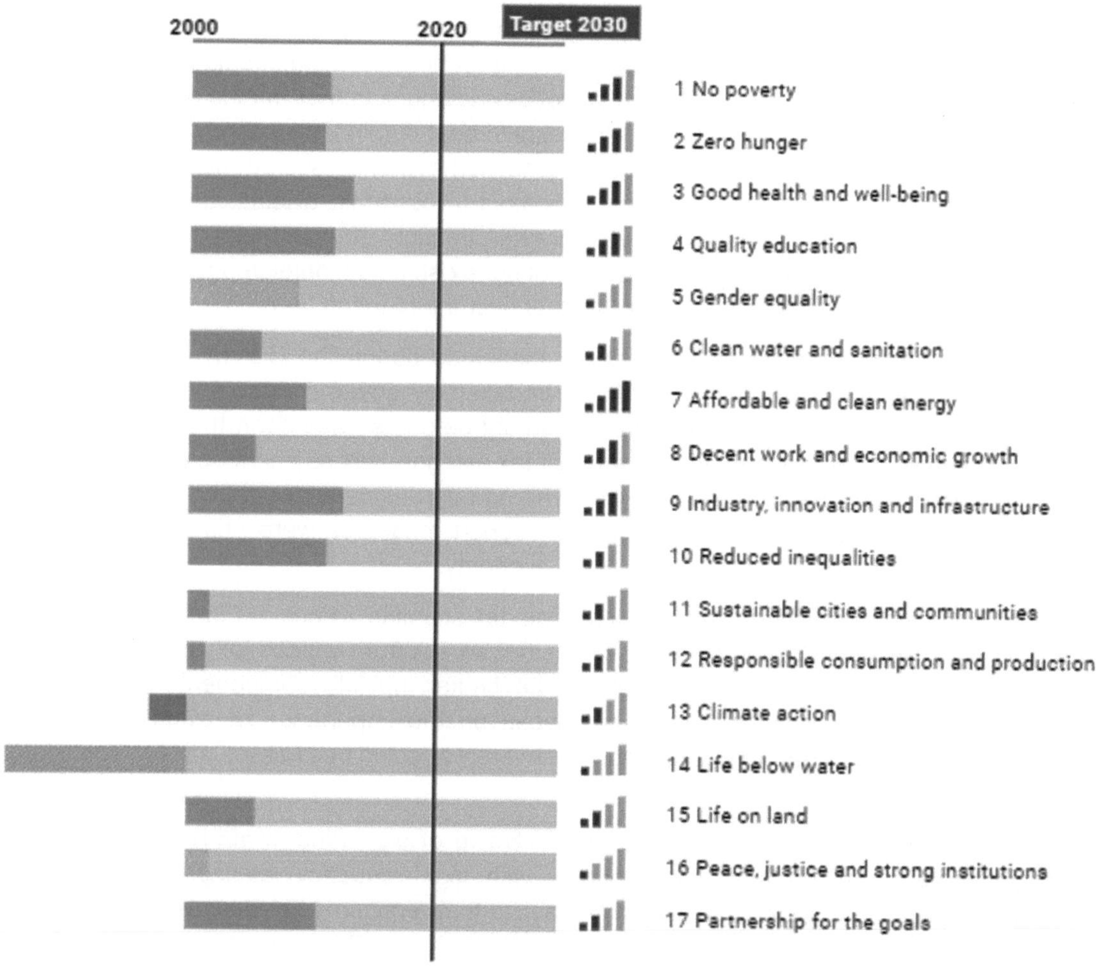

Source: (UNESCAP, 2021[9]), Asia and the Pacific SDGs Progress Report 2021.

Thus, DRM will continue to be a major strategic priority in the aftermath of COVID-19 for developing countries in Asia and the Pacific to address debt sustainability and to achieve the SDGs. In this regard, ADB considers DRM to be one of five strategic agendas to develop a prosperous, inclusive, resilient and sustainable Asia and the Pacific (ADB, 2021[10]).

While the timing of actual tax reform will vary among each economy, it is an appropriate time for developing countries in the region to begin their preparatory work through knowledge sharing and capacity building. To this end, consideration needs to be given to challenges emerging from the COVID-19 crisis, which include (i) removal of tax stimulus measures; (ii) growing income and social inequality; (iii) expansion of the informal economy (iv) addressing the tax challenges arising from the digitalisation of the economy. Other challenges include the need to finance well-functioning systems of social protection and measures that stimulate economic growth that is labour intensive, and the need to tackle climate change as well as measures to improve healthy behaviours of people.

Emerging Challenges from COVID-19 pandemic

Removal of tax measures

In the context of the pandemic, the optimal timing for the removal of the fiscal stimulus in place across countries including tax relief measures is never easy. Fiscal normalisation should be carefully calibrated and implemented in a phased manner. While many of developing countries in Asia and the Pacific may be considering reducing fiscal stimulus this year, they should bear in mind the lessons from premature fiscal consolidation after the global financial crisis. Such lessons have underscored the importance of looking closely at some of the leading, high frequency indicators to ascertain whether there are clear signs of recovery. Once visible signs of recovery and greater traction of economic growth are confirmed, governments can begin to consider easing or eliminating tax stimulus measures and strengthening DRM by restructuring tax policy to regain a balanced budget over the medium term.

According to the OECD database on country tax measures during the COVID-19 pandemic (OECD, 2021[11]), which provides a compilation of measures taken by governments of the countries covered, extension of time limits on the payment of taxes and tax deferrals have been the most widely adopted measures in the Asia and Pacific region. In the direct tax category, tax payment deferrals and tax waivers were the most used measures, whereas tax waivers and tax refunds were the most popular indirect tax measures. Available information suggests that tax support measures were primarily for the benefit of business enterprises and the production side of the economy.

Three issues need to be considered when exiting from tax stimulus. These are the what, when, and how of the exit. First, a decision must be taken as to whether an exit from various tax concessions can be put into effect simultaneously or if a withdrawal can be broken up into components of a package and implemented separately. Emphasis should be placed on the importance of avoiding the premature withdrawal of relief but of increasingly targeting it to severely affected businesses and households (OECD, 2021[12]).

Second, the government must carefully choose the timing of any withdrawal. Thus, it is necessary to monitor continuously the health of the economy with high-frequency leading/concurrent indicators, particularly for specific groups and sectors important to their economy.These indicators must fulfill two requirements: theyshould be available weekly or at least monthly and they should reflect broad macroeconomic trends. GDP estimates are the most comprehensive and obvious choice, and for fine-tuning policy responses, sectorial indices, employment trends, and consumer spending can also be tracked. It should also be kept in mind that it is not because economic activity has increased in a particular sector that businesses will be immediately viable again. It is expected that some firms will go bankrupt once their lifeline is cut. Measures like tax deferrals can be maintained for businesses that explicitly request them. Tax administrations also can be asked to develop payment plans for firms that have a large amount of deferred tax liabilities, or that are having problems surviving the crisis.

Third, the government has a choice of gradually winding down special concessions, or withdrawing them in full and going back to the normal tax structure (ADB, 2021[13]). Not withdrawing some of the tax deferral measures also creates a risk of “cliff-edge” effects (i.e., the deferred tax burden is so high that businesses decide to go bankrupt). More generally, there will be a need for policy flexibility, as continued restrictions are making conventional stimulus policies somewhat less effective and the timing of policy implementation more difficult.

Growing income and social inequality

The crisis could reverse years of progress toward eliminating poverty in developing countries in Asia and the Pacific. There are reasons to believe that the COVID-19 pandemic could worsen income inequality (Sawada and Sumulong, 2021[14]) and that efforts are needed to make tax systems more progressive to address the widening income gaps. To this end, governments could consider enhancing the progressivity of PIT systems, including through broadening the PIT base and abolishing the most regressive PIT tax expenditures, and could also consider other options to increase progressivity such as taxes on property.

Taxes on immoveable property, if well designed, are regarded as a good form of taxation for contributing to social equity because of their progressive nature. From an administrative perspective, taxes on immoveable property are also advantageous because they are difficult to avoid given the high visibility and immobility of land and buildings. Property tax can help the governments raise a more stable and predictable revenue stream. Moreover, property tax is often considered an appropriate tax to provide subnational governments with meaningful revenue autonomy in fiscally decentralised systems, and are an important revenue source to improve local service delivery. Hence, property tax can be a catalyst of local autonomy.

The revenue performance of property taxes not only remains low in developing countries in the region but also is further aggravated by rapid urbanisation in Asia-Pacific, which drives up residential property prices dramatically and will result in an increasing disparity between the actual market value of property and the assessed value captured under current property tax systems. This distorts revenue collection, which is already hampered by political capture, low-level fiscal decentralisation, institutional constraints, weak enforcement, and taxpayers' attitude to tax compliance. In combination, these factors constrain the stability and predictability of revenues for national and subnational governments.

Improving property tax management will also significantly impact the aspirations of many developing countries in Asia and the Pacific to honour the global commitments contained in the 2030 targets of the SDGs, particularly SDG 16.3 on a legal framework to ensure property rights, 16.10 on public access to information, and 17.1 on DRM. SDG localisation—described as the process of defining, implementing, and monitoring strategies locally to achieve global, national, and subnational SDGs—is required to accelerate the implementation of the SDGs and sustain it beyond 2030. It can be a key driver in addressing the critical challenges faced by countries and communities in Asia and the Pacific, which include rapid urbanisation, growing inequalities, and the impact of climate change and disasters. In this regard, improved real property valuations, poverty value and transaction databases, and land value capture policies are required.

Expansion of the informal economy

Informal economic activity is significant in the Asia and Pacific region. Most Asian revenue bodies reported in the 2018 International Survey of Revenue Administrations that the shadow economy is a concern and is rated among the higher compliance risks, with all but Viet Nam reporting a medium or higher risk rating (Figure 2.6). An examination of these ratings against the independent estimates of the size of the shadow economy would suggest that some revenue bodies may have underestimated the shadow economy risk as almost half of economies reported it as low or medium risk, while Indonesia clearly reported a focus on the shadow economy as part of its medium-term revenue strategy.

To address this risk, countries would need to define the shadow or informal economy as a first step. Often, tax administrations focus on whether firms are registrated or not, but other more subtle forms of informality such as only partly declaring income and the use of envelope wages, for instance, also fall under the informal economy and should be considered.

Although dealing with the shadow economy has in the past been especially vexed, emerging technologies enable new approaches that may support better management of unreported transactions and identification of unregistered businesses as well as under reporting or registration of workers. Maximising the use of these new capabilities, together with steps to accelerate trends away from the use of cash can be exploited to support more cost-effective monitoring and control of this risk. Strengthening system design features such as improving the revenue body's access to bulk data on financial and business transactions, facilitating information sharing (e.g., checking tax declarations with information given to the social security funds), increasing mandatory withholding and reporting, and enhanced data management capabilities, all have the potential to reduce opportunities to operate in the shadow economy.

Figure 2.6. Relative priorities of revenue bodies in Asian and the Pacific across compliance risk categories in 34 economies (2018)

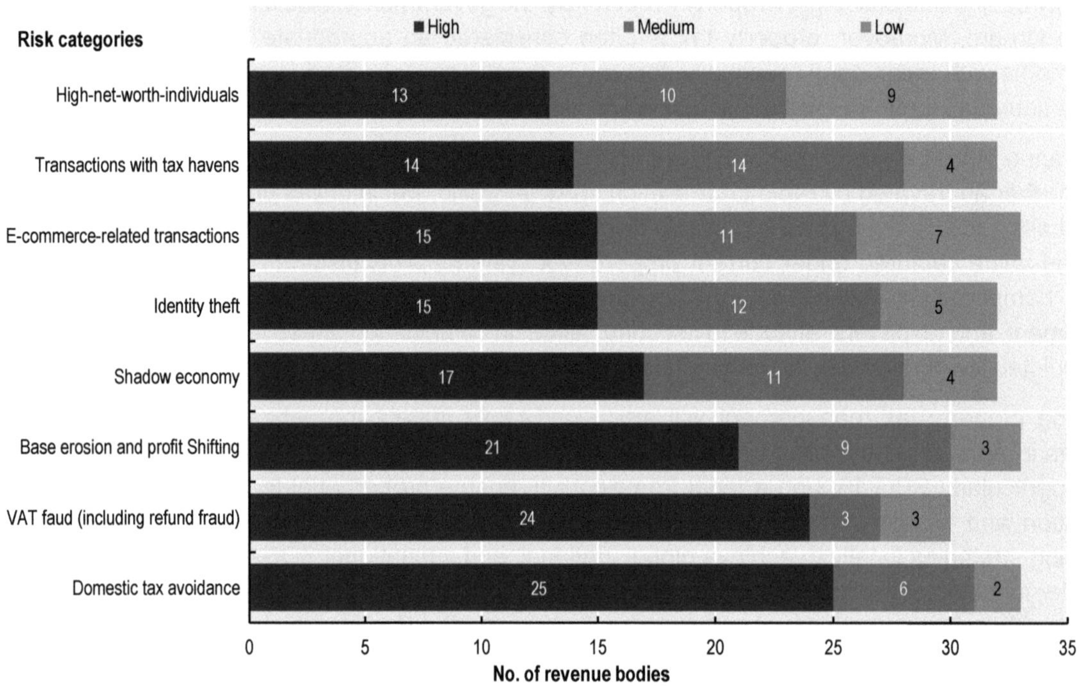

Source: 2018 International Survey on Revenue Administration

StatLink https://stat.link/0xdnwl

Addressing the tax challenges arising from the digitalisation of the economy

Addressing the tax challenges arising from digitalisation of the economy stands firmly at the top of the international tax policy and administration agenda. The existing international tax rules generally attach a taxing right to profits deriving from a physical presence in a jurisdiction. However, given globalisation and the digitalisation of the economy, businesses can, with or without the benefit of local physical operations, participate in an active and sustained manner in the economic life of a market jurisdiction. Weaknesses in the current rules create opportunities for base erosion and profit shifting (BEPS) and lead to under-taxation of certain highlight digitalised business models. This is particularly relevant to Asian and Pacific Economies where over the last decade, the digital economy is rapidly developing. According to a recent ADB study, the region accounted for about 48% of the world-wide digital economy (ADB, 2021[15]).

These challenges have been exacerbated by the increased digitalisation of the economy due to prolonged restrictions on physical movement of goods and people as a result of the COVID-19 pandemic. The OECD has been developing proposals to tackle the tax challenges of a digitalised economy based on a two-pillar approach: Pillar One proposes a new taxing right for market jurisdictions that would go beyond reference to physical presence and Pillar Two aims at creating a global minimum tax for Multinational Enterprises in order to address "remaining BEPS issues".

To tackle these challenges, exploring and reaching a multilateral, consensus-based solution will be required, so as to avoid increasing the use of uncoordinated unilateral measures, the occurrence of double taxation and undermining cross border trade and investments across Asia and the Pacific region as well as the world.

VAT is an important source of tax revenue for Asian and Pacific economies. The integrity and performance of these VAT regimes is therefore crucial for DRM in the region. The growth of e-commerce, which is expected to continue accelerating, may have significant implications for VAT policy and administration. These may notably include potentially significant threats for VAT revenues where online sales by offshore sellers remain untaxed under existing VAT systems as well as distortion of competition for compliant domestic suppliers. Economies in the region are therefore encouraged to assess the potential need for policy action to ensure that their VAT systems are adequately equipped to address the implications of e-commerce growth.

In this context, the internationally agreed standards and guidance for addressing the VAT challenges of digital trade developed by the OECD may provide the appropriate basis for VAT policy reform, as appropriate. This guidance includes rules and mechanisms to collect VAT from foreign online sellers, which have already been implemented with considerable success in more than 70 economies that have implemented them, including in developing economies. It also points in particular to the considerable opportunities created by the role of e-commerce platforms in enhancing the efficiency of VAT collection and of big data for greater visibility and traceability of economic activity and for formalisation of previously informal economic activity. It therefore holds considerable "quick-win" opportunities for DRM in Asia and the Pacific.

Economies in the region are encouraged to further consider these opportunities in light of their national circumstances, administrative capacities and policy priorities towards identifying tailored solutions that will allow them to enhance the efficiency and effectiveness of their VAT systems. To assist economies with their policy efforts in this area, the OECD is currently developing a VAT Digital Toolkit for Asia Pacific in close partnership with the World Bank Group and with the ADB as regional partner. This will provide guidance on the implementation of VAT reform to address the challenges of digital trade with a focus on the specific circumstances and design features of VAT systems in the region. It will be released by the end of the 2021.

Key approaches/tools for effective tax policy and administration reforms

Enhancing DRM is not straightforward. It requires long-standing efforts from countries, along with support from development partners. To achieve this ambitious agenda, governments need to implement tax policy and administration reforms that are specific to their circumstances and level of development. The following approach and tools will be of help in this regard.

Formulating a country-specific Medium-Term Revenue Strategy

A Medium-Term Revenue Strategy (MTRS) is a comprehensive approach to effective tax system reform to boost tax revenues over the medium-term through a country-led and whole-of-government approach (PCT, 2020[16]). The approach was developed in 2016 by the Platform for Collaboration on Tax, a partnership of the IMF, OECD, United Nations and World Bank.

An MTRS can help developing countries attain sustainable and effective tax system reforms. Such reforms often require a medium-term timeframe (5-10 years) to progressively reach the revenue objectives needed to achieve the 2030 deadline for full implementation of the SDGs. MTRSs require governments' commitment to lead the effort in reforming the tax systems, as it requires a wide range of government agencies and stakeholders beyond Ministry of Finance and Revenue Administrations. MTRSs can also serve as foundations for development coordination. In developing countries in Asia and the Pacific, the capacity to formulate and implement is limited. It is thus essential to bear in mind that external capacity development support can assist the government in establishing the MTRS (PCT, 2017[17]).

As mentioned above, Asian developing counties, like other regions, are addressing emerging challenges from the COVID-19 pandemic. The pandemic is changing the role of taxation in public policy, as tax measures are deployed to relieve the vulnerable in the immediate response to the pandemic and to ensure burden-sharing. Therefore, it is a particularly opportune time for developing countries in Asia and the Pacific to consider MTRSs.

As present, 25 countries are engaged in discussing, formulating or implementing an MTRS, of which 11 countries are from the Asia and Pacific region.

Acceleration of digital transformation of tax administration

Many tax administrations start the digitisation process by automating basic functions: electronic registration and filing. However, more countries, especially in Asia, are moving to the next stage in digital transformation: enabling real-time transaction data to flow into the tax administration directly (for example through a cash register function or an online-accounting system which is linked to the tax administration data collection system).[2] This element in the digital journey, once in operation, represents a large step towards seamless, continuous data flow which would raise compliance rates and significantly lower compliance and administrative costs.

Digital transformation and adoption in Asia and the Pacific tax administrations is as diverse as the level of capacity in each economy. Some of the globe's most technologically advanced economies are in the region (Australia, Japan, People's Republic of China, Republic of Korea, Singapore), which have integrated the use of artificial intelligence and predictive technologies and the audit and risk functions. The Republic of Korea, for example, is expanding the application of forensic and electronic audit schemes and use of big data analytics to examine potential tax avoidance by multinational enterprises and high net worth individuals. Eventually, most tax administration will embed integrated, digitised solutions and functions which can collect data from various sources, clean and filter it, and store it for risk and audit.

Tax administrations in this region are focusing on promoting e-filing and collection of digital financial statement information. In particular, economies in the Association of Southeast Asian Nations (ASEAN) are actively promoting or mandating e-filing. Many tax authorities in Asia and the Pacific are using digital solutions to improve taxpayer services, including the provision of a single platform or application for taxpayers to manage their tax compliance matters.

Proactive participation in international tax initiatives

In an increasingly integrated and globalised world, international tax cooperation is particularly relevant for developing countries in Asia and the Pacific; being able to access information from other jurisdictions is often vital for effective enforcement, while coordination on rules to regulate cross-border activities, especially of multinational enterprises (MNEs), is needed to limit opportunities for tax avoidance. While globally there has been a dramatic increase in international cooperation on tax issues since the global financial crisis in 2008,. progress in this region is still lagging. Many Asia-Pacific developing countries are still not participating in the Inclusive Framework on Base Erosion and Profit Shifting (BEPS). The rate of participation in the Global Forum on Transparency and Exchange of Information for Tax Purposes also shows room for improvement. These tendencies are also applicable to Multilateral Convention on Mutual Administrative Assistance in Tax Matters and Multilateral Convention to Implement Tax Treaty Related Measures to Prevent BEPS.

Since taxation is traditionally seen as a uniquely sovereign matter, governments may be reluctant to enter into international agreements that could potentially restrict that sovereignty. Cognisant of these tensions, many of the new tools and standards have sought to preserve sovereignty, while facilitating vital cooperation; for example the multilateral convention on mutual administrative assistance in tax matters enables exchange of information between all signatories, without any requirements to negotiate on withholding tax rates. Even where international cooperation could appear to impinge upon traditional concepts of sovereignty this is a false choice, because stepping away from international tax cooperation for the sake of protecting sovereignty will serve to erode sovereign powers by making BEPS and tax evasion easier. A failure to engage in international tax cooperation will also give rise to more unilateral tax measures, increasing the occurrence of double taxation and undermining cross-border trade and investments.

Figure 2.7. Status of participation of ADB developing member countries in international tax fora

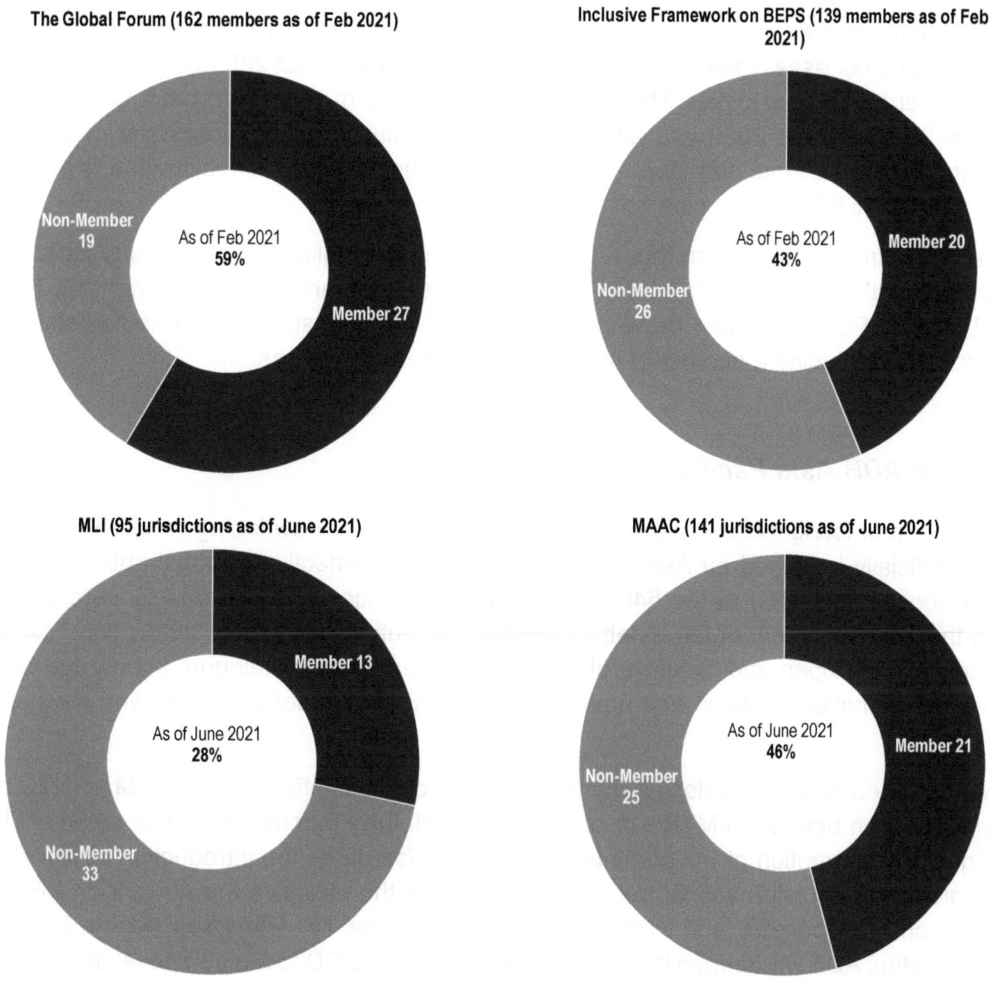

Note: : Global Forum = Global Forum on Transparency and Exchange of Information for Tax Purposes: BEPS = Base Erosion and Profit Shifting
Source: OECD

StatLink https://stat.link/37ytom

Alongside the expansion of membership of multilateral forums on tax, there has also been an increase in international capacity building initiatives, enabling Asian and Pacific countries to access expertise from both international organisations and other tax administrations (e.g. through Tax Inspectors Without

Borders). Such initiatives can have a significant impact, as shown by recent results in Mongolia (see Box 2.1)

Box 2.1. Mongolian Tax Administration issues first transfer pricing tax assessment for USD 228 million

Since 2019, the OECD, Tax Inspectors Without Borders (TIWB) and the Intergovernmental Forum on Mining, Metals and Sustainable Development (IGF) have been working with the Mongolian Tax Administration to strengthen revenue collection from the extractives sector, which contributed more than 80% of Mongolia's exports and 24% of fiscal revenues in 2019.

As a result of the mining tax audit capacity building initiatives, the Mongolian Tax Administration issued its first transfer pricing tax assessment in late 2020 for approximately USD 228 million and a denial of USD 1.5 billion in carried forward losses. The Tax Act ("tax assessment") was reported by the taxpayer's parent entity on 23 December 2020 and although the matter currently remains under dispute, this represents a significant milestone and step forward for the Mongolian Tax Administration in executing its strategy to combat BEPS in the mining sector.

The recent tax assessment builds upon focussed efforts by the Mongolian Tax Administration and the Ministry of Finance to align the country's tax rules and practices with international best practices. Having joined the OECD's BEPS Project and the Global Forum, Mongolia is successfully implementing the BEPS measures by introducing a number of international taxation provisions.

The launch of the ADB Asia Pacific Tax Hub

With the objective of promoting those key approaches and tools across developing countries in Asia and the Pacific, ADB officially launched an Asia Pacific Tax Hub as an effective regional hub on DRM and international tax cooperation (ITC) at the 54th Annual Meeting of the ADB Board of Governors in May 2021, following the announcement of the establishment of the Hub in September 2020. The Tax Hub is envisioned to serve as an open and inclusive platform for strategic policy dialogue, knowledge sharing, and development coordination between and among the ADB, ADB member countries, and development partners.

The Tax Hub will assist each ADB developing member country to define differentiated DRM and ITC goals, including three foundation blocks: an MTRS in collaboration with the Platform for Collaboration on Tax, a roadmap for digital transformation of tax administrations which facilitates the introduction of digital tools, and proactive participation in international tax initiatives such as the Inclusive Framework on BEPS and the Global Forum on Transparency and Exchange of Information for Tax Purposes (Figure 2.8). In this regard, through the Hub, ADB will deepen the collaboration with the OECD to support developing countries in Asia and the Pacific to address those emerging challenges and to stimulate proactive participation of those countries in international tax initiatives.

Figure 2.8. Key building blocks of the Tax Hub

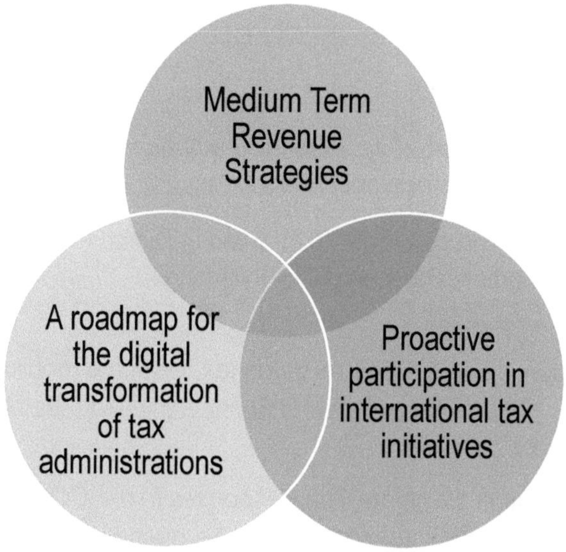

StatLink https://stat.link/uv2hif

References

ADB (2021), *ADB Annual Report 2020*, http://www.adb.org/ar2020/digital. [3]

ADB (2021), *ADB COVID-19 Policy Database*, https://covid19policy.adb.org/. [1]

ADB (2021), *Asian Development Outlook 2021: Financing a Green and Inclusive Recovery*, Asian Development Bank, Manila, Philippines, http://dx.doi.org/10.22617/FLS210163-3. [5]

ADB (2021), *Asian Economic Integration Report 2021: Making Digital Platforms Work for Asia and the Pacific*, Asian Development Bank, Manila, Philippines, http://dx.doi.org/10.22617/TCS210048-2. [15]

ADB (2021), "COVID-19 pandemic spurs Asia's focus on tax, resource mobilization reform | Asian Development Bank", https://www.adb.org/news/features/covid-19-pandemic-spurs-asia-focus-tax-resource-mobilization-reform. [4]

ADB (2021), *Exit Strategy to Ease or Eliminate Tax Responses to the COVID-19 Pandemic | Asian Development Bank*, https://www.adb.org/publications/exit-strategy-tax-responses-covid-19-pandemic (accessed on 21 June 2021). [13]

ADB (2021), *Key Indicators Database - Asian Development Bank*, https://kidb.adb.org/kidb/. [6]

ADB (2021), *Toward a Lasting and Equitable Recovery: ADB's Leadership and Country Presence during the COVID-19 Crisis - Masatsugu Asakawa | Asian Development Bank*, https://www.adb.org/news/speeches/toward-lasting-equitable-recovery-adbs-leadership-country-presence-covid-masatusugu-asakawa. [10]

ADB (2020), *The Impact of COVID-19 on Developing Asia: The Pandemic Extends into 2021 (ADB Brief No. 159)*, http://dx.doi.org/10.22617/BRF200367-2. [2]

OECD (2021), *Country tax measures during the COVID-19 pandemic*, https://www.oecd.org/tax/covid-19-tax-policy-and-other-measures.xlsm. [11]

OECD (2021), *Tax Policy Reforms 2021: Special Edition on Tax Policy during the COVID-19 Pandemic*, OECD Publishing, Paris, https://dx.doi.org/10.1787/427d2616-en. [12]

OECD (2020), *Revenue Statistics 2020*, OECD Publishing, Paris, https://dx.doi.org/10.1787/8625f8e5-en. [7]

PCT (2020), *PCT Progress Report 2020*, https://www.tax-platform.org/sites/pct/files/publications/Platform-for-Collaboration-on-Tax-PCT-Progress-Report-2020.pdf. [16]

PCT (2017), *Concept Note on the Medium-Term Revenue Strategy (MTRS)*, https://www.tax-platform.org/sites/pct/files/publications/MTRS%20Concept%20Note%20-%20Feb%206%202017.pdf. [17]

Sawada, Y. and L. Sumulong (2021), *ADBI Working Paper Series MACROECONOMIC IMPACT OF COVID-19 IN DEVELOPING ASIA Asian Development Bank Institute*, https://www.adb.org/publications/macroeconomic-impact-covid-19-developing-asia. [14]

UNESCAP (2021), *Asia and the Pacific SDG Progress Report 2021 | ESCAP*, https://www.unescap.org/kp/2021/asia-and-pacific-sdg-progress-report-2021. [9]

UNESCAP (2019), *Asia-Pacific SDG Financing Requirements and the Role of Cooperation*, https://www.unescap.org/sites/default/files/12_ESCAP-SDG%20Costing%20Cooperation.pdf. [8]

Notes

[1] According to the latest data available in the ADB Key Indicators Database, 17 out of 30 ADB developing member countries (DMCs) have experienced decrease of the ratio by more than 1% in the past 10 years, or stagnant (between -1% and 1%), while the 13 others have achieved significant progress with increase of the ratio by more than 1%.

[2] E-invoicing and real-time posting of data is a big step for tax administrations which are used to either paper or electronic filing submissions. In order for e-invoicing to work, taxpayer data—especially the tax id, name, and address must be entered exactly as was done during registration, as the first step within the tax administration system is to match the transaction to the taxpayers.

3 Tax levels and tax structure, 1990-2019

Comparative tables, 1990-2019

In all of the following tables a ("..") indicates not available. The main series in this volume cover the years 1990 to 2019.

Figures referring to 1991-99 in Table 3.1 and Table 3.2 and figures relating to 1998-99, 2001-06, 2008-09 and 2011-13 in Tables 3.5 to 3.20 have been omitted because of lack of space. Complete series are, however, available on line at OECD (2021), "Revenue Statistics - Asian and Pacific Economies: Comparative tables", OECD Tax statistics (database).

The OECD average is taken from *Revenue Statistics (2020).* Costa Rica was not an OECD Member at the time of preparation of this publication. Accordingly, Costa Rica does not appear in the list of OECD Members and is not included in the zone aggregates.

Table 3.1. Total tax revenue as percentage of GDP, 1990-2019

	1990	2000	2001	2002	2003	2004	2005	2006	2007	2008
Australia[1]	28.1	30.5	28.9	29.8	30.0	30.3	30.0	29.4	29.5	26.8
Bhutan	5.1	9.0	10.1	10.1	8.2	9.2	9.8	8.4	9.1	10.0
China[2]	..	..	..	..	..	..	..	..	16.9	17.0
Cook Islands	..	..	..	..	..	..	..	25.9	24.9	24.0
Fiji	..	..	..	..	..	..	..	..	..	22.2
Indonesia[3]	..	7.9	10.9	11.3	11.8	12.1	12.4	11.9	12.2	13.0
Japan[1]	28.2	25.8	25.9	24.9	24.5	25.2	26.2	27.0	27.5	27.4
Kazakhstan	..	19.9	22.2	20.5	22.7	21.7	25.5	26.1	26.1	27.6
Korea[1]	18.4	20.9	21.2	21.3	22.0	21.2	21.7	22.6	23.7	23.6
Lao PDR	..	..	..	..	..	..	..	..	..	..
Malaysia	18.5	14.1	18.3	18.3	16.3	15.9	15.5	15.1	14.8	15.1
Maldives	..	..	..	..	..	..	..	..	11.9	11.5
Mongolia	..	..	..	..	..	..	..	26.8	28.4	26.7
Nauru	..	..	..	..	..	..	..	..	..	..
New Zealand[1]	36.2	32.5	31.9	33.3	33.2	34.2	36.1	35.3	33.9	32.9
Papua New Guinea[4]	..	13.4	17.4	20.0	20.2	24.2	25.6	20.0	20.8	18.6
Philippines	..	15.3	15.1	14.5	14.5	14.0	14.6	15.8	15.6	15.6
Samoa	..	..	..	..	..	..	22.5	22.4	18.8	18.7
Singapore	..	15.2	15.1	12.9	12.3	12.0	11.8	11.8	13.2	14.0
Solomon Islands	..	..	..	..	..	..	..	..	15.3	16.6
Thailand	..	14.8	14.9	15.6	16.9	17.6	18.8	17.9	17.6	17.1
Tokelau	..	..	..	..	..	..	..	13.3	14.3	16.1
Vanuatu	..	16.2	16.3	16.4	16.3	16.9	17.1	17.5	19.0	19.2
Viet Nam	..	..	..	..	19.6	19.6	18.9	19.9	19.9	20.9
Africa (30) average[5]	..	..	..	..	..	..	..	..	..	..
Asia-Pacific (24) average[6, 7]	..	..	..	..	..	..	..	..	..	..
LAC average[8]	15.7	18.2	18.4	18.5	18.9	19.3	20.1	20.7	21.3	21.4
OECD average[1, 9, 10]	31.1	33.3	32.8	32.6	32.5	32.5	33.0	33.1	33.2	32.6

	2009	2010	2012	2013	2014	2015	2016	2017	2018	2019
Australia[1]	25.5	25.3	26.9	27.1	27.3	27.9	27.6	28.5	28.7	..
Bhutan	13.7	14.1	14.2	13.4	13.6	13.5	12.9	13.7	12.6	10.3
China[2]	17.1	17.8	18.7	18.6	18.5	18.1	17.5	17.4	17.0	22.1
Cook Islands	26.7	26.9	27.5	25.1	22.1	26.7	27.1	28.3	29.8	26.8
Fiji	21.6	21.6	23.8	23.7	22.7	23.6	23.1	24.2	23.5	22.2
Indonesia[3]	11.0	11.4	12.5	12.5	12.2	12.1	12.0	11.6	12.0	11.6
Japan[1]	26.0	26.5	28.2	28.9	30.3	30.7	30.7	31.4	32.0	..
Kazakhstan	21.2	23.8	23.9	22.6	21.1	15.5	14.9	16.0	17.0	16.7
Lao PDR	..	11.5	12.2	12.9	12.3	12.6	11.9	11.0	10.9	10.5
Korea[1]	22.7	22.4	23.7	23.1	23.4	23.7	24.7	25.4	26.8	27.4
Maldives	8.9	8.9	15.4	17.4	19.0	19.4	19.7	20.2	19.3	18.6
Malaysia	15.5	13.8	16.1	15.8	15.3	14.5	14.0	13.4	12.5	12.4
Mongolia	22.3	25.3	22.2	23.5	20.2	19.1	19.1	21.5	24.0	24.2
Nauru	..	..	..	..	8.4	23.2	15.7	29.0	35.4	48.2
New Zealand[1]	30.2	30.3	31.6	30.5	31.3	31.6	31.5	31.6	32.9	32.3
Papua New Guinea[4]	15.9	17.0	18.9	18.4	18.0	15.2	13.2	12.4	12.6	12.4
Philippines	14.4	14.2	15.1	15.5	16.0	16.2	16.3	16.8	17.4	18.0
Samoa	20.8	19.6	23.1	23.8	23.0	23.7	24.4	24.8	27.1	25.7
Singapore	12.4	12.5	13.5	13.2	13.4	13.1	13.0	13.8	12.9	13.3
Solomon Islands	16.5	18.9	23.4	23.3	23.0	23.1	21.6	22.5	24.1	20.4
Thailand	16.6	17.6	18.5	19.3	18.4	18.9	18.1	17.5	17.7	17.2
Tokelau	15.5	17.7	15.3	16.2	17.1	15.1	14.7	16.8	18.1	19.2
Vanuatu	17.6	16.3	16.6	17.2	17.4	16.3	15.3	17.1	17.8	17.1
Viet Nam	20.0	21.6	17.7	18.0	17.2	17.3	17.3	17.3	17.2	17.4
Africa (30) average[5]	15.0	15.1	15.8	16.1	16.4	16.5	16.4	16.5	16.6	..
Asia-Pacific (24) average[6, 7]	..	18.9	20.0	20.0	19.2	19.6	19.0	20.1	20.8	21.0
LAC average[8]	20.6	20.9	21.7	21.7	21.9	22.3	22.4	22.3	22.7	22.9
OECD average[1, 9, 10]	31.8	31.9	32.7	33.0	33.2	33.3	34.0	33.7	33.9	33.8

.. Not available

1. Australia, Japan, Korea and New Zealand are part of the OECD (37) group. Data for Australia, Japan, Korea, New Zealand and the OECD average are taken from OECD (2020), *Revenue Statistics 2020*.
2. 2007 to 2018: The tax-to-GDP ratio for China does not include revenues from social security contributions (SSCs) in these years as historical data were not available. SSCs are included in the data for China in 2019 (6.1% of GDP in that year).
3. Social security contributions data for Indonesia are only available for 2015-19 and are deemed negligible in earlier years.
4. Total revenues are not calculated for 2000 and 2001 as the data are incomplete and do not include customs revenues for these two years.
5. Represents an unweighted average for the 30 African countries included in the publication *Revenue Statistics in Africa 2020*.
6. Represents an unweighted average of the 24 Asian and Pacific economies in this publication. The Asia-Pacific (24) average should be interpreted with caution as data for social security contributions (category 2000) are not available or are partial in a few economies, including in Indonesia where SSC data are not available before 2015 and in China where SSC data are not available before 2019. The Asia-Pacific (24) average excludes Nauru prior to 2014 as data were not available. See the country tables in Chapter 4 for further information.

7. 2019: Data for 2018 are used for Australia and Japan in the calculation of the Asia-Pacific average in 2019 as data for 2019 are not available.
8. Represents an unweighted average for the 26 Latin American and Caribbean (LAC) countries included in the publication *Revenue Statistics in Latin America and the Caribbean 2021*.
9. 1990 to 2018: represents an unweighted average for the 37 OECD member countries included in the publication *Revenue Statistics 2020*.
10. 2019: calculated by applying the unweighted average percentage change for 2019 in the 35 countries providing data for that year to the overall average tax-to-GDP ratio in 2018.

StatLink https://stat.link/0qst4o

Table 3.2. Total tax revenue (excluding social security contributions) as percentage of GDP, 1990-2019

	1990	2000	2001	2002	2003	2004	2005	2006	2007	2008
Australia[1]	28.1	30.5	28.9	29.8	30.0	30.3	30.0	29.4	29.5	26.8
Bhutan	5.1	9.0	10.1	10.1	8.2	9.2	9.8	8.4	9.1	10.0
China	..	..	..	..	..	..	..	..	16.9	17.0
Cook Islands	..	..	..	..	..	..	..	25.9	24.9	24.0
Fiji	..	..	..	..	..	..	..	..	..	22.2
Indonesia	..	7.9	10.9	11.3	11.8	12.1	12.4	11.9	12.2	13.0
Japan[1]	20.7	16.7	16.5	15.4	15.1	15.7	16.6	17.1	17.5	16.8
Kazakhstan	..	19.9	22.2	20.5	22.7	21.7	25.4	25.9	25.7	27.2
Korea[1]	16.5	17.4	17.3	17.3	17.7	16.7	17.1	17.8	18.8	18.4
Lao PDR	..	..	..	..	..	..	..	..	..	..
Malaysia	18.5	13.8	18.0	18.0	16.0	15.7	15.2	14.8	14.6	14.9
Maldives	..	..	..	..	..	..	..	..	11.9	11.5
Mongolia	..	..	..	..	..	..	..	24.1	25.1	23.2
Nauru	..	..	..	..	..	..	..	..	..	..
New Zealand[1]	36.2	32.5	31.9	33.3	33.2	34.2	36.1	35.3	33.9	32.9
Papua New Guinea[2]	..	13.4	17.4	20.0	20.2	24.2	25.6	20.0	20.8	18.6
Philippines	..	13.3	13.1	12.4	12.5	12.1	12.8	14.0	13.8	13.8
Samoa	..	..	..	..	..	..	22.5	22.4	18.8	18.7
Singapore	..	15.2	15.1	12.9	12.3	12.0	11.8	11.8	13.2	14.0
Solomon Islands	..	..	..	..	..	..	..	..	15.3	16.6
Thailand	..	14.3	14.4	15.0	16.2	16.7	17.9	17.1	16.7	16.3
Tokelau	..	..	..	..	..	..	..	13.3	14.3	16.1
Vanuatu	..	16.2	16.3	16.4	16.3	16.9	17.1	17.5	19.0	19.2
Viet Nam	..	..	..	..	19.6	19.6	18.9	19.9	19.9	20.9
Africa (30) average[3]	..	..	..	..	..	..	..	..	..	..
Asia-Pacific (24) average[4, 5]	..	..	..	..	..	..	..	..	..	..
LAC average[6]	13.4	15.3	15.5	15.6	16.1	16.4	17.2	17.8	18.4	18.4
OECD average[1, 7, 8]	24.0	24.8	24.3	24.1	24.0	24.1	24.6	24.8	24.9	24.2

	2009	2010	2011	2012	2013	2014	2015	2016	2017	2018
Australia[1]	25.5	25.3	25.9	26.9	27.1	27.3	27.9	27.6	28.5	28.7
Bhutan	13.7	14.1	15.1	14.2	13.4	13.6	13.5	12.9	13.7	12.6
China	17.1	17.8	18.4	18.7	18.6	18.5	18.1	17.5	17.4	17.0
Cook Islands	26.7	26.9	24.7	27.5	25.1	22.1	26.7	27.1	28.3	29.8
Fiji	21.6	21.6	22.7	23.8	23.7	22.7	23.6	23.1	24.2	23.5
Indonesia	11.0	11.4	12.2	12.5	12.5	12.2	12.0	11.6	11.2	11.5
Japan[1]	15.3	15.6	16.1	16.5	17.1	18.3	18.6	18.3	18.8	19.2
Kazakhstan	20.7	23.2	25.0	23.3	22.0	20.5	15.0	14.4	15.5	16.4
Lao PDR	..	11.5	12.1	12.2	12.9	12.3	12.6	11.9	11.0	10.9
Korea[1]	17.4	17.2	17.6	17.8	17.0	17.1	17.4	18.3	18.8	20.0
Maldives	8.9	8.9	12.1	15.4	17.4	19.0	19.4	19.7	20.2	19.3
Malaysia	15.2	13.6	15.0	15.9	15.6	15.1	14.3	13.8	13.1	12.2
Mongolia	18.4	22.0	21.0	18.2	19.2	16.2	14.9	14.7	17.0	19.2
Nauru	..	..	..	..	..	8.4	23.2	15.7	29.0	35.4
New Zealand[1]	30.2	30.3	30.0	31.6	30.5	31.3	31.6	31.5	31.6	32.9
Papua New Guinea[2]	15.9	17.0	20.0	18.9	18.4	18.0	15.2	13.2	12.4	12.6
Philippines	12.5	12.4	12.7	13.1	13.5	13.8	14.0	14.0	14.5	15.0
Samoa	20.8	19.6	20.5	23.1	23.8	23.0	23.7	24.4	24.8	27.1
Singapore	12.4	12.5	12.9	13.5	13.2	13.4	13.1	13.0	13.8	12.9
Solomon Islands	16.5	18.9	22.2	23.4	23.3	23.0	23.1	21.6	22.5	24.1
Thailand	15.7	16.4	17.6	17.6	18.5	17.4	17.8	17.1	16.5	16.7
Tokelau	15.5	17.7	15.6	15.3	16.2	17.1	15.1	14.7	16.8	18.1
Vanuatu	17.6	16.3	16.4	16.6	17.2	17.4	16.3	15.3	17.1	17.8
Viet Nam	20.0	21.6	20.8	17.7	18.0	17.2	17.3	17.3	17.3	17.2
Africa (30) average[3]	..	14.6	15.3	15.2	15.5	15.7	15.8	15.7	15.7	15.5
Asia-Pacific (24) average[4, 5]	..	17.9	18.6	18.9	18.9	18.1	18.5	17.9	18.9	19.6
LAC average[6]	17.4	17.6	18.0	18.2	18.1	18.3	18.6	18.6	18.5	18.9
OECD average[1, 7, 8]	23.1	23.2	23.5	23.9	24.1	24.4	24.5	25.0	24.8	24.9

.. Not available

1. Australia, Japan, Korea and New Zealand are part of the OECD (37) group. Data for Australia, Japan, Korea, New Zealand and the OECD average are taken from OECD (2020), Revenue Statistics 2020.
2. Total revenues are not calculated for 2000 and 2001 as the data are incomplete and do not include customs revenues for these two years.
3. Represents an unweighted average for the 30 African countries included in the publication Revenue Statistics in Africa 2020.
4. Represents an unweighted average of the 24 Asian and Pacific economies in this publication. The Asia-Pacific (24) average excludes Nauru prior to 2014 as data were not available.
5. 2019: Data for 2018 are used for Australia and Japan in the calculation of the Asia-Pacific average in 2019 as data for 2019 are not available.
6. Represents an unweighted average for the 26 Latin American and Caribbean (LAC) countries included in the publication Revenue Statistics in Latin America and the Caribbean 2021.

7. 1990 to 2018: represents an unweighted average for the 37 OECD member countries included in the publication *Revenue Statistics 2020*.
8. 2019: calculated by applying the unweighted average percentage change for 2019 in the 35 countries providing data for that year to the overall average tax-to-GDP ratio in 2018.

StatLink https://stat.link/yuz1sc

Table 3.3. Tax revenue of main headings as percentage of GDP, 2019

	1000 Income & profits	2000 Social security	3000 Payroll	4000 Property	5000 Goods & services	6000 Other
Australia[1, 2]	17.3	0.0	1.4	2.7	7.3	0.0
Bhutan	6.1	0.0	0.0	0.0	4.2	0.0
China	5.5	6.1	0.0	1.4	9.1	0.0
Cook Islands	9.0	0.0	0.0	0.0	17.8	0.0
Fiji	6.0	0.0	0.0	0.7	15.5	0.0
Indonesia	4.9	0.5	0.0	0.2	4.7	1.3
Japan[1, 2]	10.2	12.9	0.0	2.6	6.2	0.1
Kazakhstan	6.0	0.5	1.0	0.5	8.6	0.0
Korea[2]	9.1	7.3	0.1	3.1	7.1	0.7
Lao PDR[3]	2.4	..	0.0	0.1	8.0	0.0
Malaysia[4]	8.5	0.3	0.0	0.0	3.2	0.4
Maldives	4.0	0.0	..	0.0	14.6	0.0
Mongolia	6.9	4.8	0.0	0.6	12.0	0.0
Nauru	37.9	0.0	0.0	0.0	10.3	0.0
New Zealand[2]	17.8	0.0	0.0	2.0	12.6	0.0
Papua New Guinea	7.2	0.0	0.0	0.1	5.2	0.0
Philippines	6.4	2.6	0.0	0.4	7.7	0.9
Samoa	5.7	0.0	0.0	0.0	20.1	0.0
Singapore	6.4	0.0	0.0	1.8	3.8	1.3
Solomon Islands[5]	5.9	0.0	0.0	0.1	14.4	0.0
Thailand	6.1	1.0	0.0	0.5	9.5	0.1
Tokelau	10.3	0.0	0.0	0.0	8.9	0.0
Vanuatu	0.0	0.0	0.0	0.6	16.5	0.0
Viet Nam[3]	6.3	..	0.0	0.0	11.1	0.0
Africa (30) average[1, 6]	6.2	1.4	0.1	0.3	8.7	0.1
Asia-Pacific (24) average[7]	8.6	1.6	0.1	0.7	9.9	0.2
LAC average[8]	6.2	3.9	0.2	0.9	11.4	0.4
OECD average[1, 2, 9]	11.5	9.0	0.4	1.9	10.9	0.1

.. Not available

1. Data for Australia, Japan, the Africa (30) average and the OECD average are for 2018.
2. Australia, Japan, Korea and New Zealand are part of the OECD(37) group. Data for Australia, Japan, Korea, New Zealand and the OECD average are taken from OECD (2020), *Revenue Statistics 2020*.
3. Heading 2000: SSC data are not available.
4. Heading 2000: Data are estimated.
5. The social security contributions in the Solomon Islands are null as they do not meet the social security criteria of the OECD classifications set in Annex A of the Interpretative Guide.
6. Represents an unweighted average for the 30 African countries included in the publication *Revenue Statistics in Africa 2020*.
7. Represents an unweighted average of the 24 Asian and Pacific economies in this publication. The Asia-Pacific (24) average should be interpreted with caution as data for social security contributions (category 2000) are not available or are partial in a few economies. Data for 2018 are used for Australia and Japan in the calculation as data for 2019 are not available. See the country tables in Chapter 4 for further information.
8. Represents an unweighted average for the 26 Latin American and Caribbean (LAC) countries included in the publication *Revenue Statistics in Latin America and the Caribbean 2021*.
9. Represents an unweighted average for the 37 OECD member countries included in the publication *Revenue Statistics 2020*. Data for 2018 are used as a complete breakdown in 2019 is not available.

StatLink https://stat.link/uv0t43

Table 3.4. Tax revenue of main headings as percentage of total taxation, 2019

	1000 Income & profits	2000 Social security	3000 Payroll	4000 Property	5000 Goods & services	6000 Other
Australia[1, 2]	60.2	0.0	4.8	9.5	25.5	0.0
Bhutan	59.5	0.0	-0.2	0.1	40.6	0.0
China	24.9	27.5	0.0	6.4	41.3	0.0
Cook Islands	33.6	0.0	0.0	0.0	66.4	0.0
Fiji	27.0	0.0	0.0	3.0	70.0	0.0
Indonesia	42.1	4.3	0.0	1.5	40.6	11.5
Japan[1, 2]	31.9	40.2	0.0	8.1	19.5	0.3
Kazakhstan	36.3	3.2	6.0	2.8	51.8	0.0
Korea[2]	33.2	26.7	0.3	11.4	25.8	2.5
Lao PDR[3]	22.4	..	0.0	1.2	76.4	0.0
Malaysia[4]	68.2	2.4	0.0	0.0	26.0	3.4
Maldives	21.3	0.0	..	0.2	78.5	0.0
Mongolia	28.3	19.8	0.0	2.5	49.5	0.0
Nauru	78.6	0.0	0.0	0.0	21.4	0.0
New Zealand[2]	55.0	0.0	0.0	6.2	38.9	0.0
Papua New Guinea	57.6	0.0	0.0	0.4	42.0	0.0
Philippines	35.7	14.2	0.0	2.5	42.5	5.1
Samoa	22.0	0.0	0.0	0.0	78.0	0.0
Singapore	48.1	0.0	0.0	13.2	28.8	9.9
Solomon Islands[5]	28.8	0.0	0.0	0.6	70.6	0.0
Thailand	35.6	5.9	0.0	2.7	55.1	0.7
Tokelau	53.7	0.0	0.0	0.0	46.3	0.0
Vanuatu	0.0	0.0	0.0	3.6	96.5	0.0
Viet Nam[3]	36.1	..	0.0	0.2	63.7	0.0
Africa (30) average[1, 6]	38.7	7.2	0.9	1.6	51.9	1.1
Asia-Pacific (24) average[7]	39.2	6.6	0.5	3.2	49.8	1.4
LAC average[8]	27.0	17.1	0.8	3.8	49.8	1.5
OECD average[1, 2, 9]	34.3	25.7	1.2	5.6	32.7	0.5

.. Not available

1. Data for Australia, Japan, the Africa (30) average and the OECD average are for 2018.
2. Australia, Japan, Korea and New Zealand are part of the OECD(37) group. Data for Australia, Japan, Korea, New Zealand and the OECD average are taken from OECD (2020), *Revenue Statistics 2020*.
3. Heading 2000: SSC data are not available.
4. Heading 2000: Data are estimated.
5. The social security contributions in the Solomon Islands are null as they do not meet the social security criteria of the OECD classifications set in Annex A of the Interpretative Guide.
6. Represents an unweighted average for the 30 African countries included in the publication *Revenue Statistics in Africa 2020*.
7. Represents an unweighted average of the 24 Asian and Pacific economies in this publication. The Asia-Pacific (24) average should be interpreted with caution as data for social security contributions (category 2000) are not available or are partial in a few economies. Data for 2018 are used for Australia and Japan in the calculation as data for 2019 are not available. See the country tables in Chapter 4 for further information.
8. Represents an unweighted average for the 26 Latin American and Caribbean (LAC) countries included in the publication *Revenue Statistics in Latin America and the Caribbean 2021*.
9. Represents an unweighted average for the 37 OECD member countries included in the publication *Revenue Statistics 2020*. Data for 2018 are used as a complete breakdown in 2019 is not available.

StatLink https://stat.link/canh91

Table 3.5. Taxes on income and profits (1000) as percentage of GDP

	1997	2000	2007	2010	2014	2015	2016	2017	2018	2019
Australia[1]	16.2	17.6	17.5	14.3	15.8	15.8	15.8	16.8	17.3	..
Bhutan	4.6	5.9	5.0	9.0	7.8	7.6	6.8	6.8	6.5	6.1
China	..	..	4.6	4.6	5.6	5.7	5.8	5.9	6.0	5.5
Cook Islands	..	..	9.8	10.6	5.7	9.4	9.1	10.3	11.5	9.0
Fiji	..	..	..	7.1	5.6	6.1	7.1	7.6	6.6	6.0
Indonesia	3.6	3.8	5.5	5.2	5.2	5.2	5.4	4.8	5.1	4.9
Japan[1]	9.7	9.0	10.0	8.0	9.6	9.6	9.4	9.6	10.2	..
Kazakhstan	..	8.3	14.0	9.5	7.8	6.0	5.6	5.8	6.4	6.0
Korea[1]	4.9	6.0	7.5	6.3	6.8	7.2	7.7	8.1	9.1	9.1
Lao PDR	..	..	..	2.6	2.7	2.9	2.6	2.5	2.4	2.4
Malaysia	9.8	7.7	9.9	9.1	10.9	9.0	8.3	8.0	8.6	8.5
Maldives	..	..	0.7	0.6	5.2	5.0	4.8	4.6	4.0	4.0
Mongolia	..	..	13.1	10.0	5.0	5.1	4.4	5.8	6.5	6.9
Nauru	..	..	..	..	0.0	12.1	9.2	18.8	24.8	37.9
New Zealand[1]	20.3	19.5	21.3	16.3	17.1	17.3	17.5	17.6	18.5	17.8
Papua New Guinea	..	9.6	15.1	11.8	12.1	9.9	8.1	7.5	7.7	7.2
Philippines	5.9	5.9	6.3	5.6	6.4	6.5	6.6	6.7	6.2	6.4
Samoa	..	..	4.4	4.8	5.6	5.5	5.5	5.5	6.2	5.7
Singapore	..	8.0	6.0	5.6	5.9	5.8	5.9	6.7	6.0	6.4
Solomon Islands	..	..	3.5	5.7	6.3	7.0	6.3	6.7	6.3	5.9
Thailand	..	4.7	7.0	6.4	6.7	6.6	6.2	5.9	6.0	6.1
Tokelau	..	..	6.8	9.0	8.2	7.7	8.0	9.4	8.6	10.3
Vanuatu	..	0.0	0.0	0.0	0.0	0.0	0.0	0.0	0.0	0.0
Viet Nam	..	..	9.0	8.1	6.5	6.1	5.7	5.9	6.2	6.3
Africa (30) average[2]	..	..	..	5.8	6.4	6.3	6.1	6.1	6.2	..
Asia-Pacific (24) average[3]	..	..	..	7.4	7.0	7.5	7.2	7.8	8.2	8.6
LAC average[4]	3.7	4.2	5.8	5.6	6.0	6.0	5.8	5.8	6.1	6.2
OECD average[1, 5]	11.3	11.7	11.9	10.4	11.1	11.1	11.1	11.4	11.5	..

.. Not available

1. Australia, Japan, Korea and New Zealand are part of the OECD (37) group. Data for Australia, Japan, Korea, New Zealand and the OECD average are taken from OECD (2020), *Revenue Statistics 2020*.
2. Represents an unweighted average for the 30 African countries included in the publication *Revenue Statistics in Africa 2020*.
3. Represents an unweighted average of the 24 Asian and Pacific economies in this publication. Data for 2018 are used for Australia and Japan in the calculation as data for 2019 are not available. See the country tables in Chapter 4 for further information.
4. Represents an unweighted average for the 26 Latin American and Caribbean (LAC) countries included in the publication *Revenue Statistics in Latin America and the Caribbean 2021*.
5. Represents an unweighted average for the 37 OECD member countries included in the publication *Revenue Statistics 2020*.

StatLink https://stat.link/6ki4bo

Table 3.6. Taxes on income and profits (1000) as percentage of total taxation

	1997	2000	2007	2010	2014	2015	2016	2017	2018	2019
Australia[1]	56.6	57.9	59.3	56.5	57.8	56.6	57.2	58.8	60.2	..
Bhutan	53.6	65.7	55.2	64.0	57.5	55.8	52.7	49.8	51.7	59.5
China[2]	..	..	..	..	..	..	..	..	..	24.9
Cook Islands	..	..	39.2	39.4	25.6	35.0	33.5	36.6	38.6	33.6
Fiji	..	..	..	32.6	24.7	25.8	30.6	31.5	28.1	27.0
Indonesia	47.2	47.7	45.1	45.8	42.5	43.1	44.7	41.0	42.2	42.1
Japan[1]	37.0	34.8	36.4	30.2	31.8	31.2	30.6	30.7	31.9	..
Kazakhstan	..	41.4	53.7	40.0	37.2	38.8	37.3	36.0	37.9	36.3
Korea[1]	26.2	28.8	31.8	28.0	29.1	30.3	31.2	32.1	34.1	33.2
Lao PDR	..	..	..	22.7	22.3	22.7	21.9	23.1	22.3	22.4
Malaysia	49.8	54.6	66.6	66.1	71.0	61.9	59.3	60.1	68.5	68.2
Maldives	..	..	5.9	6.9	27.4	26.0	24.4	22.6	20.7	21.3
Mongolia	..	..	46.1	39.5	24.6	26.5	22.8	26.9	26.8	28.3
Nauru	..	..	..	..	0.0	52.2	58.7	64.9	70.2	78.6
New Zealand[1]	59.8	60.0	62.9	53.8	54.6	54.9	55.6	55.6	56.3	55.0
Papua New Guinea	..	71.7	73.0	69.4	67.0	65.2	61.4	60.9	61.3	57.6
Philippines	36.6	38.6	40.4	39.2	39.8	40.3	40.4	39.8	35.4	35.7
Samoa	..	..	23.6	24.7	24.4	23.1	22.8	22.1	23.0	22.0
Singapore	..	52.8	45.4	44.7	44.2	44.7	44.9	48.3	46.6	48.1
Solomon Islands	..	..	23.1	30.3	27.4	30.1	29.1	29.6	26.3	28.8
Thailand	..	31.8	39.6	36.5	36.6	34.9	34.4	33.4	34.1	35.6
Tokelau	..	..	47.8	51.1	48.1	51.1	54.6	55.8	47.3	53.7
Vanuatu	..	0.0	0.0	0.0	0.0	0.0	0.0	0.0	0.0	0.0
Viet Nam	..	..	45.1	37.5	37.7	35.4	32.7	34.1	36.2	36.1
Africa (30) average[3]	..	..	..	39.1	40.2	39.1	38.1	38.1	38.7	..
Asia-Pacific (24) average[4]	..	..	..	39.0	36.1	38.5	38.3	38.9	39.1	39.2
LAC average[5]	21.2	22.2	26.8	26.3	27.0	26.7	26.4	26.3	26.9	27.0
OECD average[1, 6]	33.7	34.5	35.7	32.6	33.3	33.6	33.1	33.9	34.3	..

.. Not available

1. Australia, Japan, Korea and New Zealand are part of the OECD (37) group. Data for Australia, Japan, Korea, New Zealand and the OECD average are taken from OECD (2020), *Revenue Statistics 2020*.
2. 2007 to 2018: Data for China are not included in this table as historical data on revenues from social security contributions are not available.
3. Represents an unweighted average for the 30 African countries included in the publication *Revenue Statistics in Africa 2020*.
4. Represents an unweighted average of the 24 Asian and Pacific economies in this publication. The Asia-Pacific (24) average should be interpreted with caution as data for social security contributions (category 2000) are not available or are partial in a few economies. Data for 2018 are used for Australia and Japan in the calculation as data for 2019 are not available. See the country tables in Chapter 4 for further information.
5. Represents an unweighted average for the 26 Latin American and Caribbean (LAC) countries included in the publication *Revenue Statistics in Latin America and the Caribbean 2021*.
6. Represents an unweighted average for the 37 OECD member countries included in the publication *Revenue Statistics 2020*.

StatLink https://stat.link/36e1g2

Table 3.7. Social security contributions (2000) as percentage of GDP

	1997	2000	2007	2010	2014	2015	2016	2017	2018	2019
Australia[1]	0.0	0.0	0.0	0.0	0.0	0.0	0.0	0.0	0.0	..
Bhutan	0.0	0.0	0.0	0.0	0.0	0.0	0.0	0.0	0.0	0.0
China[2]	..	..	..	..	..	..	..	..	..	6.1
Cook Islands	..	..	0.0	0.0	0.0	0.0	0.0	0.0	0.0	0.0
Fiji	..	..	..	0.0	0.0	0.0	0.0	0.0	0.0	0.0
Indonesia[3]	..	..	..	..	..	0.1	0.4	0.4	0.4	0.5
Japan[1]	9.0	9.1	10.0	10.9	12.0	12.1	12.4	12.5	12.9	..
Kazakhstan	..	0.0	0.4	0.6	0.6	0.6	0.6	0.5	0.5	0.5
Korea[1]	2.7	3.5	4.9	5.2	6.3	6.3	6.5	6.5	6.8	7.3
Lao PDR	..	..	..	..	..	..	..	..	..	..
Malaysia[4]	..	0.3	0.3	0.2	0.2	0.2	0.3	0.3	0.3	0.3
Maldives	..	..	0.0	0.0	0.0	0.0	0.0	0.0	0.0	0.0
Mongolia	..	..	3.2	3.3	3.9	4.2	4.4	4.5	4.8	4.8
Nauru	..	..	..	..	0.0	0.0	0.0	0.0	0.0	0.0
New Zealand[1]	0.0	0.0	0.0	0.0	0.0	0.0	0.0	0.0	0.0	0.0
Papua New Guinea	..	0.0	0.0	0.0	0.0	0.0	0.0	0.0	0.0	0.0
Philippines	1.3	2.0	1.8	1.8	2.2	2.3	2.3	2.2	2.4	2.6
Samoa	..	..	0.0	0.0	0.0	0.0	0.0	0.0	0.0	0.0
Singapore	..	0.0	0.0	0.0	0.0	0.0	0.0	0.0	0.0	0.0
Solomon Islands[5]	..	..	0.0	0.0	0.0	0.0	0.0	0.0	0.0	0.0
Thailand	..	0.5	0.9	1.2	1.0	1.1	1.0	1.0	1.0	1.0
Tokelau	..	..	0.0	0.0	0.0	0.0	0.0	0.0	0.0	0.0
Vanuatu	..	0.0	0.0	0.0	0.0	0.0	0.0	0.0	0.0	0.0
Viet Nam	..	..	..	..	..	..	..	..	..	..
Africa (30) average[6]	..	..	..	1.3	1.3	1.3	1.3	1.4	1.4	..
Asia-Pacific (24) average[7]	..	..	..	1.2	1.3	1.3	1.3	1.3	1.4	1.6
LAC average[8]	2.7	2.9	2.9	3.3	3.6	3.8	3.8	3.8	3.8	3.9
OECD average[1, 9]	8.6	8.4	8.3	8.7	8.8	8.8	9.0	8.9	9.0	..

.. Not available

1. Australia, Japan, Korea and New Zealand are part of the OECD (37) group. Data for Australia, Japan, Korea, New Zealand and the OECD average are taken from OECD (2020), Revenue Statistics 2020.
2. 2007 to 2018: Data for China are not included in this table as historical data on revenues from social security contributions are not available.
3. Social security contributions data for Indonesia are only available for 2015 to 2019 and are deemed negligible in earlier years.
4. Heading 2000: Data are estimated for 2019.
5. The social security contributions in the Solomon Islands are null as they do not meet the social security criteria of the OECD classifications set in Annex A of the Interpretative Guide.
6. Represents an unweighted average for the 30 African countries included in the publication Revenue Statistics in Africa 2020.
7. Represents an unweighted average of the 24 Asian and Pacific economies in this publication. The Asia-Pacific (24) average should be interpreted with caution as data for social security contributions (category 2000) are not available or are partial in a few economies. Data for 2018 are used for Australia and Japan in the calculation as data for 2019 are not available. See the country tables in Chapter 4 for further information.
8. Represents an unweighted average for the 26 Latin American and Caribbean (LAC) countries included in the publication Revenue Statistics in Latin America and the Caribbean 2021.
9. Represents an unweighted average for the 37 OECD member countries included in the publication Revenue Statistics 2020.

StatLink https://stat.link/uoj08y

Table 3.8. Social security contributions (2000) as percentage of total taxation

	1997	2000	2007	2010	2014	2015	2016	2017	2018	2019
Australia[1]	0.0	0.0	0.0	0.0	0.0	0.0	0.0	0.0	0.0	..
Bhutan	0.0	0.0	0.0	0.0	0.0	0.0	0.0	0.0	0.0	0.0
China[2]	..	..	..	..	..	..	..	..	..	27.5
Cook Islands	..	..	0.0	0.0	0.0	0.0	0.0	0.0	0.0	0.0
Fiji	..	..	..	0.0	0.0	0.0	0.0	0.0	0.0	0.0
Indonesia[3]	..	..	..	..	..	0.6	3.2	3.4	3.6	4.3
Japan[1]	34.3	35.2	36.5	41.1	39.7	39.4	40.4	39.9	40.2	..
Kazakhstan	..	0.0	1.5	2.5	2.7	3.8	3.8	3.2	3.2	3.2
Korea[1]	14.2	16.7	20.7	23.3	26.9	26.6	26.2	25.7	25.4	26.7
Lao PDR	..	..	..	..	..	..	..	..	..	..
Malaysia[4]	..	2.0	1.7	1.8	1.6	1.7	1.8	1.9	2.4	2.4
Maldives	..	..	0.0	0.0	0.0	0.0	0.0	0.0	0.0	0.0
Mongolia	..	..	11.4	13.1	19.4	22.0	23.2	21.0	20.1	19.8
Nauru	..	..	..	..	0.0	0.0	0.0	0.0	0.0	0.0
New Zealand[1]	0.0	0.0	0.0	0.0	0.0	0.0	0.0	0.0	0.0	0.0
Papua New Guinea	..	0.0	0.0	0.0	0.0	0.0	0.0	0.0	0.0	0.0
Philippines	8.1	13.1	11.8	12.7	13.5	14.1	14.0	13.4	13.7	14.2
Samoa	..	..	0.0	0.0	0.0	0.0	0.0	0.0	0.0	0.0
Singapore	..	0.0	0.0	0.0	0.0	0.0	0.0	0.0	0.0	0.0
Solomon Islands[5]	..	..	0.0	0.0	0.0	0.0	0.0	0.0	0.0	0.0
Thailand	..	3.7	5.1	7.1	5.3	5.6	5.6	5.7	5.7	5.9
Tokelau	..	..	0.0	0.0	0.0	0.0	0.0	0.0	0.0	0.0
Vanuatu	..	0.0	0.0	0.0	0.0	0.0	0.0	0.0	0.0	0.0
Viet Nam	..	..	..	..	..	..	..	..	..	..
Africa (30) average[6]	..	..	..	7.1	7.3	7.3	7.5	7.6	7.2	..
Asia-Pacific (24) average[7]	..	..	..	5.3	5.5	5.4	5.6	5.4	5.4	6.6
LAC average[8]	15.2	15.8	14.1	15.7	16.5	16.6	16.7	17.0	16.9	17.1
OECD average[1, 9]	25.1	24.8	24.4	26.4	25.9	25.7	25.7	25.6	25.7	..

.. Not available

1. Australia, Japan, Korea and New Zealand are part of the OECD (37) group. Data for Australia, Japan, Korea, New Zealand and the OECD average are taken from OECD (2020), *Revenue Statistics 2020*.
2. 2007 to 2018: Data for China are not included in this table as historical data on revenues from social security contributions are not available.
3. Social security contributions data for Indonesia are only available for 2015 to 2019 and are deemed negligible in earlier years.
4. Heading 2000: Data are estimated for 2019.
5. The social security contributions in the Solomon Islands are null as they do not meet the social security criteria of the OECD classifications set in Annex A of the Interpretative Guide.
6. Represents an unweighted average for the 30 African countries included in the publication *Revenue Statistics in Africa 2020*.
7. Represents an unweighted average of the 24 Asian and Pacific economies in this publication. The Asia-Pacific (24) average should be interpreted with caution as data for social security contributions (category 2000) are not available or are partial in a few economies. Data for 2018 are used for Australia and Japan in the calculation as data for 2019 are not available. See the country tables in Chapter 4 for further information.
8. Represents an unweighted average for the 26 Latin American and Caribbean (LAC) countries included in the publication *Revenue Statistics in Latin America and the Caribbean 2021*.
9. Represents an unweighted average for the 37 OECD member countries included in the publication *Revenue Statistics 2020*.

StatLink https://stat.link/aujx1l

Table 3.9. Taxes on property (4000) as percentage of GDP

	1997	2000	2007	2010	2014	2015	2016	2017	2018	2019
Australia[1]	2.6	2.7	2.6	2.4	2.8	3.0	3.0	2.9	2.7	..
Bhutan	0.0	0.0	0.1	0.0	0.0	0.0	0.0	0.0	0.0	0.0
China	..	..	1.6	1.3	1.5	1.7	1.5	1.5	1.4	1.4
Cook Islands	..	..	0.0	0.0	0.0	0.0	0.0	0.0	0.0	0.0
Fiji	..	..	..	0.0	0.7	0.7	0.8	0.7	0.8	0.7
Indonesia	0.3	0.3	0.7	0.6	0.3	0.3	0.2	0.2	0.2	0.2
Japan[1]	2.9	2.7	2.5	2.6	2.6	2.5	2.6	2.6	2.6	..
Kazakhstan	..	0.8	0.6	0.6	0.5	0.6	0.5	0.5	0.5	0.5
Korea[1]	2.4	2.6	3.0	2.5	2.6	2.9	2.9	3.0	3.1	3.1
Lao PDR	..	..	..	0.1	0.1	0.1	0.1	0.1	0.1	0.1
Malaysia[2]	0.0	0.0	..	..	0.0	0.0	0.0	0.0	0.0	0.0
Maldives	..	..	0.1	0.0	0.1	0.1	0.0	0.1	0.0	0.0
Mongolia	..	..	0.6	0.5	0.5	0.5	0.5	0.6	0.5	0.6
Nauru	..	..	..	..	0.0	0.0	0.0	0.0	0.0	0.0
New Zealand[1]	1.8	1.7	1.8	2.0	2.0	2.0	1.9	1.9	1.9	2.0
Papua New Guinea	..	0.5	0.3	0.2	0.2	0.1	0.1	0.1	0.1	0.1
Philippines	0.2	0.5	0.4	0.4	0.5	0.5	0.4	0.5	0.4	0.4
Samoa	..	..	0.1	0.0	0.0	0.0	0.0	0.0	0.0	0.0
Singapore	..	1.7	2.3	1.8	1.8	1.7	1.7	1.9	1.8	1.8
Solomon Islands	..	..	0.2	0.1	0.1	0.2	0.2	0.1	0.1	0.1
Thailand	..	0.3	0.2	0.2	0.5	0.5	0.4	0.5	0.5	0.5
Tokelau	..	..	0.0	0.0	0.0	0.0	0.0	0.0	0.0	0.0
Vanuatu	..	0.5	0.8	0.7	0.5	0.5	0.4	0.5	0.6	0.6
Viet Nam	..	..	0.1	0.1	0.0	0.0	0.0	0.0	0.0	0.0
Africa (30) average[3]	..	..	..	0.4	0.4	0.4	0.4	0.3	0.3	..
Asia-Pacific (24) average[4]	..	..	..	0.7	0.7	0.7	0.7	0.7	0.7	0.7
LAC average[5]	0.7	0.7	1.0	0.8	0.9	0.9	0.8	0.9	0.8	0.9
OECD average[1, 6]	1.7	1.7	1.8	1.7	1.9	1.9	2.3	1.9	1.9	..

.. Not available

1. Australia, Japan, Korea and New Zealand are part of the OECD (37) group. Data for Australia, Japan, Korea, New Zealand and the OECD average are taken from OECD (2020), Revenue Statistics 2020.
2. Figures do not include tax revenues from local governments (Quit Rent and Assessment tax), which are unavailable.
3. Represents an unweighted average for the 30 African countries included in the publication Revenue Statistics in Africa 2020.
4. Represents an unweighted average of the 24 Asian and Pacific economies in this publication. Data for 2018 are used for Australia and Japan in the calculation as data for 2019 are not available. See the country tables in Chapter 4 for further information.
5. Represents an unweighted average for the 26 Latin American and Caribbean (LAC) countries included in the publication Revenue Statistics in Latin America and the Caribbean 2021.
6. Represents an unweighted average for the 37 OECD member countries included in the publication Revenue Statistics 2020.

StatLink https://stat.link/ma9f15

Table 3.10. Taxes on property (4000) as percentage of total taxation

	1997	2000	2007	2010	2014	2015	2016	2017	2018	2019
Australia[1]	9.2	8.8	9.0	9.4	10.2	10.7	10.8	10.0	9.5	..
Bhutan	0.4	0.3	0.6	0.1	0.1	0.4	0.3	0.2	0.2	0.1
China[2]	..	..	..	..	..	..	..	..	..	6.4
Cook Islands	..	..	0.0	0.0	0.0	0.0	0.0	0.0	0.0	0.0
Fiji	..	..	..	0.0	3.3	3.1	3.3	2.9	3.3	3.0
Indonesia	4.2	3.7	6.1	5.2	2.2	2.4	1.6	1.4	1.4	1.5
Japan[1]	11.2	10.5	9.0	9.7	8.5	8.2	8.3	8.2	8.1	..
Kazakhstan	..	4.1	2.2	2.4	2.3	3.6	3.3	3.0	2.8	2.8
Korea[1]	12.7	12.4	12.8	11.3	11.0	12.4	11.6	11.7	11.6	11.4
Lao PDR	..	..	..	1.1	0.9	0.9	0.7	0.7	1.1	1.2
Malaysia[3]	0.0	0.0	..	..	0.0	0.0	0.0	0.0	0.0	0.0
Maldives	..	..	0.4	0.4	0.3	0.3	0.2	0.7	0.3	0.2
Mongolia	..	..	2.0	1.9	2.6	2.6	2.7	2.6	2.2	2.5
Nauru	..	..	..	..	0.0	0.0	0.0	0.0	0.0	0.0
New Zealand[1]	5.4	5.3	5.3	6.6	6.3	6.2	6.1	6.0	5.8	6.2
Papua New Guinea	..	3.4	1.4	1.0	1.3	0.6	0.9	0.5	1.0	0.4
Philippines	0.9	3.1	2.9	2.9	2.8	2.8	2.7	2.8	2.6	2.5
Samoa	..	..	0.5	0.0	0.0	0.0	0.0	0.0	0.0	0.0
Singapore	..	11.2	17.1	14.5	13.2	13.0	13.0	14.1	14.0	13.2
Solomon Islands	..	..	1.1	0.6	0.6	0.8	0.7	0.5	0.5	0.6
Thailand	..	2.2	1.2	1.3	2.6	2.7	2.3	2.8	2.7	2.7
Tokelau	..	..	0.0	0.0	0.0	0.0	0.0	0.0	0.0	0.0
Vanuatu	..	3.2	4.4	4.4	3.1	3.0	2.9	3.0	3.1	3.6
Viet Nam	..	..	0.3	0.3	0.2	0.2	0.2	0.2	0.2	0.2
Africa (30) average[4]	..	..	..	1.9	1.8	1.9	1.8	1.6	1.6	..
Asia-Pacific (24) average[5]	..	..	..	3.5	3.1	3.2	3.1	3.1	3.1	3.2
LAC average[6]	3.8	3.7	4.9	4.0	4.1	4.0	3.8	3.8	3.7	3.8
OECD average[1, 7]	5.2	5.5	5.6	5.5	5.8	5.8	6.6	5.9	5.6	..

.. Not available

1. Australia, Japan, Korea and New Zealand are part of the OECD (37) group. Data for Australia, Japan, Korea, New Zealand and the OECD average are taken from OECD (2020), *Revenue Statistics 2020*.
2. 2007 to 2018: Data for China are not included in this table as historical data on revenues from social security contributions are not available.
3. Figures do not include tax revenues from local governments (Quit Rent and Assessment tax), which are unavailable.
4. Represents an unweighted average for the 30 African countries included in the publication *Revenue Statistics in Africa 2020*.
5. Represents an unweighted average of the 24 Asian and Pacific economies in this publication. The Asia-Pacific (24) average should be interpreted with caution as data for social security contributions (category 2000) are not available or are partial in a few economies. Data for 2018 are used for Australia and Japan in the calculation as data for 2019 are not available. See the country tables in Chapter 4 for further information.
6. Represents an unweighted average for the 26 Latin American and Caribbean (LAC) countries included in the publication *Revenue Statistics in Latin America and the Caribbean 2021*.
7. Represents an unweighted average for the 37 OECD member countries included in the publication *Revenue Statistics 2020*.

StatLink https://stat.link/hnv3ap

Table 3.11. Taxes on goods and services (5000) as percentage of GDP

	1997	2000	2007	2010	2014	2015	2016	2017	2018	2019
Australia[1]	7.9	8.8	8.0	7.3	7.3	7.7	7.5	7.5	7.3	..
Bhutan	3.8	2.9	3.9	4.9	5.8	5.9	6.1	6.9	6.0	4.2
China	..	..	10.7	11.9	11.5	10.7	10.2	10.0	9.6	9.1
Cook Islands	..	..	15.1	16.3	16.5	17.4	18.0	17.9	18.3	17.8
Fiji	..	..	..	14.6	16.3	16.8	15.3	15.9	16.1	15.5
Indonesia	3.6	3.5	5.1	4.7	5.4	5.2	4.8	5.0	5.0	4.7
Japan[1]	4.5	5.0	4.9	5.0	6.0	6.4	6.3	6.6	6.2	..
Kazakhstan	..	6.9	8.8	11.9	11.1	7.2	7.2	8.2	8.5	8.6
Korea[1]	8.1	8.0	7.4	7.5	7.0	6.7	7.0	7.0	7.0	7.1
Lao PDR	..	..	..	8.7	9.4	9.6	9.2	8.4	8.3	8.0
Malaysia	8.9	5.6	4.1	3.9	3.6	4.8	5.0	4.7	3.2	3.2
Maldives	..	..	11.2	8.3	13.7	14.3	14.9	15.5	15.3	14.6
Mongolia	..	..	11.5	11.5	10.8	9.3	9.8	10.7	12.2	12.0
Nauru	..	..	..	..	8.4	11.1	6.5	10.2	10.5	10.3
New Zealand[1]	11.8	11.3	10.7	12.0	12.2	12.3	12.1	12.2	12.5	12.6
Papua New Guinea	..	3.3	5.3	5.0	5.7	5.2	5.0	4.8	4.7	5.2
Philippines	8.1	6.4	6.3	5.9	6.4	6.3	6.4	6.8	7.5	7.7
Samoa	..	..	14.3	14.7	17.4	18.2	18.8	19.3	20.9	20.1
Singapore	..	4.7	4.3	4.3	4.2	4.1	4.1	3.9	3.8	3.8
Solomon Islands	..	..	11.6	13.1	16.6	16.0	15.1	15.7	17.6	14.4
Thailand	..	9.2	9.4	9.6	10.1	10.6	10.3	10.1	10.0	9.5
Tokelau	..	..	7.4	8.6	8.8	7.4	6.7	7.4	9.5	8.9
Vanuatu	..	15.7	18.2	15.6	16.8	15.8	14.8	16.6	17.3	16.5
Viet Nam	..	..	10.9	13.4	10.7	11.1	11.6	11.4	11.0	11.1
Africa (30) average[2]	..	..	..	7.8	8.3	8.5	8.6	8.7	8.7	..
Asia-Pacific (24) average[3]	..	..	..	9.5	10.1	10.0	9.7	10.1	10.4	9.9
LAC average[4]	9.9	10.1	11.0	10.5	10.9	11.1	11.3	11.3	11.4	11.4
OECD average[1, 5]	10.9	10.8	10.7	10.6	10.8	10.9	11.0	11.0	10.9	..

.. Not available

1. Australia, Japan, Korea and New Zealand are part of the OECD (37) group. Data for Australia, Japan, Korea, New Zealand and the OECD average are taken from OECD (2020), *Revenue Statistics 2020*.
2. Represents an unweighted average for the 30 African countries included in the publication *Revenue Statistics in Africa 2020*.
3. Represents an unweighted average of the 24 Asian and Pacific economies in this publication. Data for 2018 are used for Australia and Japan in the calculation as data for 2019 are not available. See the country tables in Chapter 4 for further information.
4. Represents an unweighted average for the 26 Latin American and Caribbean (LAC) countries included in the publication *Revenue Statistics in Latin America and the Caribbean 2021*.
5. Represents an unweighted average for the 37 OECD member countries included in the publication *Revenue Statistics 2020*.

StatLink https://stat.link/erz3xa

Table 3.12. Taxes on goods and services (5000) as percentage of total taxation

	1997	2000	2007	2010	2014	2015	2016	2017	2018	2019
Australia[1]	27.5	28.8	27.0	29.0	26.9	27.6	27.1	26.3	25.5	..
Bhutan	44.9	32.2	42.7	34.8	42.2	43.5	47.4	50.0	47.8	40.6
China[2]	..	..	..	..	..	..	..	..	..	41.3
Cook Islands	..	..	60.8	60.6	74.4	65.0	66.5	63.4	61.4	66.4
Fiji	..	..	..	67.4	72.0	71.2	66.2	65.6	68.6	70.0
Indonesia	47.6	44.7	41.7	41.8	44.4	43.3	39.8	42.7	41.8	40.6
Japan[1]	17.2	19.3	18.0	18.7	19.8	21.0	20.4	21.0	19.5	..
Kazakhstan	..	34.7	33.8	50.2	52.7	46.5	48.1	51.1	50.2	51.8
Korea[1]	42.7	38.4	31.3	33.7	30.0	28.0	28.1	27.7	26.3	25.8
Lao PDR	..	..	..	76.2	76.9	76.4	77.4	76.2	76.6	76.4
Malaysia	45.2	39.8	27.9	28.4	23.6	33.0	35.6	34.8	25.8	26.0
Maldives	..	..	93.7	92.7	72.3	73.7	75.4	76.7	79.0	78.5
Mongolia	..	..	40.4	45.5	53.4	48.9	51.3	49.6	50.8	49.5
Nauru	..	..	..	..	100.0	47.8	41.3	35.1	29.8	21.4
New Zealand[1]	34.8	34.7	31.7	39.6	39.2	38.9	38.4	38.4	37.9	38.9
Papua New Guinea	..	24.9	25.5	29.6	31.5	34.3	37.5	38.5	37.6	42.0
Philippines	50.2	42.0	40.7	41.3	40.0	39.0	39.1	40.3	43.0	42.5
Samoa	..	..	76.0	75.3	75.6	76.9	77.2	77.9	77.0	78.0
Singapore	..	31.1	32.9	34.4	31.3	31.7	31.8	28.5	29.5	28.8
Solomon Islands	..	..	75.8	69.1	72.0	69.1	70.1	69.8	73.1	70.6
Thailand	..	61.9	53.4	54.4	54.9	56.2	56.9	57.4	56.7	55.1
Tokelau	..	..	52.2	48.9	51.9	48.9	45.4	44.2	52.7	46.3
Vanuatu	..	96.8	95.6	95.6	96.9	97.0	97.1	97.0	96.9	96.5
Viet Nam	..	..	54.6	62.1	62.0	64.4	67.1	65.7	63.6	63.7
Africa (30) average[3]	..	..	..	51.9	50.2	51.2	52.2	52.3	51.9	..
Asia-Pacific (24) average[4]	..	..	..	51.3	54.1	51.4	51.5	51.2	50.9	49.8
LAC average[5]	58.0	56.6	51.8	51.2	50.1	50.4	50.6	50.7	50.3	49.8
OECD average[1, 6]	33.9	33.6	32.6	33.8	33.2	33.2	33.0	33.0	32.7	..

.. Not available

1. Australia, Japan, Korea and New Zealand are part of the OECD (37) group. Data for Australia, Japan, Korea, New Zealand and the OECD average are taken from OECD (2020), *Revenue Statistics 2020*.
2. 2007 to 2018: Data for China are not included in this table as historical data on revenues from social security contributions are not available.
3. Represents an unweighted average for the 30 African countries included in the publication *Revenue Statistics in Africa 2020*.
4. Represents an unweighted average of the 24 Asian and Pacific economies in this publication. The Asia-Pacific (24) average should be interpreted with caution as data for social security contributions (category 2000) are not available or are partial in a few economies. Data for 2018 are used for Australia and Japan in the calculation as data for 2019 are not available. See the country tables in Chapter 4 for further information.
5. Represents an unweighted average for the 26 Latin American and Caribbean (LAC) countries included in the publication *Revenue Statistics in Latin America and the Caribbean 2021*.
6. Represents an unweighted average for the 37 OECD member countries included in the publication *Revenue Statistics 2020*.

StatLink https://stat.link/jay467

Table 3.13. Taxes on general consumption (5110) as percentage of GDP

	1997	2000	2007	2010	2014	2015	2016	2017	2018	2019
Australia[1]	2.4	3.7	3.9	3.5	3.6	3.7	3.6	3.6	3.4	..
Bhutan	1.3	1.5	1.6	2.1	2.5	2.6	2.5	2.6	2.7	2.8
China[2]	..	..	8.8	9.1	8.6	7.8	7.6	7.6	7.3	6.7
Cook Islands	..	..	10.8	11.0	11.6	12.5	12.5	12.6	13.3	13.0
Fiji	..	..	..	8.7	9.3	9.8	7.5	7.8	7.6	7.5
Indonesia	2.7	2.3	3.6	3.4	3.9	3.7	3.3	3.5	3.6	3.4
Japan[1]	1.9	2.3	2.4	2.5	3.7	4.2	4.1	4.1	4.1	..
Kazakhstan	..	4.4	4.9	3.1	3.0	2.3	3.2	3.1	3.3	3.9
Korea[1]	3.6	3.6	3.8	3.9	4.0	3.6	3.9	4.1	4.1	4.3
Lao PDR	..	..	..	3.3	3.6	4.3	3.6	3.5	3.4	3.3
Malaysia	2.2	1.7	1.0	1.0	1.0	2.7	3.3	3.2	1.7	1.0
Maldives	..	..	0.0	0.0	7.9	9.6	9.3	9.4	9.4	8.7
Mongolia	..	..	5.3	5.9	6.2	4.5	4.8	5.8	6.8	6.7
Nauru	..	..	..	..	0.0	0.0	0.0	0.0	0.0	0.0
New Zealand[1]	8.3	8.1	8.0	9.3	9.5	9.5	9.4	9.5	9.7	9.8
Papua New Guinea	..	3.3	2.3	2.3	2.9	2.7	2.5	2.2	2.1	2.4
Philippines[3]	1.7	1.5	2.0	1.8	2.1	2.1	2.2	2.2	2.0	2.1
Samoa	..	..	7.2	6.9	9.3	9.6	9.4	9.9	10.9	10.7
Singapore	..	1.3	2.2	2.4	2.5	2.4	2.5	2.3	2.2	2.2
Solomon Islands	..	..	11.6	6.3	7.6	7.0	6.2	6.6	6.9	5.8
Thailand	..	3.4	3.6	3.7	4.0	3.9	3.9	3.8	3.9	3.5
Tokelau	..	..	0.0	0.0	0.0	0.0	0.0	0.0	0.0	0.0
Vanuatu	..	9.1	10.9	6.3	7.3	7.0	6.4	7.3	8.2	7.6
Viet Nam	..	..	5.6	7.2	6.1	6.0	6.0	6.3	6.2	6.0
Africa (30) average[4]	..	..	..	4.4	5.0	5.0	5.0	5.0	5.1	..
Asia-Pacific (24) average[5]	..	..	..	4.5	5.0	5.1	4.9	5.0	5.1	5.0
LAC average[6]	5.4	5.5	6.8	6.4	7.1	7.2	7.3	7.2	7.3	7.2
OECD average[1, 7]	6.6	6.6	6.8	6.7	6.9	6.9	7.0	7.0	7.1	..

.. Not available

1. Australia, Japan, Korea and New Zealand are part of the OECD (37) group. Data for Australia, Japan, Korea, New Zealand and the OECD average are taken from OECD (2020), *Revenue Statistics 2020*.
2. 2007 to 2018: Revenues from import excise tax and refund of excise tax for export are included under heading 5111 as they cannot be separated from revenues from import VAT and refunds of VAT for export and VAT represents the majority of the revenues.
3. The data exclude revenue from VAT on imports. This revenue could not be distinguished from revenue from other import duties and is currently classified under heading 5120 (taxes on specific goods and services).
4. Represents an unweighted average for the 30 African countries included in the publication *Revenue Statistics in Africa 2020*.
5. Represents an unweighted average of the 24 Asian and Pacific economies in this publication. Data for 2018 are used for Australia and Japan in the calculation as data for 2019 are not available. See the country tables in Chapter 4 for further information.
6. Represents an unweighted average for the 26 Latin American and Caribbean (LAC) countries included in the publication *Revenue Statistics in Latin America and the Caribbean 2021*.
7. Represents an unweighted average for the 37 OECD member countries included in the publication *Revenue Statistics 2020*.

StatLink https://stat.link/d95kn3

Table 3.14. Taxes on general consumption (5110) as percentage of total taxation

	1997	2000	2007	2010	2014	2015	2016	2017	2018	2019
Australia[1]	8.4	12.0	13.1	13.8	13.1	13.3	13.2	12.5	12.0	..
Bhutan	15.4	16.7	18.0	15.1	18.3	19.3	19.3	19.1	21.7	26.8
China[2]	..	..	..	..	..	..	..	..	..	30.2
Cook Islands	..	..	43.4	41.1	52.4	46.6	46.1	44.4	44.6	48.5
Fiji	..	..	..	40.4	41.0	41.3	32.4	32.3	32.2	33.8
Indonesia	35.5	29.4	29.2	29.6	31.9	30.4	27.8	30.5	30.3	29.0
Japan[1]	7.2	9.1	8.8	9.6	12.2	13.7	13.3	13.0	12.8	..
Kazakhstan	..	22.2	18.8	13.1	14.3	14.8	21.3	19.2	19.4	23.2
Korea[1]	18.9	17.0	15.8	17.5	17.2	15.3	15.8	16.0	15.3	15.7
Lao PDR	..	..	..	28.6	29.4	33.9	30.5	31.8	31.4	31.5
Malaysia	11.1	11.9	6.7	7.2	6.5	18.9	23.6	24.2	13.4	8.2
Maldives	..	..	0.0	0.0	41.9	49.5	47.1	46.7	48.6	46.9
Mongolia	..	..	18.9	23.4	30.6	23.7	25.0	27.0	28.2	27.5
Nauru	..	..	..	..	0.0	0.0	0.0	0.0	0.0	0.0
New Zealand[1]	24.5	24.9	23.5	30.7	30.4	30.2	29.9	30.2	29.6	30.4
Papua New Guinea	..	24.9	11.1	13.3	15.9	17.9	19.1	18.0	16.4	18.9
Philippines[3]	10.6	9.5	12.9	13.0	13.2	13.0	13.5	13.1	11.3	11.5
Samoa	..	..	38.2	35.0	40.3	40.4	38.5	40.0	40.1	41.7
Singapore	..	8.3	16.8	19.6	18.9	18.6	18.9	16.5	16.8	16.5
Solomon Islands	..	..	75.8	33.3	32.9	30.1	28.8	29.4	28.8	28.6
Thailand	..	23.1	20.6	20.8	21.9	20.8	21.5	21.9	22.2	20.6
Tokelau	..	..	0.0	0.0	0.0	0.0	0.0	0.0	0.0	0.0
Vanuatu	..	56.4	57.1	38.8	42.2	42.8	41.6	42.5	45.8	44.6
Viet Nam	..	..	28.1	33.3	35.6	34.7	34.6	36.2	36.1	34.4
Africa (30) average[4]	..	..	..	29.7	29.7	29.7	29.9	30.2	30.2	..
Asia-Pacific (24) average[5]	..	..	..	21.7	24.3	24.8	24.4	24.5	24.2	24.7
LAC average[6]	29.5	28.7	30.4	30.1	31.5	31.5	32.0	31.7	31.9	31.4
OECD average[1, 7]	20.5	20.4	20.7	21.3	21.3	21.1	20.9	21.2	21.2	..

.. Not available

1. Australia, Japan, Korea and New Zealand are part of the OECD (37) group. Data for Australia, Japan, Korea, New Zealand and the OECD average are taken from OECD (2020), *Revenue Statistics 2020*.
2. 2007 to 2018: Data for China are not included in this table as historical data on revenues from social security contributions are not available.
3. The data exclude revenue from VAT on imports. This revenue could not be distinguished from revenue from other import duties and is currently classified under heading 5120 (taxes on specific goods and services).
4. Represents an unweighted average for the 30 African countries included in the publication *Revenue Statistics in Africa 2020*.
5. Represents an unweighted average of the 24 Asian and Pacific economies in this publication. The Asia-Pacific (24) average should be interpreted with caution as data for social security contributions (category 2000) are not available or are partial in a few economies. Data for 2018 are used for Australia and Japan in the calculation as data for 2019 are not available. See the country tables in Chapter 4 for further information.
6. Represents an unweighted average for the 26 Latin American and Caribbean (LAC) countries included in the publication *Revenue Statistics in Latin America and the Caribbean 2021*.
7. Represents an unweighted average for the 37 OECD member countries included in the publication *Revenue Statistics 2020*.

StatLink https://stat.link/t45cwp

Table 3.15. Taxes on specific goods and services (5120) as percentage of GDP

	1997	2000	2007	2010	2014	2015	2016	2017	2018	2019
Australia[1]	4.0	4.3	3.3	3.0	2.9	2.9	2.8	2.9	2.8	..
Bhutan	2.5	1.4	2.2	2.8	3.3	3.1	3.4	4.0	3.0	1.2
China[2]	..	..	1.8	2.5	2.5	2.5	2.2	2.2	2.0	2.2
Cook Islands	..	..	4.1	5.0	4.6	4.7	5.3	5.1	4.8	4.6
Fiji	..	..	..	5.8	7.0	7.0	7.8	8.0	8.5	8.0
Indonesia	0.9	1.2	1.5	1.4	1.5	1.6	1.4	1.4	1.4	1.3
Japan[1]	2.1	2.0	2.0	1.9	1.8	1.8	1.7	2.1	1.7	..
Kazakhstan	..	2.1	3.1	8.3	7.7	4.6	3.7	4.8	4.9	4.5
Korea[1]	4.1	4.1	3.4	3.4	2.5	2.6	2.6	2.6	2.5	2.4
Lao PDR	..	..	..	4.3	4.7	4.1	4.5	3.7	4.3	4.1
Malaysia	5.4	2.9	2.5	2.4	2.2	1.6	1.3	1.0	1.2	1.8
Maldives	..	..	11.0	8.1	5.6	4.6	5.4	5.9	5.7	5.7
Mongolia	..	..	4.9	4.8	3.8	4.1	4.1	3.8	4.6	4.5
Nauru	..	..	..	..	7.7	10.3	6.0	9.7	9.8	9.6
New Zealand[1]	2.8	2.5	2.0	1.9	1.9	1.9	1.8	1.8	1.9	1.9
Papua New Guinea	..	..	3.0	2.8	2.8	2.5	2.4	2.5	2.7	2.9
Philippines[3]	6.3	4.9	4.2	3.9	4.2	4.1	4.1	4.5	5.4	5.5
Samoa	..	..	7.1	7.9	8.1	8.7	9.4	9.4	10.0	9.4
Singapore	..	2.0	1.3	1.3	1.3	1.3	1.2	1.2	1.1	1.2
Solomon Islands	..	..	6.2	6.7	8.9	8.9	8.8	8.9	10.6	8.4
Thailand	..	5.5	5.5	5.7	5.0	5.4	5.3	5.3	5.1	5.1
Tokelau	..	..	7.4	8.6	8.8	7.4	6.7	7.4	9.5	8.9
Vanuatu	..	6.5	7.3	6.7	5.9	6.2	5.9	6.4	6.4	6.1
Viet Nam	..	..	4.8	5.6	4.1	4.6	5.0	4.6	4.2	4.4
Africa (30) average[4]	..	..	..	3.2	3.2	3.4	3.5	3.5	3.4	..
Asia-Pacific (24) average[5]	..	..	..	4.6	4.5	4.4	4.3	4.6	4.8	4.5
LAC average[6]	4.2	4.3	3.9	3.7	3.4	3.6	3.6	3.7	3.7	3.8
OECD average[1, 7]	3.7	3.6	3.3	3.3	3.3	3.3	3.4	3.3	3.2	..

.. Not available

1. Australia, Japan, Korea and New Zealand are part of the OECD (37) group. Data for Australia, Japan, Korea, New Zealand and the OECD average are taken from OECD (2020), *Revenue Statistics 2020*.
2. 2007 to 2018: Revenues from import excise tax and refund of excise tax for export are included under heading 5111 as they cannot be separated from revenues from import VAT and refunds of VAT for export and VAT represents the majority of the revenues.
3. The data include revenues from VAT on imports, usually classified under heading 5110 (taxes on general consumption). This revenue could not be distinguished from revenue from other import duties.
4. Represents an unweighted average for the 30 African countries included in the publication *Revenue Statistics in Africa 2020*.
5. Represents an unweighted average of the 24 Asian and Pacific economies in this publication. Data for 2018 are used for Australia and Japan in the calculation as data for 2019 are not available. See the country tables in Chapter 4 for further information.
6. Represents an unweighted average for the 26 Latin American and Caribbean (LAC) countries included in the publication *Revenue Statistics in Latin America and the Caribbean 2021*.
7. Represents an unweighted average for the 37 OECD member countries included in the publication *Revenue Statistics 2020*.

StatLink https://stat.link/mbi8p3

Table 3.16. Taxes on specific goods and services (5120) as percentage of total taxation

	1997	2000	2007	2010	2014	2015	2016	2017	2018	2019
Australia[1]	13.8	14.1	11.3	11.9	10.5	10.4	10.0	10.1	9.9	..
Bhutan	29.4	15.5	24.7	19.6	23.9	22.6	26.4	29.2	24.2	11.9
China[2]	..	..	..	..	..	..	..	..	..	9.9
Cook Islands	..	..	16.3	18.6	20.6	17.7	19.5	18.1	16.1	17.3
Fiji	..	..	..	26.9	30.9	29.8	33.7	33.2	36.3	36.1
Indonesia	12.1	15.3	12.4	12.2	12.6	12.9	12.0	12.2	11.6	11.6
Japan[1]	7.9	7.9	7.1	7.2	6.0	5.8	5.7	6.6	5.3	..
Kazakhstan	..	10.3	12.1	35.1	36.3	29.5	24.9	30.2	29.1	26.8
Korea[1]	21.6	19.7	14.5	15.1	10.8	10.9	10.5	10.1	9.4	8.7
Lao PDR	..	..	..	37.8	38.6	32.9	37.9	33.7	39.3	38.8
Malaysia	27.5	20.5	17.1	17.3	14.1	11.0	9.0	7.8	9.4	14.4
Maldives	..	..	92.2	90.8	29.8	23.5	27.6	29.3	29.8	30.9
Mongolia	..	..	17.3	19.0	18.6	21.3	21.6	17.8	18.9	18.8
Nauru	..	..	..	..	91.6	44.6	38.2	33.3	27.8	19.9
New Zealand[1]	8.2	7.5	5.9	6.4	6.1	6.1	5.9	5.7	5.8	5.8
Papua New Guinea	..	..	14.4	16.3	15.6	16.4	18.4	20.5	21.2	23.0
Philippines[3]	39.1	32.0	27.0	27.6	26.2	25.5	25.1	26.6	31.2	30.5
Samoa	..	..	37.8	40.2	35.3	36.5	38.7	38.0	36.9	36.3
Singapore	..	13.0	10.1	10.3	9.5	10.0	9.2	8.8	8.7	8.7
Solomon Islands	..	..	40.7	35.3	38.4	38.4	40.6	39.8	43.9	41.3
Thailand	..	37.0	31.5	32.1	27.1	28.3	29.0	30.0	28.8	29.4
Tokelau	..	..	52.2	48.9	51.9	48.9	45.4	44.2	52.7	46.3
Vanuatu	..	40.4	38.6	40.8	33.7	38.1	38.7	37.6	36.0	35.4
Viet Nam	..	..	24.2	26.2	24.1	26.6	29.0	26.3	24.2	25.5
Africa (30) average[4]	..	..	..	20.9	19.7	20.7	21.4	21.2	20.8	..
Asia-Pacific (24) average	..	..	..	27.1	26.6	23.8	24.2	23.9	24.2	22.6
LAC average[5]	27.0	26.4	19.8	19.2	16.6	17.0	16.8	17.2	16.7	16.6
OECD average[1, 6]	11.5	11.4	10.1	10.6	10.0	10.1	10.1	9.9	9.6	..

.. Not available

1. Australia, Japan, Korea and New Zealand are part of the OECD (37) group. Data for Australia, Japan, Korea, New Zealand and the OECD average are taken from OECD (2020), Revenue Statistics 2020.
2. 2007 to 2018: Data for China are not included in this table as historical data on revenues from social security contributions are not available.
3. The data include revenues from VAT on imports, usually classified under heading 5110 (taxes on general consumption). This revenue could not be distinguished from revenue from other import duties.
4. Represents an unweighted average for the 30 African countries included in the publication Revenue Statistics in Africa 2020.
5. Represents an unweighted average for the 26 Latin American and Caribbean (LAC) countries included in the publication Revenue Statistics in Latin America and the Caribbean 2021.
6. Represents an unweighted average for the 37 OECD member countries included in the publication Revenue Statistics 2020.

StatLink https://stat.link/znyrmk

Table 3.17. Gross domestic product for tax reporting years at market prices, in national currency

	1997	2000	2007	2010	2014	2015	2016	2017	2018	2019
Australia[1, 2]	588	705	1 177	1 417	1 625	1 661	1 764	1 850	1 947	..
Bhutan[2]	14 226	20 460	50 862	76 860	122 500	136 911	152 390	163 456	172 759	178 370
China	7 972	10 028	27 009	41 212	64 356	68 886	74 640	83 204	91 928	98 652
Cook Islands	..	..	314 585	339 219	409 195	439 214	465 766	504 258	548 693	528 123
Fiji	3 275	3 572	5 440	6 024	9 167	9 822	10 327	11 065	11 651	11 874
Indonesia	754 614	1 520 683	4 323 057	6 864 133	10 569 705	11 526 333	12 401 729	13 589 826	14 838 312	15 833 943
Japan[1]	533 393	528 447	530 923	499 429	518 235	532 786	536 851	547 548	548 122	..
Kazakhstan	1 672	2 600	12 850	21 816	39 676	40 884	46 971	54 379	61 820	69 533
Lao PDR	..	..	..	61 997	106 797	117 252	129 279	140 698	152 414	164 017
Korea	544 082	651 634	1 089 660	1 322 611	1 562 929	1 658 020	1 740 780	1 835 698	1 893 497	1 913 964
Maldives	..	..	23 915	33 129	56 867	63 147	67 300	72 873	81 994	88 827
Malaysia	282	356	665	821	1 106	1 177	1 250	1 372	1 447	1 511
Mongolia	933	1 224	4 957	9 757	22 227	23 150	23 943	27 876	32 411	37 281
Nauru[2]	..	..	29 000	54 000	114 000	104 000	137 000	145 000	160 000	166 000
New Zealand[1]	105	122	189	206	245	258	275	293	304	308
Papua New Guinea	10 701	9 736	28 304	38 752	57 131	60 139	65 038	72 522	79 159	84 554
Philippines	2 773	3 698	7 198	9 399	13 207	13 944	15 132	16 557	18 265	19 516
Samoa[2, 3]	733	796	1 758	1 742	1 911	2 089	2 110	2 108	2 108	2 161
Singapore[4]	150	169	278	336	405	426	450	480	512	509
Solomon Islands	..	..	5 347	7 279	9 850	10 345	10 957	11 703	12 522	12 834
Thailand[5]	4 695	4 989	8 846	10 621	13 132	13 589	14 345	15 246	16 164	16 816
Tokelau[2, 6]	..	..	8 399	9 597	12 355	14 222	14 838	15 000	15 739	15 800
Vanuatu	31 606	37 627	53 926	67 912	79 109	82 798	87 250	94 887	100 771	106 740
Viet Nam	313 623	441 646	1 246 769	2 157 828	3 937 856	4 192 862	4 502 733	5 005 975	5 542 332	6 037 348

.. Not available

Note: All units are in billions except for Bhutan, Cook Islands, Fiji, Maldives, Nauru, Papua New Guinea, Samoa, Solomon Islands, Tokelau, Vanuatu and Viet Nam. Due to the size of their economies, the GDP figures for Cook Islands, Nauru and Tokelau are expressed in thousands while they are in millions for Bhutan, Fiji, Maldives, Papua New Guinea, Samoa, Solomon Islands and Vanuatu.

1. The year Y is calculated (at annual rate) as the average of: Q2(Y) to Q1(Y+1) for Japan; and Q3(Y) to Q2(Y+1) for Australia and New Zealand.
2. Data are reported on a fiscal year basis beginning 1st July. For example, the data for 2019 represent the period from July 2019 to June 2020.
3. The year Y is calculated using the formula GDP(Y)/2+GDP(Y-1)/2. This is done in order to make the value of the GDP correspond more closely to a July(Y-1)-to-June(Y) fiscal year.
4. Data are on a fiscal year basis ending 31st March. For example, the data for 2019 represent 1 April 2019 to 31 March 2020.
5. Data are on a fiscal year basis ending 30th September. For example, the data for 2019 represents 1 October 2018 to 30 September 2019.
6. 2019: Data are provisional.

Source: OECD National Accounts data for Australia, Indonesia, Japan, Korea and New Zealand; National Statistical Offices for China, Cook Islands, Fiji, Kazakhstan, Lao PDR, Malaysia, Maldives, Mongolia, Philippines, Singapore, Thailand, Tokelau and Viet Nam; Asian Development Bank's Key Indicators Database for Papua New Guinea, Solomon Islands and Vanuatu; IMF *World Economic Outlook* (WEO) April 2021 data for Bhutan. Data for 2018 and 2019 were estimated for the Solomon Islands and Vanuatu, using the GDP growth rates of the IMF's *World Economic Outlook* (WEO) April 2021 edition.

StatLink https://stat.link/vcameq

Table 3.18. Gross domestic product for tax reporting years at market prices, in millions of US dollars at market exchange rates

	1997	2000	2007	2010	2014	2015	2016	2017	2018	2019
Australia[1, 2]	436 263	408 375	985 048	1 299 443	1 464 338	1 247 832	1 310 918	1 417 660	1 454 629	..
Bhutan[2]	398	469	1 151	1 648	1 993	2 148	2 254	2 537	2 548	2 569
China	961 602	1 211 332	3 550 328	6 087 192	10 475 625	11 061 573	11 233 314	12 310 491	13 894 908	14 279 903
Cook Islands	..	..	231	244	339	306	324	358	380	348
Fiji	2 268	1 678	3 378	3 140	4 857	4 682	4 930	5 353	5 581	5 497
Indonesia	259 373	180 566	472 983	755 256	891 051	860 741	932 066	1 015 488	1 042 680	1 120 141
Japan[1]	4 408 334	4 900 526	4 508 703	5 690 809	4 896 054	4 403 106	4 934 168	4 880 842	4 963 170	..
Kazakhstan	22 166	18 292	104 850	148 047	221 416	184 388	137 289	166 806	179 340	181 667
Lao PDR	..	..	..	7 504	13 266	14 363	15 905	17 056	18 133	18 881
Korea	572 412	576 341	1 172 370	1 144 691	1 484 173	1 465 577	1 499 910	1 623 599	1 721 070	1 642 473
Maldives	..	..	1 868	2 588	3 690	4 098	4 367	4 729	5 321	5 764
Malaysia	100 169	93 790	193 550	255 018	338 066	301 355	301 255	319 109	358 712	364 684
Mongolia	1 181	1 137	4 235	7 185	12 227	11 750	11 159	11 426	13 138	13 997
Nauru[2]	..	..	24	50	103	78	102	111	120	115
New Zealand[1]	69 286	55 432	138 914	148 372	203 188	179 756	191 225	208 260	210 017	203 078
Papua New Guinea	7 442	3 499	9 545	14 251	23 211	21 723	20 759	22 743	24 035	24 960
Philippines	94 106	83 667	155 980	208 369	297 484	306 446	318 627	328 481	346 842	376 796
Samoa[2, 3]	286	256	649	686	823	862	807	831	837	826
Singapore[4]	100 936	97 930	184 360	246 080	319 713	310 154	325 593	347 480	379 378	372 888
Solomon Islands	..	..	699	903	1 338	1 311	1 381	1 458	1 566	1 579
Thailand[5]	149 701	124 127	256 347	335 010	404 354	396 635	406 545	449 365	500 081	541 564
Tokelau[2, 6]	..	..	6	7	10	10	10	11	11	10
Vanuatu	273	273	527	681	817	774	798	880	928	924
Viet Nam	26 892	31 176	77 520	112 825	185 759	191 288	201 326	220 376	240 766	259 924

.. Not available

Note: This table is produced based on GDP data in national currency from Table 3.17 and exchange rate data from Table 3.20.

1. The year Y is calculated (at annual rate) as the average of: Q2(Y) to Q1(Y+1) for Japan; and Q3(Y) to Q2(Y+1) for Australia and New Zealand.
2. Data are reported on a fiscal year basis beginning 1st July. For example, the data for 2019 represent the period from July 2019 to June 2020.
3. The year Y is calculated using the formula GDP(Y)/2+GDP(Y-1)/2. This is done in order to make the value of the GDP correspond more closely to a July(Y-1)-to-June(Y) fiscal year.
4. Data are on a fiscal year basis ending 31st March. For example, the data for 2019 represent 1 April 2019 to 31 March 2020.
5. Data are on a fiscal year basis ending 30th September. For example, the data for 2019 represents 1 October 2018 to 30 September 2019.
6. 2019: Data are provisional.

StatLink https://stat.link/8ledap

Table 3.19. Total tax revenue in millions of US dollars at market exchange rates

	1997	2000	2007	2010	2014	2015	2016	2017	2018	2019
Australia	125 058	124 385	290 788	328 349	399 343	348 153	362 049	404 006	417 175	..
Bhutan	34	42	104	232	272	290	291	348	321	265
China[1]	..	..	599 678	1 081 331	1 939 874	2 005 974	1 961 814	2 135 982	2 364 024	3 154 303
Cook Islands	..	..	58	66	75	82	88	101	113	93
Fiji	..	..	..	680	1 102	1 105	1 140	1 296	1 312	1 221
Indonesia	19 709	14 213	57 818	85 766	108 382	104 245	111 934	117 917	124 842	129 793
Japan	1 153 894	1 263 376	1 241 967	1 509 609	1 482 193	1 351 487	1 516 233	1 531 474	1 589 706	..
Kazakhstan	..	3 643	27 329	35 169	46 682	28 652	20 478	26 658	30 416	30 294
Lao PDR	..	..	..	860	1 630	1 803	1 894	1 883	1 971	1 981
Korea	108 274	120 547	278 198	256 154	347 014	347 879	371 149	411 689	460 420	449 659
Maldives	..	..	223	231	700	794	861	955	1 026	1 072
Malaysia	19 726	13 180	28 674	35 259	51 794	43 775	42 264	42 679	44 872	45 392
Mongolia	..	..	1 201	1 819	2 465	2 244	2 129	2 461	3 157	3 391
Nauru	..	..	..	..	9	18	16	32	42	56
New Zealand	23 510	18 037	47 059	44 906	63 532	56 824	60 268	65 820	69 065	65 619
Papua New Guinea	..	469	1 981	2 417	4 176	3 302	2 747	2 818	3 031	3 105
Philippines	15 201	12 770	24 304	29 501	47 563	49 780	51 815	55 153	60 267	67 963
Samoa	..	..	122	134	189	204	197	206	227	212
Singapore	..	14 865	24 305	30 691	42 705	40 476	42 488	48 057	49 080	49 586
Solomon Islands	..	..	107	171	308	303	298	328	377	323
Thailand	..	18 414	45 006	59 001	74 221	74 958	73 566	78 798	88 414	93 324
Tokelau	..	..	1	1	2	2	2	2	2	2
Vanuatu	..	44	100	111	142	126	122	151	166	158
Viet Nam	..	..	15 444	24 361	31 962	33 096	34 833	38 216	41 444	45 355

.. Not available

Note: This table is produced based on total tax revenues from Chapter 4 and exchange rate data from Table 3.20.

1. 2007 to 2018: The figures for China do not include revenue from social security contributions as detailed data were not available.

StatLink https://stat.link/27qc59

Table 3.20. Exchange rates used, national currency per US dollar

	1997	2000	2007	2010	2014	2015	2016	2017	2018	2019
Australia	1.35	1.73	1.20	1.09	1.11	1.33	1.35	1.31	1.34	..
Bhutan	35.77	43.64	44.19	46.65	61.47	63.75	67.62	64.44	67.79	69.44
China	8.29	8.28	7.61	6.77	6.14	6.23	6.64	6.76	6.62	6.91
Cook Islands	1.51	2.21	1.36	1.39	1.21	1.43	1.44	1.41	1.45	1.52
Fiji	1.44	2.13	1.61	1.92	1.89	2.10	2.10	2.07	2.09	2.16
Indonesia	2 909.38	8 421.78	9 139.99	9 088.49	11 862.06	13 391.17	13 305.63	13 382.56	14 230.93	14 135.67
Japan	121.00	107.84	117.76	87.76	105.85	121.00	108.80	112.18	110.44	..
Kazakhstan	75.44	142.13	122.55	147.36	179.19	221.73	342.13	326.00	344.71	382.75
Lao PDR	1 251.52	8 217.50	9 596.76	8 261.35	8 050.37	8 163.50	8 128.03	8 249.35	8 405.27	8 686.67
Korea	950.51	1 130.64	929.45	1 155.43	1 053.06	1 131.31	1 160.59	1 130.64	1 100.19	1 165.29
Maldives	11.77	11.77	12.80	12.80	15.41	15.41	15.41	15.41	15.41	15.41
Malaysia	2.81	3.80	3.44	3.22	3.27	3.91	4.15	4.30	4.04	4.14
Mongolia	789.73	1 076.44	1 170.40	1 357.90	1 817.94	1 970.31	2 145.53	2 439.78	2 467.05	2 663.54
Nauru	1.35	1.73	1.20	1.09	1.11	1.33	1.35	1.31	1.34	1.44
New Zealand	1.51	2.21	1.36	1.39	1.21	1.43	1.44	1.41	1.45	1.52
Papua New Guinea	1.44	2.78	2.97	2.72	2.46	2.77	3.13	3.19	3.29	3.39
Philippines	29.47	44.19	46.15	45.11	44.40	45.50	47.49	50.40	52.66	51.80
Samoa	2.56	3.12	2.71	2.54	2.32	2.42	2.61	2.54	2.52	2.62
Singapore	1.49	1.72	1.51	1.36	1.27	1.38	1.38	1.38	1.35	1.36
Solomon Islands	3.72	5.09	7.65	8.07	7.36	7.89	7.93	8.03	8.00	8.13
Thailand	31.36	40.19	34.51	31.70	32.48	34.26	35.29	33.93	32.32	31.05
Tokelau	1.51	2.21	1.36	1.39	1.21	1.43	1.44	1.41	1.45	1.52
Vanuatu	115.87	137.87	102.33	99.70	96.86	107.00	109.31	107.77	108.53	115.57
Viet Nam	11 662.21	14 166.28	16 083.20	19 125.36	21 198.72	21 919.14	22 365.38	22 715.58	23 019.60	23 227.33

.. Not available

Source: OECD National Accounts data for Australia, the Cook Islands, Indonesia, Japan, Korea, Nauru and New Zealand; IMF's World Economic Outlook (April 2021) for the Bhutan, China, Fiji, Kazakhstan, Lao PDR, Malaysia, Maldives, Mongolia, Nauru, Papua New Guinea, Philippines, Samoa, Singapore, Solomon Islands, Thailand, Viet Nam and Vanuatu.

StatLink https://stat.link/hdebz2

4 Country tables, tax revenues, 1990-2019

Country tax revenue tables, 1990-2019

In all of the following tables a ("..") indicates not available. The main series in this volume cover the years 1990 to 2019.

Figures referring to 1998-99, 2001-06, 2008-09 and 2011-13 in Tables 4.1 to 4.24 have been omitted because of lack of space. Full time series can be accessed at https://stats.oecd.org/ within the theme Public Sector, Taxation and Market Regulation/Taxation/Revenue Statistics Asian and Pacific Economies.

Table 4.1. Australia: Details of tax revenue

Million AUD

	1997	2000	2007	2010	2014	2015	2016	2017	2018	2019
Total tax revenue	**168 582**	**214 752**	**347 545**	**357 958**	**443 049**	**463 350**	**487 078**	**527 181**	**558 453**	..
1000 Taxes on income, profits and capital gains	**95 367**	**124 427**	**206 134**	**202 184**	**255 966**	**262 357**	**278 764**	**310 041**	**336 239**	..
1100 Of individuals	70 782	80 991	127 587	138 163	183 023	191 747	198 534	212 520	229 499	..
1110 On income and profits	69 212	80 991	127 587	138 163	183 023	191 747	198 534	212 520	229 499	..
1120 On capital gains	1 570	0	0	0	0	0	0	0	0	..
1200 Corporate	24 585	43 436	78 547	64 021	72 943	70 610	80 230	97 521	106 740	..
1210 On profits	22 253	43 436	78 547	64 021	72 943	70 610	80 230	97 521	106 740	..
Income tax on companies	21 242	42 221	76 655	62 549	71 224	68 779	78 254	95 539	104 641	..
Dividend and interest taxes	693	846	1 892	1 472	1 719	1 831	1 976	1 982	2 099	..
Other withholding taxes	318	369	0	0	0	0	0	0	0	..
1220 On capital gains	2 332	0	0	0	0	0	0	0	0	..
1300 Unallocable between 1100 and 1200	0	0	0	0	0	0	0	0	0	..
2000 Social security contributions	**0**	**0**	**0**	**0**	**0**	**0**	**0**	**0**	**0**	..
2100 Employees	0	0	0	0	0	0	0	0	0	..
2110 On a payroll basis	..	..	..	..	..	..	..	..	..	..
2120 On an income tax basis	..	..	..	..	..	..	..	..	..	..
2200 Employers	0	0	0	0	0	0	0	0	0	..
2210 On a payroll basis	..	..	..	..	..	..	..	..	..	..
2220 On an income tax basis	..	..	..	..	..	..	..	..	..	..
2300 Self-employed or non-employed	0	0	0	0	0	0	0	0	0	..
2310 On a payroll basis	..	..	..	..	..	..	..	..	..	..
2320 On an income tax basis	..	..	..	..	..	..	..	..	..	..
2400 Unallocable between 2100, 2200 and 2300	0	0	0	0	0	0	0	0	0	..
2410 On a payroll basis	..	..	..	..	..	..	..	..	..	..
2420 On an income tax basis	..	..	..	..	..	..	..	..	..	..
3000 Taxes on payroll and workforce	**11 277**	**9 624**	**16 407**	**18 492**	**22 776**	**23 354**	**23 799**	**25 520**	**26 923**	..
4000 Taxes on property	**15 505**	**18 825**	**31 156**	**33 526**	**45 293**	**49 641**	**52 585**	**52 967**	**53 142**	..
4100 Recurrent taxes on immovable property	7 739	9 067	15 615	19 907	25 062	27 093	29 232	30 305	32 694	..
4110 Households	..	..	..	..	..	..	..	..	..	..
4120 Others	..	..	..	..	..	..	..	..	..	..
4200 Recurrent taxes on net wealth	0	0	0	0	0	0	0	0	0	..
4210 Individual	..	..	..	..	..	..	..	..	..	..
4220 Corporate	..	..	..	..	..	..	..	..	..	..
4300 Estate, inheritance and gift taxes	0	0	0	0	0	0	0	0	0	..
4310 Estate and inheritance taxes	..	..	..	..	..	..	..	..	..	..
Estate duty central government	..	..	..	..	..	..	..	..	..	..
St. and loc. estate probate and succession	..	..	..	..	..	..	..	..	..	..
4320 Gift taxes	..	..	..	..	..	..	..	..	..	..
4400 Taxes on financial and capital transactions	7 766	9 758	15 541	13 619	20 231	22 548	23 353	22 662	20 448	..
4500 Non-recurrent taxes	0	0	0	0	0	0	0	0	0	..
4510 On net wealth	..	..	..	..	..	..	..	..	..	..
4520 Other non-recurrent taxes	..	..	..	..	..	..	..	..	..	..
4600 Other recurrent taxes on property	0	0	0	0	0	0	0	0	0	..
5000 Taxes on goods and services	**46 433**	**61 876**	**93 848**	**103 756**	**119 014**	**127 998**	**131 930**	**138 653**	**142 149**	..
5100 Taxes on production, sale, transfer, etc.	37 359	56 178	84 851	92 007	104 528	110 185	113 155	118 867	122 064	..
5110 General taxes	14 085	25 830	45 486	49 329	57 830	61 815	64 251	65 700	66 829	..
5111 Value added taxes	0	23 854	44 381	48 093	56 462	60 312	62 727	64 062	65 147	..
5112 Sales tax	14 085	1 976	1 105	1 236	1 368	1 503	1 524	1 638	1 682	..
5113 Other	0	0	0	0	0	0	0	0	0	..
5120 Taxes on specific goods and services	23 274	30 348	39 365	42 678	46 698	48 370	48 904	53 167	55 235	..
5121 Excise duties	14 449	19 768	24 357	26 689	24 506	22 541	22 773	23 673	24 497	..
Excises central government	13 573	19 019	23 526	25 803	23 799	21 625	21 895	22 763	23 488	..
Statutory corporate payments	258	295	231	452	209	405	335	346	446	..
Primary production charges	618	454	600	434	498	511	543	564	563	..
5122 Profits of fiscal monopolies	0	0	0	0	0	0	0	0	0	..
5123 Customs and import duties	3 637	4 606	6 070	5 828	10 884	14 046	14 196	15 690	15 944	..
Customs duties central government	3 637	4 606	6 070	5 828	10 884	14 046	14 196	15 690	15 944	..
5124 Taxes on exports	6	0	10	11	12	11	11	0	0	..
Customs duties on coal exports	0	..	0	0	0	0	0	0	0	..
Other	6	..	10	11	12	11	11	..	..	..
5125 Taxes on investment goods	0	0	0	0	0	0	0	0	0	..
5126 Taxes on specific services	5 182	5 974	8 928	10 150	11 296	11 772	11 924	13 804	14 794	..
Taxes race meetings	601	300	358	366	290	257	225	265	411	..
Poker machines	1 760	2 074	3 009	3 125	3 480	3 684	3 717	3 881	3 986	..
Lotteries	330	890	1 118	1 147	1 270	1 369	1 293	1 330	1 632	..
Levies on fire insurance companies	521	574	937	1 232	739	786	803	812	806	..
Other	1 970	2 136	3 506	4 280	5 517	5 676	5 886	7 516	7 959	..
5127 Other taxes on internat. trade and transactions	0	0	0	0	0	0	0	0	0	..
5128 Other taxes	0	0	0	0	0	0	0	0	0	..

	1997	2000	2007	2010	2014	2015	2016	2017	2018	2019
5130 Unallocable between 5110 and 5120	0	0	0	0	0	0	0	0	0	..
5200 Taxes on use of goods and perform activities	9 074	5 698	8 997	11 749	14 486	17 813	18 775	19 786	20 085	..
5210 Recurrent taxes	8 956	5 698	8 997	11 749	14 486	17 813	18 775	19 786	20 085	..
5211 Paid by households: motor vehicles	2 188	3 908	6 196	7 229	9 155	9 586	9 930	7 781	7 990	..
5212 Paid by others: motor vehicles	1 350	125	189	232	308	318	344	3 005	2 996	..
Fees on motor vehicle registry	1 287	0	0	0	0	0	0	1 766	1 788	..
Drivers licences	0	0	0	0	0	0	0	0	0	..
Stamp duty on vehicle registry	63	125	189	232	308	318	344	1 239	1 208	..
5213 Paid in respect of other goods	5 418	1 665	2 611	4 288	5 022	7 910	8 501	9 000	9 099	..
Broadcasting tv licences	329	210	288	150	185	128	0	52	52	..
Business franchise lic. tobac. fuel	3 992	227	0	0	0	1	0	1	0	..
Other taxes	565	1 129	2 321	4 136	4 815	7 760	8 478	8 911	9 002	..
Liquor taxes	532	97	2	1	23	22	23	36	45	..
Dog licenses	0	0	0	0	0	0	0	0	0	..
5220 Non-recurrent taxes	118	0	0	0	0	0	0	0	0	..
5300 Unallocable between 5100 and 5200	0	0	0	0	0	0	0	0	0	..
6000 Other taxes	**0**	**0**	**0**	**0**	**0**	**0**	**0**	**0**	**0**	**..**
6100 Paid solely by business	..	..	..	..	..	..	..	..	..	..
6200 Other	..	..	..	..	..	..	..	..	..	..

Note: Data are on a fiscal year basis beginning 1st July.

From 1998 taxes are recorded on an accrual basis; prior to that they were on a cash basis.

Direct taxes paid by public trading enterprises are excluded from receipts.

The figures for total tax revenue do not match the published totals in Taxation Revenue Australia. The latter is based on an accrual IMF GFS methodology and there are some differences between that and the OECD equivalent.

Heading 5213 includes radio and television licenses fees, though these are usually not regarded as a tax revenue in the OECD list.

Headings for non-wastable tax credits 1110 and 1210 include the private health insurance tax offset, family benefit, baby bonus tax offsets (paid during the 2003-04 budget year), film tax offset, and research and development tax offsets. The estimation of non-wastable credits into the expenditure and transfer components is in accordance with the OECD guidelines on the treatment and the data for this memorandum item has been provided by the Australian Taxation Office.

Source: Australian Bureau of Statistics.

StatLink https://stat.link/uyk3dj

Table 4.2. Bhutan: Details of tax revenue

Million BTN

	1997	2000	2007	2010	2014	2015	2016	2017	2018	2019
Total tax revenue	**1 209**	**1 851**	**4 613**	**10 816**	**16 718**	**18 518**	**19 649**	**22 404**	**21 746**	**18 398**
1000 Taxes on income, profits and capital gains	**648**	**1 217**	**2 547**	**6 925**	**9 610**	**10 337**	**10 355**	**11 167**	**11 240**	**10 941**
1100 Of individuals	24	66	265	705	1 536	1 764	953	1 335	1 543	2 291
1110 On income and profits	24	66	265	705	1 536	1 764	953	1 335	1 543	..
Salary income	..	..	..	..	..	1 617	696	1 111	1 270	..
Rental income	..	..	..	..	..	32	34	37	43	..
Dividends and interest	..	..	..	..	..	92	125	106	122	..
Other income	..	..	..	..	..	23	97	80	108	..
1120 On capital gains	..	..	..	..	..	..	..	..	..	..
1200 Corporate	624	1 151	2 283	6 220	8 074	8 573	9 402	9 832	9 697	8 651
1210 On profits	624	1 151	2 283	6 220	8 074	8 573	9 402	9 832	9 697	..
Corporate income tax	559	920	1 818	5 110	6 489	7 430	8 149	9 014	9 022	..
Druk Holdings and Investments (DHI)	0	0	0	1 372	1 569	..	..	..	..	..
Druk Green Power Corporation Limited (DGPC)	0	0	878	1 953	2 134	..	..	..	..	..
Bhutan Power Corporation Limited (BPC)	0	0	109	346	415	..	..	..	..	..
Others	559	920	831	1 439	2 370	..	..	..	..	..
Business income tax	65	232	465	1 110	1 585	1 143	1 254	818	674	..
1220 On capital gains of corporates	..	..	..	..	..	..	..	..	..	..
1300 Unallocable between 1100 and 1200	0	0	0	0	0	0	0	0	0	0
2000 Social security contributions	**0**	**0**	**0**	**0**	**0**	**0**	**0**	**0**	**0**	**0**
2100 Employees	..	..	..	..	..	..	..	..	..	..
2110 On a payroll basis	..	..	..	..	..	..	..	..	..	..
2120 On an income tax basis	..	..	..	..	..	..	..	..	..	..
2200 Employers	..	..	..	..	..	..	..	..	..	..
2210 On a payroll basis	..	..	..	..	..	..	..	..	..	..
2220 On an income tax basis	..	..	..	..	..	..	..	..	..	..
2300 Self-employed or non-employed	..	..	..	..	..	..	..	..	..	..
2310 On a payroll basis	..	..	..	..	..	..	..	..	..	..
2320 On an income tax basis	..	..	..	..	..	..	..	..	..	..
2400 Unallocable between 2100, 2200 and 2300	..	..	..	..	..	..	..	..	..	..
2410 On a payroll basis	..	..	..	..	..	..	..	..	..	..
2420 On an income tax basis	..	..	..	..	..	..	..	..	..	..
3000 Taxes on payroll and workforce	**13**	**22**	**58**	**105**	**32**	**57**	**-80**	**-9**	**74**	**-32**
Health contribution	13	22	58	105	32	57	-80	-9	74	-32
4000 Taxes on property	**4**	**5**	**25**	**6**	**8**	**67**	**55**	**34**	**33**	**27**
4100 Recurrent taxes on immovable property	4	5	25	6	8	4	3	7	7	5
4110 Households	4	5	25	6	8	4	3	7	7	5
4120 Others	0	0	0	0	0	0	0	0	0	0
4200 Recurrent taxes on net wealth	0	0	0	0	0	0	0	0	0	0
4210 Individual	..	..	..	..	..	..	..	..	..	..
4220 Corporate	..	..	..	..	..	..	..	..	..	..
4300 Estate, inheritance and gift taxes	0	0	0	0	0	0	0	0	0	0
4310 Estate and inheritance taxes	..	..	..	..	..	..	..	..	..	..
4320 Gift taxes	..	..	..	..	..	..	..	..	..	..
4400 Taxes on financial and capital transactions	0	0	0	0	0	63	52	28	25	22
4500 Other non-reccurrent taxes on property	0	0	0	0	0	0	0	0	0	0
4510 On net wealth	..	..	..	..	..	..	..	..	..	..
4520 Other non-recurrent taxes	..	..	..	..	..	..	..	..	..	..
4600 Other recurrent taxes on property	0	0	0	0	0	0	0	0	0	0
5000 Taxes on goods and services	**542**	**596**	**1 969**	**3 760**	**7 048**	**8 056**	**9 318**	**11 212**	**10 399**	**7 462**
5100 Taxes on production, sale, transfer, etc	542	596	1 969	3 760	7 048	7 765	8 974	10 816	9 978	7 117
5110 General taxes on goods and services	186	309	831	1 636	3 060	3 575	3 796	4 270	4 714	4 922
5111 Value added taxes	0	0	0	0	0	0	0	0	0	0
5112 Sales tax	186	309	831	1 636	3 060	3 575	3 796	4 270	4 714	4 922
Goods and commodities	..	..	..	..	..	1 979	1 710	1 315	1 370	1 486
Beer	..	..	..	..	..	767	952	1 137	1 212	1 438
Vehicles	..	..	..	..	..	0	0	540	643	757
Petroleum products	..	..	..	..	..	234	434	414	522	296
Hotels and restaurants	..	..	..	..	..	318	393	448	500	440
Telecom services	..	..	..	..	..	178	179	223	252	323
Cement	..	..	..	..	..	50	70	92	97	97
Aerated water	..	..	..	..	..	26	35	76	94	85
Entertainment services	..	..	..	..	..	23	23	26	25	0
5113 Other	0	0	0	0	0	0	0	0	0	0
5120 Taxes on specific goods and services	356	287	1 138	2 124	3 987	4 190	5 178	6 546	5 264	2 196
5121 Excises	266	130	878	1 605	2 687	2 483	3 580	4 834	3 406	803
Distillery products	104	130	153	321	481	539	663	885	906	680
Excise duty refund from India	162	0	725	1 284	2 206	1 944	2 917	3 949	2 500	123
5122 Profits of fiscal monopolies	0	0	0	0	0	0	0	0	0	0

	1997	2000	2007	2010	2014	2015	2016	2017	2018	2019
5123 Customs and import duties	65	139	237	483	1 242	1 605	1 472	1 712	1 704	1 280
Customs duty on goods and commodities and customs service charge	..	..	..	..	..	597	563	773	678	468
Fuel	..	..	..	..	..	348	411	405	525	401
Motor vehicles	..	..	..	..	..	659	499	534	501	411
5124 Taxes on exports	19	13	0	0	0	0	0	0	0	0
5125 Taxes on investment goods	0	0	0	0	0	0	0	0	0	0
5126 Taxes on specific services	5	5	23	35	59	103	126	0	154	112
5127 Other taxes on internat. trade and transactions	0	0	0	0	0	0	0	0	0	0
5128 Other taxes	0	0	0	0	0	0	0	0	0	0
5130 Unallocable between 5110 and 5120	0	0	0	0	0	0	0	0	0	0
5200 Taxes on use of goods and to perform activities	0	0	0	0	0	291	344	395	422	345
5210 Recurrent taxes	..	..	..	..	..	259	303	323	351	290
5211 Paid by households: motor vehicles	..	..	..	..	..	172	198	214	238	193
5212 Paid by others: motor vehicles	..	..	..	..	..	0	0	0	0	0
5213 Paid in respect of other goods	..	..	..	..	..	87	105	110	114	97
5220 Non-recurrent taxes	..	..	..	..	..	32	41	72	70	54
5300 Unallocable between 5100 and 5200	0	0	0	0	0	0	0	0	0	0
6000 Other taxes	**1**	**11**	**13**	**20**	**20**	**0**	**0**	**0**	**0**	**0**
6100 Paid solely by business	..	..	..	..	..	..	..	..	..	..
6200 Other	..	..	..	..	..	..	..	..	..	..

Note: Data are reported on a fiscal year basis beginning 1st July. For example, the data for 2019 represent the period from July 2019 to June 2020.
The data are on a cash basis.
Heading 1000: Detailed breakdown of income taxes is not available for 2019 at the time of publication and the numbers may include fines and penalties which are not considered tax revenues by the OECD.
Source: Ministry of Finance, Bhutan.

StatLink https://stat.link/jipwea

Table 4.3. China: Details of tax revenue

Billion CNY

	1997	2000	2007	2010	2014	2015	2016	2017	2018	2019
Total tax revenue	..	..	**4 562**	**7 321**	**11 917**	**12 492**	**13 035**	**14 437**	**15 640**	**21 791**
1000 Taxes on income, profits and capital gains	..	..	**1 237**	**1 896**	**3 593**	**3 958**	**4 315**	**4 899**	**5 484**	**5 416**
1100 Of individuals	..	..	319	484	738	862	1 009	1 197	1 387	1 039
1110 On income and profits	..	..	..	..	..	..	..	..	..	..
1120 On capital gains	..	..	..	..	..	..	..	..	..	..
1200 Corporate	..	..	918	1 412	2 856	3 097	3 306	3 703	4 097	4 377
Enterprise income tax	..	..	878	1 284	2 464	2 713	2 885	3 212	3 532	3 730
Land appreciation tax	..	..	40	128	391	383	421	491	564	647
1210 On profits	..	..	..	..	..	..	..	..	..	..
1220 On capital gains of corporates	..	..	..	..	..	..	..	..	..	..
1300 Unallocable between 1100 and 1200	..	..	0	0	0	0	0	0	0	0
2000 Social security contributions	..	..	..	..	..	..	..	..	..	**5 999**
2100 Employees	..	..	..	..	..	..	..	..	..	..
2110 On a payroll basis	..	..	..	..	..	..	..	..	..	..
2120 On an income tax basis	..	..	..	..	..	..	..	..	..	..
2200 Employers	..	..	..	..	..	..	..	..	..	..
2210 On a payroll basis	..	..	..	..	..	..	..	..	..	..
2220 On an income tax basis	..	..	..	..	..	..	..	..	..	..
2300 Self-employed or non-employed	..	..	..	..	..	..	..	..	..	..
2310 On a payroll basis	..	..	..	..	..	..	..	..	..	..
2320 On an income tax basis	..	..	..	..	..	..	..	..	..	..
2400 Unallocable between 2100, 2200 and 2300	..	..	..	..	..	..	..	..	..	5 999
2410 On a payroll basis	..	..	..	..	..	..	..	..	..	..
2420 On an income tax basis	..	..	..	..	..	..	..	..	..	..
3000 Taxes on payroll and workforce	..	..	**0**	**0**	**0**	**0**	**0**	**0**	**0**	**0**
4000 Taxes on property	..	..	**443**	**540**	**938**	**1 153**	**1 099**	**1 208**	**1 321**	**1 386**
4100 Recurrent taxes on immovable property	..	..	96	190	384	419	448	496	528	518
4110 Households	..	..	0	0	0	0	0	0	0	0
4120 Others	..	..	96	190	384	419	448	496	528	518
House property tax	..	..	58	89	185	205	222	260	289	299
Urban and town land use tax	..	..	39	100	199	214	226	236	239	220
4200 Recurrent taxes on net wealth	..	..	0	0	0	0	0	0	0	0
4210 Individual	..	..	..	..	..	..	..	..	..	..
4220 Corporate	..	..	..	..	..	..	..	..	..	..
4300 Estate, inheritance and gift taxes	..	..	0	0	0	0	0	0	0	0
4310 Estate and inheritance taxes	..	..	..	..	..	..	..	..	..	..
4320 Gift taxes	..	..	..	..	..	..	..	..	..	..
4400 Taxes on financial and capital transactions	..	..	347	351	554	734	651	712	793	868
Stamp tax on securities transactions	..	..	201	54	67	255	125	107	98	123
Other stamp duties	..	..	26	50	87	89	96	114	122	123
Deed tax	..	..	121	246	400	390	430	491	573	621
4500 Other non-reccurrent taxes on property	..	..	0	0	0	0	0	0	0	0
4510 On net wealth	..	..	..	..	..	..	..	..	..	..
4520 Other non-recurrent taxes	..	..	..	..	..	..	..	..	..	..
4600 Other recurrent taxes on property	..	..	0	0	0	0	0	0	0	0
5000 Taxes on goods and services	..	..	**2 882**	**4 885**	**7 386**	**7 381**	**7 621**	**8 329**	**8 836**	**8 990**
5100 Taxes on production, sale, transfer, etc	..	..	2 855	4 769	7 121	7 105	7 345	8 081	8 601	8 736
5110 General taxes on goods and services	..	..	2 373	3 730	5 535	5 397	5 688	6 284	6 734	6 581
5111 Value added taxes	..	..	1 715	2 614	3 757	3 466	4 538	6 284	6 734	6 581
Domestic VAT	..	..	1 547	2 109	3 086	3 111	4 071	5 638	6 153	6 235
Import VAT	..	..	615	1 049	1 443	1 253	1 278	1 597	1 688	1 512
Urban maintenance and construction tax	..	..	116	189	364	389	403	436	484	482
Refund of VAT for export	..	..	-563	-733	-1 136	-1 287	-1 215	-1 387	-1 591	-1 648
5112 Sales tax	..	..	0	0	0	0	0	0	0	0
5113 Other	..	..	658	1 116	1 778	1 931	1 150	0	0	0
Business tax	..	..	658	1 116	1 778	1 931	1 150	0	0	0
5120 Taxes on specific goods and services	..	..	483	1 039	1 586	1 707	1 658	1 797	1 867	2 155
5121 Excises	..	..	313	794	1 193	1 348	1 302	1 362	1 420	1 684
Domestic excise tax	..	..	221	607	891	1 054	1 022	1 023	1 063	1 256
Import excise tax	..	..	0	0	0	0	0	0	0	69
Motor vehicles purchase tax	..	..	88	179	289	279	267	328	345	350
Leaf tobacco tax	..	..	5	8	14	14	13	12	11	11
Refund of excise tax for export	..	..	0	0	0	0	0	0	0	-2
5122 Profits of fiscal monopolies	..	..	0	0	0	0	0	0	0	0
5123 Customs and import duties	..	..	143	203	284	256	260	300	285	289
5124 Taxes on exports	..	..	0	0	0	0	0	0	0	0
5125 Taxes on investment goods	..	..	0	0	0	0	0	0	0	0
5126 Taxes on specific services	..	..	0	0	0	0	0	0	0	0
5127 Other taxes on internat. trade and transactions	..	..	0	0	0	0	0	0	0	0

	1997	2000	2007	2010	2014	2015	2016	2017	2018	2019
5128 Other taxes	..	..	26	42	108	103	95	135	163	182
Resources tax	..	..	26	42	108	103	95	135	163	182
5130 Unallocable between 5110 and 5120	..	..	0	0	0	0	0	0	0	0
5200 Taxes on use of goods and to perform activities	..	..	27	116	265	276	276	248	235	254
5210 Recurrent taxes	..	..	7	24	54	61	68	77	83	88
Vehicle and vessel tax	..	..	7	24	54	61	68	77	83	88
5211 Paid by households: motor vehicles	..	..	..	..	..	..	..	..	..	..
5212 Paid by others: motor vehicles	..	..	..	..	..	..	..	..	..	..
5213 Paid in respect of other goods	..	..	..	..	..	..	..	..	..	..
5220 Non-recurrent taxes	..	..	20	92	210	214	208	170	152	166
Cultivated land use tax	..	..	19	89	206	210	203	165	132	139
Vessel tonnage tax	..	..	2	3	5	5	5	5	5	5
Environmental protection tax	..	..	0	0	0	0	0	0	15	22
5300 Unallocable between 5100 and 5200	..	..	0	0	0	0	0	0	0	0
6000 Other taxes	**..**	**..**	**0**	**0**	**0**	**0**	**0**	**0**	**0**	**0**
6100 Paid solely by business	..	..	..	..	..	..	..	..	..	..
6200 Other	..	..	..	..	..	..	..	..	..	..

Note: Year ending 31st December.
The data are on a cash basis.
Heading 2000: Social security contribution data for China include contributions from old-age insurance, medical insurance, unemployment insurance and employment injury insurance. The figures also include contributions to individual accounts, which are not considered as tax revenues by the OECD.
Heading 2000, 2007 to 2018: SSC data are not available.
Heading 5111: In years prior to 2019, import VAT also included import excise tax as they cannot be distinguished. Similarly, before 2019, refund of VAT for export also included refund of excise tax for export as they cannot be distinguished. In both cases, the VAT portions accounted for the majority of combined revenues. The heading "Urban maintenance and construction tax" is a surtax of both VAT and excises, but it is not possible to distinguish revenues between the two sources. It is classified under heading 5111 as VAT is the main source of revenues. A small portion of urban maintenance and construction tax should be attributed to the central government. This portion is identified in 2019 but it is not possible to separate the central and local portions in previous years.
Source: Ministry of Finance of China.

StatLink https://stat.link/n1vgh9

Table 4.4. Cook Islands: Details of tax revenue

Thousand NZD

	1997	2000	2007	2010	2014	2015	2016	2017	2018	2019
Total tax revenue	..	..	**78 330**	**91 161**	**90 572**	**117 445**	**126 010**	**142 539**	**163 423**	**141 406**
1000 Taxes on income, profits and capital gains	..	..	**30 685**	**35 916**	**23 213**	**41 090**	**42 210**	**52 127**	**63 029**	**47 495**
1100 Of individuals	..	..	22 163	26 277	14 189	27 696	26 055	30 039	38 432	30 025
1110 On income and profits	..	..	22 163	26 277	14 189	27 696	26 055	30 039	38 432	30 025
Net Income Tax	..	..	22 163	26 361	11 963	24 768	24 298	28 197	36 929	28 757
Withholding Tax	..	..	0	-84	2 226	2 928	1 757	1 842	1 504	1 268
1120 On capital gains	..	..	0	0	0	0	0	0	0	0
1200 Corporate	..	..	8 523	9 638	9 024	13 394	16 155	22 089	24 596	17 470
1210 On profits	..	..	8 523	9 638	9 024	13 394	16 155	22 089	24 596	17 470
1220 On capital gains of corporates	..	..	0	0	0	0	0	0	0	0
1300 Unallocable between 1100 and 1200	..	..	0	0	0	0	0	0	0	0
2000 Social security contributions	..	..	**0**	**0**	**0**	**0**	**0**	**0**	**0**	**0**
2100 Employees	..	..	..	..	..	..	..	..	..	..
2110 On a payroll basis	..	..	..	..	..	..	..	..	..	..
2120 On an income tax basis	..	..	..	..	..	..	..	..	..	..
2200 Employers	..	..	..	..	..	..	..	..	..	..
2210 On a payroll basis	..	..	..	..	..	..	..	..	..	..
2220 On an income tax basis	..	..	..	..	..	..	..	..	..	..
2300 Self-employed or non-employed	..	..	..	..	..	..	..	..	..	..
2310 On a payroll basis	..	..	..	..	..	..	..	..	..	..
2320 On an income tax basis	..	..	..	..	..	..	..	..	..	..
2400 Unallocable between 2100, 2200 and 2300	..	..	..	..	..	..	..	..	..	..
2410 On a payroll basis	..	..	..	..	..	..	..	..	..	..
2420 On an income tax basis	..	..	..	..	..	..	..	..	..	..
3000 Taxes on payroll and workforce	..	..	**0**	**0**	**0**	**0**	**0**	**0**	**0**	**0**
4000 Taxes on property	..	..	**0**	**0**	**0**	**0**	**0**	**0**	**0**	**0**
4100 Recurrent taxes on immovable property	..	..	..	..	..	..	..	..	..	..
4110 Households	..	..	..	..	..	..	..	..	..	..
4120 Others	..	..	..	..	..	..	..	..	..	..
4200 Recurrent taxes on net wealth	..	..	..	..	..	..	..	..	..	..
4210 Individual	..	..	..	..	..	..	..	..	..	..
4220 Corporate	..	..	..	..	..	..	..	..	..	..
4300 Estate, inheritance and gift taxes	..	..	..	..	..	..	..	..	..	..
4310 Estate and inheritance taxes	..	..	..	..	..	..	..	..	..	..
4320 Gift taxes	..	..	..	..	..	..	..	..	..	..
4400 Taxes on financial and capital transactions	..	..	..	..	..	..	..	..	..	..
4500 Other non-reccurrent taxes on property	..	..	..	..	..	..	..	..	..	..
4510 On net wealth	..	..	..	..	..	..	..	..	..	..
4520 Other non-recurrent taxes	..	..	..	..	..	..	..	..	..	..
4600 Other recurrent taxes on property	..	..	..	..	..	..	..	..	..	..
5000 Taxes on goods and services	..	..	**47 645**	**55 246**	**67 359**	**76 355**	**83 800**	**90 411**	**100 394**	**93 911**
5100 Taxes on production, sale, transfer, etc	..	..	46 772	54 398	66 142	75 495	82 703	89 199	99 252	93 095
5110 General taxes on goods and services	..	..	33 973	37 444	47 459	54 708	58 140	63 330	72 958	68 579
5111 Value added taxes	..	..	33 955	37 381	47 453	54 659	58 124	63 330	72 958	68 579
VAT revenues (gross)	..	..	41 689	45 454	62 549	67 855	70 574	82 054	86 189	82 242
VAT refunds	..	..	-5 043	-4 365	-7 507	-7 433	-7 796	-9 965	-3 697	-3 959
VAT on Crown Appropriations	..	..	-2 692	-3 707	-7 589	-5 763	-4 653	-8 759	-9 535	-9 704
5112 Sales tax	..	..	0	0	0	0	0	0	0	0
5113 Other	..	..	18	63	6	49	16	0	0	0
5120 Taxes on specific goods and services	..	..	12 799	16 955	18 682	20 787	24 564	25 869	26 294	24 516
5121 Excises	..	..	0	0	0	0	0	0	0	0
5122 Profits of fiscal monopolies	..	..	0	0	0	0	0	0	0	0
5123 Customs and import duties	..	..	9 810	11 052	10 536	12 320	14 330	15 098	14 566	15 407
5124 Taxes on exports	..	..	0	0	0	0	0	0	0	0
5125 Taxes on investment goods	..	..	0	0	0	0	0	0	0	0
5126 Taxes on specific services	..	..	2 989	5 903	8 146	8 468	10 234	10 771	11 729	9 109
5127 Other taxes on internat. trade and transactions	..	..	0	0	0	0	0	0	0	0
5128 Other taxes	..	..	0	0	0	0	0	0	0	0
5130 Unallocable between 5110 and 5120	..	..	0	0	0	0	0	0	0	0
5200 Taxes on use of goods and to perform activities	..	..	873	847	1 217	860	1 097	1 212	1 142	816
5210 Recurrent taxes	..	..	218	207	186	229	209	291	271	323
5211 Paid by households: motor vehicles	..	..	0	0	0	0	0	0	0	0
5212 Paid by others: motor vehicles	..	..	0	0	0	0	0	0	0	0
5213 Paid in respect of other goods	..	..	218	207	186	229	209	291	271	323
5220 Non-recurrent taxes	..	..	655	640	1 032	631	888	922	871	493
5300 Unallocable between 5100 and 5200	..	..	0	0	0	0	0	0	0	0
6000 Other taxes	..	..	**0**	**0**	**0**	**0**	**0**	**0**	**0**	**0**
6100 Paid solely by business	..	..	..	..	..	..	..	..	..	..
6200 Other	..	..	..	..	..	..	..	..	..	..

Note: Data are reported on a fiscal year basis beginning 1st July. For example, the data for 2019 represent the period from July 2019 to June 2020.
The data are on a cash basis.
Figures exclude tax revenues collected by sub-national governments as the data are not available.
Source: Ministry of Finance and Economic Management of the Cook Islands.

StatLink https://stat.link/3tzglr

Table 4.5. Fiji: Details of tax revenue

Million FJD

	1997	2000	2007	2010	2014	2015	2016	2017	2018	2019
Total tax revenue	..	..	..	**1 304**	**2 080**	**2 318**	**2 387**	**2 679**	**2 739**	**2 637**
1000 Taxes on income, profits and capital gains	..	..	..	**426**	**514**	**598**	**730**	**845**	**769**	**712**
1100 Of individuals	..	..	..	184	209	211	222	231	224	202
1110 On income and profits	..	..	..	184	166	187	198	200	177	182
PAYE	..	..	..	184	140	159	167	167	146	152
Social responsibility tax	..	..	..	0	8	8	11	10	8	7
Fringe benefit tax	..	..	..	0	19	20	21	24	22	23
1120 On capital gains	..	..	..	0	43	24	23	31	47	20
1200 Corporate	..	..	..	242	305	386	508	614	545	510
1210 On profits	..	..	..	242	305	386	508	614	545	510
Company Tax	..	..	..	161	208	291	348	445	385	358
Dividend and Withholding	..	..	..	73	85	85	105	121	120	119
Provisional tax	..	..	..	11	11	10	49	59	61	68
Other income taxes	..	..	..	30	30	45	44	49	57	49
Income tax refunds	..	..	..	-34	-28	-45	-38	-60	-78	-83
1220 On capital gains of corporates	..	..	..	0	0	0	0	0	0	0
1300 Unallocable between 1100 and 1200	..	..	..	0	0	0	0	0	0	0
2000 Social security contributions	..	..	..	**0**	**0**	**0**	**0**	**0**	**0**	**0**
2100 Employees	..	..	..	..	..	..	..	..	..	..
2110 On a payroll basis	..	..	..	..	..	..	..	..	..	..
2120 On an income tax basis	..	..	..	..	..	..	..	..	..	..
2200 Employers	..	..	..	..	..	..	..	..	..	..
2210 On a payroll basis	..	..	..	..	..	..	..	..	..	..
2220 On an income tax basis	..	..	..	..	..	..	..	..	..	..
2300 Self-employed or non-employed	..	..	..	..	..	..	..	..	..	..
2310 On a payroll basis	..	..	..	..	..	..	..	..	..	..
2320 On an income tax basis	..	..	..	..	..	..	..	..	..	..
2400 Unallocable between 2100, 2200 and 2300	..	..	..	..	..	..	..	..	..	..
2410 On a payroll basis	..	..	..	..	..	..	..	..	..	..
2420 On an income tax basis	..	..	..	..	..	..	..	..	..	..
3000 Taxes on payroll and workforce	..	..	..	**0**	**0**	**0**	**0**	**0**	**0**	**0**
4000 Taxes on property	..	..	..	**0**	**68**	**71**	**78**	**78**	**92**	**79**
4100 Recurrent taxes on immovable property	..	..	..	..	0	0	0	0	0	0
4110 Households	..	..	..	..	..	..	..	..	..	..
4120 Others	..	..	..	..	..	..	..	..	..	..
4200 Recurrent taxes on net wealth	..	..	..	..	0	0	0	0	0	0
4210 Individual	..	..	..	..	..	..	..	..	..	..
4220 Corporate	..	..	..	..	..	..	..	..	..	..
4300 Estate, inheritance and gift taxes	..	..	..	..	0	0	0	0	0	0
4310 Estate and inheritance taxes	..	..	..	..	..	..	..	..	..	..
4320 Gift taxes	..	..	..	..	..	..	..	..	..	..
4400 Taxes on financial and capital transactions	..	..	..	..	68	71	78	78	92	79
4500 Other non-reccurrent taxes on property	..	..	..	..	0	0	0	0	0	0
4510 On net wealth	..	..	..	..	..	..	..	..	..	..
4520 Other non-recurrent taxes	..	..	..	..	..	..	..	..	..	..
4600 Other recurrent taxes on property	..	..	..	..	0	0	0	0	0	0
5000 Taxes on goods and services	..	..	..	**878**	**1 498**	**1 650**	**1 580**	**1 757**	**1 879**	**1 846**
5100 Taxes on production, sale, transfer, etc	..	..	..	877	1 496	1 648	1 578	1 755	1 877	1 844
5110 General taxes on goods and services	..	..	..	526	852	958	774	864	882	892
5111 Value added taxes	..	..	..	496	794	893	653	744	789	804
VAT revenues (gross)	..	..	..	646	1 102	1 204	943	987	1 049	1 014
VAT refunds	..	..	..	-150	-308	-311	-290	-243	-259	-210
5112 Sales tax	..	..	..	0	0	0	0	0	0	0
5113 Other	..	..	..	31	58	65	121	121	93	88
5120 Taxes on specific goods and services	..	..	..	350	644	690	804	890	995	952
5121 Excises	..	..	..	88	139	145	246	313	394	370
Environmental levy	..	..	..	0	0	0	67	108	161	166
Import excises	..	..	..	20	43	43	47	54	61	41
Domestic excises	..	..	..	81	98	106	134	154	174	167
Other excises	..	..	..	5	2	2	2	2	2	2
Rebates	..	..	..	-17	-6	-6	-5	-5	-4	-6
5122 Profits of fiscal monopolies	..	..	..	0	0	0	0	0	0	0
5123 Customs and import duties	..	..	..	252	365	392	398	419	441	420
5124 Taxes on exports	..	..	..	9	10	10	10	10	9	8
5125 Taxes on investment goods	..	..	..	0	0	0	0	0	0	0
5126 Taxes on specific services	..	..	..	0	130	143	150	148	150	154
5127 Other taxes on internat. trade and transactions	..	..	..	0	0	0	0	0	0	0
5128 Other taxes	..	..	..	0	0	0	0	0	0	0
5130 Unallocable between 5110 and 5120	..	..	..	0	0	0	0	0	0	0

	1997	2000	2007	2010	2014	2015	2016	2017	2018	2019
5200 Taxes on use of goods and to perform activities	..	..	..	2	2	2	2	2	2	2
5210 Recurrent taxes	..	..	..	2	2	1	1	2	2	2
5211 Paid by households: motor vehicles	..	..	..	0	0	0	0	0	0	0
5212 Paid by others: motor vehicles	..	..	..	0	0	0	0	0	0	0
5213 Paid in respect of other goods	..	..	..	2	2	1	1	2	2	2
5220 Non-recurrent taxes	..	..	..	0	0	0	0	0	0	0
5300 Unallocable between 5100 and 5200	..	..	..	0	0	0	0	0	0	0
6000 Other taxes	**..**	**..**	**..**	**0**	**0**	**0**	**0**	**0**	**0**	**0**
6100 Paid solely by business	..	..	..	..	..	..	..	..	..	..
6200 Other	..	..	..	..	..	..	..	..	..	..

Note: Year ending 31st December.
The data are on a cash basis.
Figures exclude tax revenues collected by sub-national governments as the data are not available.
The resource tax and the tourist VAT refund registration fee (about 0.6% of GDP in 2019) are not included in tax revenues. These revenues are considered as non-tax revenue in accordance with the OECD classification, as set out in the Interpretative Guide in Annex A.
Source: Revenue and Customs Service of Fiji.

StatLink https://stat.link/pf9jrn

Table 4.6. Indonesia: Details of tax revenue

Billion IDR

	1997	2000	2007	2010	2014	2015	2016	2017	2018	2019
Total tax revenue	**57 340**	**119 697**	**528 453**	**779 484**	**1 285 635**	**1 395 962**	**1 489 357**	**1 578 033**	**1 776 622**	**1 834 711**
1000 Taxes on income, profits and capital gains	**27 062**	**57 073**	**238 431**	**357 046**	**546 181**	**602 308**	**666 212**	**646 793**	**749 977**	**772 266**
1100 Of individuals	..	..	77 250	62 221	121 566	132 761	131 307	139 030	160 775	179 373
1110 On income and profits	..	..	..	59 540	117 447	128 550	127 267	135 002	156 418	172 444
1120 On capital gains	..	..	..	2 682	4 119	4 211	4 040	4 028	4 357	6 929
1200 Corporate	..	..	161 181	294 824	424 614	469 547	534 905	507 764	589 202	592 893
1210 On profits	..	..	..	287 843	410 181	434 471	492 908	497 491	577 862	585 031
1220 On capital gains	..	..	..	6 981	14 434	35 076	41 998	10 273	11 340	7 862
1300 Unallocable between 1100 and 1200	27 062	57 073	0	0	0	0	0	0	0	0
2000 Social security contributions	**..**	**..**	**..**	**..**	**..**	**7 715**	**47 220**	**54 401**	**63 643**	**79 631**
2100 Employees	..	..	..	..	..	1 590	1 829	2 121	2 494	2 814
2110 On a payroll basis	..	..	..	..	..	..	..	..	..	..
2120 On an income tax basis	..	..	..	..	..	..	..	..	..	..
2200 Employers	..	..	..	..	..	3 505	4 108	4 650	5 322	5 926
2210 On a payroll basis	..	..	..	..	..	..	..	..	..	..
2220 On an income tax basis	..	..	..	..	..	..	..	..	..	..
2300 Self-employed or non-employed	..	..	..	..	..	..	..	..	..	..
2310 On a payroll basis	..	..	..	..	..	..	..	..	..	..
2320 On an income tax basis	..	..	..	..	..	..	..	..	..	..
2400 Unallocable between 2100, 2200 and 2300	..	..	..	..	..	2 620	41 283	47 630	55 827	70 891
2410 On a payroll basis	..	..	..	..	..	..	..	..	..	..
2420 On an income tax basis	..	..	..	..	..	..	..	..	..	..
3000 Taxes on payroll and workforce	**0**	**0**	**0**	**0**	**0**	**0**	**0**	**0**	**0**	**0**
4000 Taxes on property	**2 413**	**4 456**	**32 161**	**40 537**	**28 400**	**33 826**	**23 885**	**21 854**	**24 901**	**26 744**
4100 Recurrent taxes on immovable property	2 413	3 525	23 724	28 581	23 476	29 250	19 443	16 770	19 445	21 146
4110 Households	..	..	..	..	..	..	..	..	..	..
4120 Others	..	..	..	..	..	..	..	..	..	..
4200 Recurrent taxes on net wealth	0	0	0	0	0	0	0	0	0	0
4210 Individual	..	..	..	..	..	..	..	..	..	..
4220 Corporate	..	..	..	..	..	..	..	..	..	..
4300 Estate, inheritance and gift taxes	0	0	0	0	0	0	0	0	0	0
4310 Estate and inheritance taxes	..	..	..	..	..	..	..	..	..	..
4320 Gift taxes	..	..	..	..	..	..	..	..	..	..
4400 Taxes on financial and capital transactions	0	931	8 438	11 956	4 924	4 576	4 441	5 083	5 456	5 598
Tax on acquisition of land and buildings	..	931	8 438	11 956	4 924	4 576	4 441	5 083	5 456	5 598
4500 Non-recurrent taxes	0	0	0	0	0	0	0	0	0	0
4510 On net wealth	..	..	..	..	..	..	..	..	..	..
4520 Other non-recurrent taxes	..	..	..	..	..	..	..	..	..	..
4600 Other recurrent taxes on property	0	0	0	0	0	0	0	0	0	0
5000 Taxes on goods and services	**27 274**	**53 547**	**220 143**	**325 685**	**571 303**	**603 869**	**592 291**	**674 209**	**743 395**	**745 592**
5100 Taxes on production, sale, transfer, etc	27 274	53 547	220 143	325 685	571 303	603 869	592 291	674 209	743 395	745 592
5110 General taxes	20 351	35 232	154 527	230 605	409 570	424 288	413 295	481 707	537 924	532 116
5111 Value added taxes	20 351	35 232	154 527	218 133	393 463	410 391	395 616	464 477	520 390	515 972
5112 Sales tax	0	0	0	12 472	16 107	13 897	17 680	17 230	17 534	16 144
5113 Other	0	0	0	0	0	0	0	0	0	0
5120 Taxes on specific goods and services	6 923	18 315	65 616	95 080	161 734	179 581	178 996	192 502	205 470	213 476
5121 Excises	4 263	11 287	44 679	66 166	118 086	144 641	143 525	153 288	159 589	172 422
5122 Profits of fiscal monopolies	0	0	0	0	0	0	0	0	0	0
5123 Customs and import duties	2 579	6 697	16 699	20 017	32 319	31 213	32 472	35 066	39 117	37 527
5124 Taxes on exports	81	331	4 237	8 898	11 329	3 727	2 999	4 147	6 765	3 527
5125 Taxes on investment goods	0	0	0	0	0	0	0	0	0	0
5126 Taxes on specific services	0	0	0	0	0	0	0	0	0	0
5127 Other taxes on internat. trade and transactions	0	0	0	0	0	0	0	0	0	0
5128 Other taxes	0	0	0	0	0	0	0	0	0	0
5130 Unallocable between 5110 and 5120	0	0	0	0	0	0	0	0	0	0
5200 Taxes on use of goods and to perform activities	0	0	0	0	0	0	0	0	0	0
5210 Recurrent taxes	..	..	..	..	..	..	..	..	..	..
5211 Paid by households: motor vehicles	..	..	..	..	..	..	..	..	..	..
5212 Paid by others: motor vehicles	..	..	..	..	..	..	..	..	..	..
5213 Paid in respect of other goods	..	..	..	..	..	..	..	..	..	..
5220 Non-recurrent taxes	..	..	..	..	..	..	..	..	..	..
5300 Unallocable between 5100 and 5200	0	0	0	0	0	0	0	0	0	0
6000 Other taxes	**591**	**4 621**	**37 718**	**56 216**	**139 750**	**148 244**	**159 748**	**180 775**	**194 707**	**210 479**
6100 Paid solely by business	0	0	0	0	0	0	0	0	0	0
6200 Other	591	4 621	37 718	56 216	139 750	148 244	159 748	180 775	194 707	210 479
Other local level	0	3 784	34 981	56 177	138 769	147 829	157 166	180 101	194 190	208 938
Other non local level	591	837	2 738	39	981	416	2 582	674	517	1 541

Note: Year ending 31st December.
The data are on a cash basis.
Revenue data in 2016 and 2017 include revenues from the "Tax Amnesty" policy which will not be repeated in the following year.
Revenue data since 2008 have been updated based on more detailed classification provided by the government.
Heading 2000: Social security contribution data are obtained from BPJS Kesehatan and BPJS Ketenagakerjaan. The government of Indonesia does not consider social security contributions as part of tax revenues.
Heading 2100: Includes Death Benefit (JK), a life insurance with payment for participants upon the death of their wives/husbands/children or for families upon the death of participants.
Heading 2200: Includes Work Accident Insurance (JKK) which provides protection against the risks of work-related accidents.
Heading 2400: Includes Pension Insurance (JP), and mandatory contributions from BPJS Health for formal workers. Data in 2015 only include Pension Insurance (JP). Contributions from the BPJS Health for 2018 and 2019 are estimated.
Heading 6200: Other non local level tax revenues have been classified under central government in this edition. They were previously under local government.

Source: Fiscal Policy Agency, Ministry of Finance; BPJS Kesehatan (Social Security Administrator for Health); BPJS Ketenagakerjaan (Employees Social Security System).

StatLink https://stat.link/eoxs4u

Table 4.7. Japan: Details of tax revenue

Billion JPY

	1997	2000	2007	2010	2014	2015	2016	2017	2018	2019
Total tax revenue	**139 617**	**136 236**	**146 248**	**132 484**	**156 886**	**163 533**	**164 970**	**171 806**	**175 564**	**107 393**
1000 Taxes on income, profits and capital gains	**51 673**	**47 398**	**53 174**	**40 034**	**49 939**	**50 969**	**50 448**	**52 658**	**56 083**	**56 704**
1100 Of individuals	29 809	28 677	28 600	24 663	29 655	30 847	30 670	32 325	33 492	33 512
1110 On income and profits	29 809	28 677	28 600	24 663	29 655	30 847	30 670	32 325	33 492	33 512
Income tax	19 183	18 789	16 080	12 984	17 139	18 178	17 978	19 276	20 316	20 354
Prefectural inhabitants tax	3 183	3 621	5 008	4 699	5 215	5 252	5 128	5 376	4 863	4 751
Municipal inhabitants tax	7 172	6 044	7 294	6 795	7 114	7 224	7 365	7 471	8 106	8 196
Enterprise tax	271	223	218	184	186	194	198	203	207	211
1120 On capital gains	0	0	0	0	0	0	0	0	0	0
1200 Corporate	21 864	18 721	24 573	15 372	20 284	20 122	19 778	20 333	22 591	23 193
1210 On profits	21 864	18 721	24 573	15 372	20 284	20 122	19 778	20 333	22 591	23 193
Corporation tax	13 477	11 747	14 744	8 968	11 464	10 832	10 332	11 995	12 318	12 858
Prefectural inhabitants tax	1 026	879	1 206	777	963	859	763	762	835	824
Municipal inhabitants tax	2 532	2 176	3 015	1 954	2 445	2 324	2 392	2 224	2 427	2 409
Enterprise tax	4 830	3 918	5 608	2 253	3 017	3 510	4 395	3 991	4 243	4 278
Local special corporate tax	0	0	0	1 420	2 395	2 081	1 782	1 858	2 088	2 136
Local corporate tax	0	0	0	0	1	516	629	654	681	688
1220 On capital gains	0	0	0	0	0	0	0	0	0	0
1300 Unallocable between 1100 and 1200	0	0	0	0	0	0	0	0	0	0
2000 Social security contributions	**47 861**	**47 968**	**53 325**	**54 461**	**62 252**	**64 465**	**66 622**	**68 616**	**70 588**	**..**
2100 Employees	19 682	19 830	21 975	23 593	27 168	28 224	29 312	32 578	33 656	..
2110 On a payroll basis	19 682	19 830	21 975	23 593	27 168	28 224	29 312	32 578	33 656	..
2120 On an income tax basis	0	0	0	0	0	0	0	0	0	..
2200 Employers	22 826	22 456	24 243	24 674	28 374	29 479	30 540	31 648	32 664	..
2210 On a payroll basis	22 826	22 456	24 243	24 674	28 374	29 479	30 540	31 648	32 664	..
2220 On an income tax basis	0	0	0	0	0	0	0	0	0	..
2300 Self-employed or non-employed	5 352	5 683	7 108	6 194	6 710	6 763	6 771	4 390	4 268	..
2310 On a payroll basis	5 352	5 683	7 108	6 194	6 710	6 763	6 771	4 390	4 268	..
2320 On an income tax basis	0	0	0	0	0	0	0	0	0	..
2400 Unallocable between 2100, 2200 and 2300	0	0	0	0	0	0	0	0	0	..
2410 On a payroll basis	..	..	..	..	..	..	..	..	..	..
2420 On an income tax basis	..	..	..	..	..	..	..	..	..	..
3000 Taxes on payroll and workforce	**0**	**0**	**0**	**0**	**0**	**0**	**0**	**0**	**0**	**0**
4000 Taxes on property	**15 679**	**14 294**	**13 138**	**12 878**	**13 306**	**13 400**	**13 772**	**14 073**	**14 196**	**14 304**
4100 Recurrent taxes on immovable property	10 410	10 414	9 949	10 225	10 016	10 005	10 165	10 323	10 386	10 604
Prefectural property tax	8	11	14	5	2	2	3	4	11	8
Municipal property tax	8 822	9 041	8 729	8 961	8 769	8 755	9 077	9 025	9 083	9 279
City planning tax	1 326	1 318	1 202	1 256	1 244	1 244	1 262	1 277	1 291	1 317
Special landholding tax	94	43	4	3	2	3	7	1	0	0
Water and land utilization tax	0	0	0	0	0	0	0	0	0	0
Land value tax	160	1	0	0	0	0	0	0	0	0
4110 Households	..	..	..	..	..	..	..	..	..	..
4120 Others	..	..	..	..	..	..	..	..	..	..
4200 Recurrent taxes on net wealth	0	0	0	0	0	0	0	0	0	0
4210 Individual	..	..	..	..	..	..	..	..	..	..
4220 Corporate	..	..	..	..	..	..	..	..	..	..
4300 Estate, inheritance and gift taxes	2 413	1 782	1 503	1 250	1 883	1 968	2 131	2 292	2 333	2 232
4310 Estate and inheritance taxes	..	..	..	..	..	..	..	..	..	..
Inheritance tax	..	..	..	..	..	..	..	..	..	..
4320 Gift taxes	..	..	..	..	..	..	..	..	..	..
Tax on gifts	..	..	..	..	..	..	..	..	..	..
4400 Taxes on financial and capital transactions	2 856	2 099	1 686	1 403	1 407	1 426	1 476	1 458	1 477	1 468
Bourse tax	40	0	0	0	0	0	0	0	0	0
Securities transaction	404	0	0	0	0	0	0	0	0	0
Bank of Japan note issue tax	0	0	0	0	0	0	0	0	0	0
Stamp revenues	1 681	1 532	1 202	1 024	1 035	1 050	1 079	1 052	1 073	1 049
Real property acquisition tax	731	567	485	379	372	377	397	407	404	419
4500 Non-recurrent taxes	0	0	0	0	0	0	0	0	0	0
4510 On net wealth	..	..	..	..	..	..	..	..	..	..
4520 Other non-recurrent taxes	..	..	..	..	..	..	..	..	..	..
4600 Other recurrent taxes on property	0	0	0	0	0	0	0	0	0	0
5000 Taxes on goods and services	**24 058**	**26 227**	**26 256**	**24 730**	**30 991**	**34 286**	**33 711**	**36 031**	**34 252**	**35 938**
5100 Taxes on production, sale, transfer, etc.	21 132	23 180	23 241	22 160	28 587	31 871	31 254	33 582	31 754	33 401
5110 General taxes	10 112	12 350	12 841	12 675	19 135	22 400	21 931	22 249	22 496	24 231
5111 Value added taxes	10 112	12 350	12 841	12 675	19 135	22 400	21 931	22 249	22 496	24 231
5112 Sales tax	0	0	0	0	0	0	0	0	0	0
5113 Other	0	0	0	0	0	0	0	0	0	0
5120 Taxes on specific goods and services	11 021	10 830	10 400	9 485	9 452	9 470	9 323	11 333	9 258	9 169

	1997	2000	2007	2010	2014	2015	2016	2017	2018	2019
5121 Excise duties	9 764	9 837	9 374	8 622	8 308	8 351	8 316	10 241	8 121	8 070
Liquor tax	1 962	1 816	1 524	1 389	1 328	1 338	1 320	1 304	1 275	1 271
Sugar excises	0	0	0	0	0	0	0	0	0	0
Local gasoline tax	276	296	302	294	266	264	261	256	251	246
Gasoline tax	2 583	2 769	2 820	2 750	2 486	2 465	2 434	2 396	2 348	2 303
Liquefied petroleum gas tax	29	28	27	24	19	18	17	17	15	14
Aviation fuel tax	104	104	104	89	67	66	66	67	68	67
Commodity tax	0	0	0	0	0	0	0	0	0	0
Playing-card tax	0	0	0	0	0	0	0	0	0	0
Prefectural tobacco tax	248	282	278	256	155	153	149	141	139	142
Municipal tobacco tax	799	865	853	788	950	936	911	862	850	871
Timber delivery tax	0	0	0	0	0	0	0	0	0	0
Mineral product tax	2	2	2	2	2	2	2	2	2	2
Electricity and gas tax	0	0	0	0	0	0	0	0	0	0
Diesel oil tax	1 331	1 208	1 034	918	936	925	933	949	958	958
Vehicle acquisition tax	562	464	425	192	86	137	146	190	198	94
Promotion of power resources development tax	354	375	352	349	321	316	320	326	322	330
Petroleum and coal tax	497	489	513	502	631	630	702	691	701	707
Tobacco tax	1 018	876	925	908	919	954	914	864	861	889
Special tobacco tax	0	264	214	163	142	148	141	134	125	126
5122 Profits of fiscal monopolies	0	0	0	0	0	0	0	0	0	0
Monopoly profits	..	..	..	..	..	..	..	..	..	..
5123 Customs and import duties	1 012	877	941	786	1 073	1 049	939	1 024	1 071	1 034
Customs duty	1 012	877	941	786	1 073	1 049	939	1 024	1 071	1 034
5124 Taxes on exports	0	0	0	0	0	0	0	0	0	0
5125 Taxes on investment goods	0	0	0	0	0	0	0	0	0	0
5126 Taxes on specific services	245	116	85	77	70	70	68	67	66	65
Travel tax	0	0	0	0	0	0	0	0	0	0
Admission tax	0	0	0	0	0	0	0	0	0	0
Local entertainment tax	0	0	0	0	0	0	0	0	0	0
Golf course utilization tax	98	81	60	55	48	48	46	45	43	42
Meal and lodging tax	0	0	0	0	0	0	0	0	0	0
Special local consumption tax	125	12	0	0	0	0	0	0	0	0
Bathing tax	22	23	25	22	22	23	22	23	22	23
5127 Other taxes on internat. trade and transactions	0	0	0	0	0	0	0	0	0	0
5128 Other taxes	0	0	0	0	0	0	0	0	0	0
5130 Unallocable between 5110 and 5120	0	0	0	0	0	0	0	0	0	0
5200 Taxes on use of goods and perform activities	2 926	3 047	3 015	2 570	2 404	2 416	2 457	2 450	2 498	2 537
5210 Recurrent taxes	2 905	3 027	2 993	2 548	2 382	2 393	2 435	2 427	2 475	2 512
Automobile tax	1 705	1 765	1 717	1 616	1 556	1 543	1 535	1 541	1 550	1 591
Light vehicle tax	113	125	164	178	195	200	238	249	258	269
Motor vehicle tonnage tax	1 084	1 134	1 110	753	629	649	660	637	665	651
Hunter licence tax	2	2	0	0	0	0	0	0	0	0
Hunting tax	1	1	2	2	2	1	1	1	1	1
Mine lot tax	1	1	0	0	0	0	0	0	0	0
5211 Paid by households: motor vehicles	..	..	..	..	..	..	..	..	..	..
5212 Paid by others: motor vehicles	..	..	..	..	..	..	..	..	..	..
5213 Paid in respect of other goods	..	..	..	..	..	..	..	..	..	..
5220 Non-recurrent taxes	21	20	22	21	23	22	22	22	23	25
5300 Unallocable between 5100 and 5200	0	0	0	0	0	0	0	0	0	0
6000 Other taxes	**346**	**348**	**356**	**381**	**399**	**413**	**418**	**427**	**445**	**447**
6100 Paid solely by business	325	324	313	330	356	361	366	371	378	384
Business office tax	325	324	313	330	356	361	366	371	378	384
6200 Other	22	24	43	52	43	52	52	56	67	63
Taxes not in local tax law	21	24	43	52	43	52	52	56	65	63
Other	0	0	0	0	0	0	0	0	2	0

Note: Data are on a fiscal year basis beginning 1st April.

From 1990, data are on accrual basis.

The figures for different groups of taxes are reported on different reporting bases, namely: Social security contributions (heading 2000): in principle accrual basis, Central government taxes: accrual basis (revenues accrued during the fiscal year plus cash receipts collected before the end of May (the end of April until 1977), Local government taxes: accrual basis (due to be paid during the fiscal year and cash receipts collected before the end of May).

The Japanese authorities take the view that the Enterprise tax (classified in 1100 and 1200) and the Mineral product tax (classified in 5121) should be classified in heading 6000 since under articles 72 and 519 of the Local Tax Law these taxes are regarded as levies on the business or mining activity itself.

Heading 2000 includes some unidentifiable voluntary contributions.

Heading 2300: Includes contibutions to the National pension, National Health Insurance and the Farmer's pension fund. Contributions to the Farmer's pension fund are not available for the years before 1999.

Heading 4100: Municipal property tax, includes Prefectural property tax from 1990 to 1994 because data is not available to provide a breakdown.

Heading 5121: Municipal tobacco tax, includes Prefectural tobacco tax from 1990 to 1994 because data is not available to provide a breakdown.

Heading 5121: In sub-item Petroleum and coal tax, the data before 2003 refer to petroleum tax.

Source: Tax Bureau, Ministry of Finance.

StatLink https://stat.link/ax0k2m

Table 4.8. Kazakhstan: Details of tax revenue

Million KZT

	1997	2000	2007	2010	2014	2015	2016	2017	2018	2019
Total tax revenue	..	**517 777**	**3 349 317**	**5 182 379**	**8 365 069**	**6 352 963**	**7 006 053**	**8 690 678**	**10 484 416**	**11 594 940**
1000 Taxes on income, profits and capital gains	..	**214 545**	**1 797 785**	**2 072 357**	**3 113 992**	**2 467 977**	**2 610 413**	**3 128 907**	**3 972 562**	**4 204 258**
1100 Of individuals	..	51 016	221 025	312 332	552 280	598 807	691 778	750 212	838 394	876 324
1110 On income and profits	..	51 016	221 025	312 332	552 280	598 807	691 778	750 212	838 394	876 324
From non-foreign citizens	..	51 016	221 025	276 089	492 913	566 974	688 023	744 662	831 567	869 181
From foreign citizens	..	0	0	36 243	59 367	31 832	3 755	5 550	6 828	7 143
1120 On capital gains	..	..	..	..	..	..	..	..	..	..
1200 Corporate	..	163 529	1 576 760	1 760 025	2 561 712	1 869 170	1 918 635	2 378 695	3 134 167	3 327 934
1210 On profits	..	163 529	1 576 760	1 760 025	2 561 712	1 869 170	1 918 635	2 378 695	3 134 167	3 327 934
From non-oil companies	..	163 529	766 979	847 057	1 172 635	1 236 561	1 445 066	1 545 293	1 703 353	1 975 134
From oil companies	..	0	0	0	0	0	0	0	0	0
From oil companies to National Fund	..	0	809 782	912 968	1 389 077	632 609	473 569	833 402	1 430 814	1 352 800
1220 On capital gains	..	..	..	..	..	..	..	..	..	..
1300 Unallocable between 1100 and 1200	..	0	0	0	0	0	0	0	0	0
2000 Social security contributions	..	**0**	**49 904**	**131 041**	**225 948**	**240 590**	**264 710**	**280 537**	**330 852**	**369 835**
2100 Employees	..	..	..	..	..	..	..	..	..	..
2110 On a payroll basis	..	..	..	..	..	..	..	..	..	..
2120 On an income tax basis	..	..	..	..	..	..	..	..	..	..
2200 Employers	..	..	..	..	..	..	..	..	..	..
2210 On a payroll basis	..	..	..	..	..	..	..	..	..	..
2220 On an income tax basis	..	..	..	..	..	..	..	..	..	..
2300 Self-employed or non-employed	..	..	..	..	..	..	..	..	..	..
2310 On a payroll basis	..	..	..	..	..	..	..	..	..	..
2320 On an income tax basis	..	..	..	..	..	..	..	..	..	..
2400 Unallocable between 2100, 2200 and 2300	..	..	49 904	131 041	225 948	240 590	264 710	280 537	330 852	369 835
2410 On a payroll basis	..	..	..	..	..	..	..	..	..	..
2420 On an income tax basis	..	..	..	..	..	..	..	..	..	..
3000 Taxes on payroll and workforce	..	**99 082**	**295 733**	**253 830**	**427 985**	**464 674**	**530 440**	**576 607**	**618 505**	**696 635**
The social tax	..	99 082	295 733	253 830	427 985	464 674	530 440	576 607	618 505	696 635
4000 Taxes on property	..	**21 013**	**73 822**	**124 632**	**192 063**	**226 853**	**227 862**	**257 012**	**298 617**	**322 481**
4100 Recurrent taxes on immovable property	..	20 504	71 592	122 146	188 331	224 752	226 815	255 868	298 455	322 481
4110 Households	..	3 230	2 936	4 402	9 385	10 164	11 906	3 922	22 374	29 386
4120 Others	..	17 274	68 655	117 744	178 946	214 588	214 909	251 946	276 082	293 095
Uniform land tax	..	235	428	762	876	833	944	1 004	1 036	1 055
Property tax	..	13 699	59 140	104 745	165 795	200 710	200 685	236 542	269 534	292 040
Land tax	..	3 340	9 086	12 238	12 275	13 045	13 281	14 401	5 512	0
4200 Recurrent taxes on net wealth	..	0	0	0	0	0	0	0	0	0
4210 Individual	..	..	..	..	..	..	..	..	..	..
4220 Corporate	..	..	..	..	..	..	..	..	..	..
4300 Estate, inheritance and gift taxes	..	0	0	0	0	0	0	0	0	0
4310 Estate and inheritance taxes	..	..	..	..	..	..	..	..	..	..
4320 Gift taxes	..	..	..	..	..	..	..	..	..	..
4400 Taxes on financial and capital transactions	..	509	2 231	2 486	3 732	2 101	1 047	1 143	161	0
4500 Non-recurrent taxes	..	0	0	0	0	0	0	0	0	0
4510 On net wealth	..	..	..	..	..	..	..	..	..	..
4520 Other non-recurrent taxes	..	..	..	..	..	..	..	..	..	..
4600 Other recurrent taxes on property	..	0	0	0	0	0	0	0	0	0
5000 Taxes on goods and services	..	**179 452**	**1 131 164**	**2 600 514**	**4 405 005**	**2 952 727**	**3 372 218**	**4 437 419**	**5 259 064**	**6 000 743**
5100 Taxes on production, sale, transfer, etc	..	168 678	1 032 930	2 497 709	4 237 236	2 816 629	3 238 137	4 285 158	5 080 971	5 799 325
5110 General taxes	..	115 159	629 279	677 229	1 197 258	943 051	1 495 682	1 664 699	2 034 314	2 693 127
5111 Value added taxes	..	115 159	629 279	677 229	1 197 258	943 051	1 495 682	1 664 699	2 034 314	2 693 127
Domestic VAT	..	75 625	137 290	197 358	333 943	203 247	525 318	532 864	800 800	1 221 658
Domestic VAT to National Fund	..	0	0	0	0	0	0	0	0	0
VAT on imported goods	..	39 534	464 361	435 869	789 302	667 404	860 801	1 017 876	1 124 959	1 338 188
Other VAT	..	0	27 628	44 002	74 013	72 399	109 563	113 959	108 554	133 281
5112 Sales tax	..	0	0	0	0	0	0	0	0	0
5113 Other	..	0	0	0	0	0	0	0	0	0
5120 Taxes on specific goods and services	..	53 519	403 651	1 820 480	3 039 978	1 873 579	1 742 455	2 620 458	3 046 657	3 106 198
5121 Excises	..	19 285	58 753	61 423	147 057	161 068	205 231	255 994	311 856	343 409
Alcohol	..	12 939	18 189	15 691	38 788	36 345	40 712	58 793	79 874	75 013
Tobacco	..	5 182	10 953	22 903	78 695	98 346	121 403	137 791	163 140	195 093
Petroleum product	..	1 164	20 970	20 966	25 221	26 216	42 042	58 146	67 504	71 761
Automobiles	..	0	8 641	1 864	4 352	931	0	0	0	0
Others	..	0	0	0	0	-770	1 075	1 265	1 338	1 542
5122 Profits of fiscal monopolies	..	0	0	0	0	0	0	0	0	0
5123 Customs and import duties	..	18 471	150 355	354 487	279 313	189 522	266 484	296 905	331 629	372 223
5124 Taxes on exports	..	0	611	492 870	1 513 573	920 175	807 011	1 154 883	1 586 728	1 647 138
Taxes on exports	..	..	0	22 060	778 853	692 855	688 122	904 476	1 099 662	1 215 970
Taxes on exports to National Fund	..	..	611	470 810	734 720	227 320	118 889	250 408	487 066	431 168

	1997	2000	2007	2010	2014	2015	2016	2017	2018	2019
5125 Taxes on investment goods	..	0	0	0	0	0	0	0	0	0
5126 Taxes on specific services	..	0	6 184	14 566	21 036	24 798	25 856	27 144	43 076	38 673
Telecommunication	..	..	3 624	5 535	6 167	8 151	8 124	8 286	8 596	9 281
Placement of outdoor advertisements	..	..	2 560	3 723	5 981	6 076	5 855	5 510	5 615	6 047
Gambling business	..	..	0	3 693	7 598	9 231	10 518	11 746	26 846	21 003
Others	..	..	0	1 614	1 291	1 340	1 359	1 602	2 018	2 341
5127 Other taxes on internat. trade and transactions	..	0	0	0	0	0	0	0	0	0
5128 Other taxes	..	15 763	187 748	897 133	1 078 999	578 015	437 873	885 532	773 369	704 755
Production of useful minerals of non-oil sector companies	..	15 763	16 510	122 128	122 909	118 073	159 276	259 183	308 717	365 225
Production of useful minerals of oil sector companies	..	0	0	0	0	0	0	0	0	0
Production of useful minerals of oil sector co. to National Fund	..	0	171 238	775 005	956 090	459 942	278 597	626 350	464 652	339 530
5130 Unallocable between 5110 and 5120	..	0	0	0	0	0	0	0	0	0
5200 Taxes on use of goods and perform activities	..	10 774	98 234	102 806	167 769	136 098	134 081	152 261	178 093	201 419
5210 Recurrent taxes	..	5 901	11 382	26 327	38 930	42 319	46 879	59 981	67 191	73 032
5211 Paid by households: motor vehicles	..	3 930	8 099	21 565	31 656	34 466	38 572	51 271	57 814	63 210
5212 Paid by others: motor vehicles	..	1 971	3 241	4 697	7 188	7 812	8 307	8 710	9 377	9 823
5213 Paid in respect of other goods	..	0	42	65	86	41	0	0	0	0
5220 Non-recurrent taxes	..	4 873	86 852	76 478	128 840	93 779	87 202	92 280	110 902	128 386
Emissions into the environment	..	0	70 958	57 982	97 712	63 379	67 216	72 529	87 126	100 810
Others	..	4 873	15 894	18 497	31 128	30 399	19 985	19 752	23 776	27 577
5300 Unallocable between 5100 and 5200	..	0	0	0	0	0	0	0	0	0
6000 Other taxes	**..**	**3 684**	**909**	**6**	**75**	**141**	**410**	**10 198**	**4 816**	**988**
6100 Paid solely by business	..	0	0	0	0	0	0	0	0	0
6200 Other	..	3 684	909	6	75	141	410	10 198	4 816	988

Note: Year ending 31st December.

Data are on a cash basis.

The share of the Republic of Kazakhstan under production sharing contracts of oil companies, the bonuses of oil and non-oil sector companies, the levy for the use of the radio-frequency spectrum, the payment to compensate for historic costs as well as certain other items are classified as non-tax revenues according to the OECD Interpretative Guide, but are considered as tax revenues in Kazakhstan.

Headings 1210, 5124 and 5128: These categories includes revenues that are paid to the National Fund of the Republic of Kazakhstan. This fund was created in 2000 as a stabilisation fund and includes revenues levied from oil and gas companies.

Heading 2000: Social security contribution data since 2018 have also included contributions to compulsory social health insurance in this edition. Social security contribution revenues are not considered as tax revenues in Kazakhstan, but are considered as tax revenues under the OECD Interpretative Guide, subject to certain criteria.

Heading 4120: The uniform land tax is a presumptive tax for farmers and peasants' households. Such payers are not obliged to pay personal income tax, land tax, environmental fees, transport tax, property tax and other mandatory payments to the budget. The uniform land tax is levied on the value of land in use.

Source: Ministry of Finance of the Republic of Kazakhstan.

StatLink https://stat.link/6zuos5

Table 4.9. Korea: Details of tax revenue

Billion KRW

	1997	2000	2007	2010	2014	2015	2016	2017	2018	2019
Total tax revenue	**102 916**	**136 295**	**258 571**	**295 968**	**365 428**	**393 559**	**430 752**	**465 470**	**506 548**	**523 985**
1000 Taxes on income, profits and capital gains	**26 916**	**39 254**	**82 239**	**82 905**	**106 353**	**119 151**	**134 503**	**149 420**	**172 976**	**174 040**
1100 Of individuals	16 543	19 950	43 276	42 098	59 457	67 600	75 711	83 121	93 274	91 714
1110 On income and profits	14 586	18 569	31 984	33 935	51 410	55 744	62 028	67 987	75 251	75 613
Income tax	0	0	0	0	0	0	0	0	0	0
Dividends and interest income tax	0	0	4 682	4 425	4 628	4 561	4 125	4 517	4 982	5 577
Wages and salaries income tax	0	0	14 124	15 517	25 359	27 055	30 994	34 034	38 000	38 466
Other income tax	0	0	2 607	2 986	3 805	4 467	5 346	5 333	5 975	6 640
Global income tax	12 911	16 128	6 151	6 369	11 486	12 784	14 348	16 049	17 483	16 778
Defence tax on income tax	0	0	0	0	0	0	0	0	0	0
Education tax on income tax	0	0	0	0	0	0	0	0	0	0
Rural dev. tax on interest, bus. Inc. & cap. gains relief	149	156	160	179	115	105	109	104	111	139
Inhabitant tax on income tax (local)	1 526	2 285	4 260	4 459	6 017	6 772	7 106	7 950	8 700	8 013
1120 On capital gains	1 957	1 381	11 292	8 163	8 047	11 856	13 683	15 134	18 023	16 101
Capital gains tax	1 957	1 381	11 292	8 163	8 047	11 856	13 683	15 134	18 023	16 101
1200 Corporate	10 158	19 271	38 963	40 807	46 896	51 551	58 792	66 299	79 702	82 326
1210 On profits	10 158	19 271	38 963	40 807	46 896	51 551	58 792	66 299	79 702	82 326
Corporation tax - withholding	5 501	8 577	8 360	9 095	12 172	12 317	11 986	11 990	13 174	14 168
Corporation tax - final returns	3 924	9 302	27 057	28 173	30 478	32 713	40 130	47 187	57 763	58 006
Defence tax on corporation tax	0	0	0	0	0	0	0	0	0	0
Inhabitant tax on corporation tax (local)	733	1 142	3 152	3 094	3 882	6 217	6 270	6 785	8 307	9 729
Rural development tax corporate income	0	251	394	445	364	304	406	337	458	423
Excess profit tax	0	0	0	0	0	0	0	0	0	0
1220 On capital gains	0	0	0	0	0	0	0	0	0	0
Capital gains tax	..	..	..	..	..	..	..	..	..	..
1300 Unallocable between 1100 and 1200	215	33	0	0	0	0	0	0	0	0
Business income tax	0	0	..	..	..	..	..	..	..	..
Real estate income tax	0	0	..	..	..	..	..	..	..	..
Defence tax on real estate & business income	0	0	..	..	..	..	..	..	..	..
Rural dev. tax on bus. inc. & cap. gains relief	211	30	..	..	..	..	..	..	..	..
Inhabitant tax before 1990 (local)	1	0	..	..	..	..	..	..	..	..
Farm land tax (local)	3	3	..	..	..	..	..	..	..	..
Inhabitant tax on farm land tax (local)	0	0	..	..	..	..	..	..	..	..
2000 Social security contributions	**14 583**	**22 759**	**53 588**	**69 090**	**98 184**	**104 693**	**112 658**	**119 676**	**128 660**	**140 071**
2100 Employees	6 376	8 578	21 773	28 213	41 355	44 281	48 077	51 125	55 257	60 682
Veterans' relief fund	0	0	0	0	0	0	0	0	0	0
Soldiers' annuity fund	0	0	0	0	0	0	0	0	0	0
Unemployment assurance	264	598	1 164	1 358	2 866	3 076	3 251	3 418	3 666	4 027
National welfare pension fund	3 597	4 325	9 338	11 004	14 823	15 821	16 862	17 864	19 090	20 630
Social benefit fund	0	0	0	0	0	0	0	0	0	0
Health Insurance	1 149	2 066	8 180	11 783	18 492	19 868	21 470	22 814	24 920	27 911
Teachers' pensions	219	279	581	868	1 081	1 125	1 410	1 507	1 595	1 678
Government employees pensions	1 013	1 144	2 202	2 878	3 593	3 876	4 533	4 934	5 371	5 796
Military personal pensions	134	166	308	322	500	515	551	588	615	640
2110 On a payroll basis	..	8 578	21 773	28 213	41 355	44 281	48 077	51 125	55 257	60 682
2120 On an income tax basis	..	0	0	0	0	0	0	0	0	0
2200 Employers	5 901	9 409	23 557	30 856	44 806	47 846	51 190	54 063	58 712	63 780
Ind. works' insurance fund	1 819	1 876	4 431	4 632	5 797	6 062	6 283	6 429	7 346	7 539
Soldiers' annuity fund	0	0	0	0	0	0	0	0	0	0
Pneumoconiosis fund	0	0	0	0	0	0	0	0	0	0
Unemployment insurance	653	1 449	2 474	2 860	5 150	5 499	5 790	6 082	6 517	7 063
Veterans' relief fund	0	0	0	0	0	0	0	0	0	0
National welfare pension fund	1 814	4 340	9 383	11 052	14 909	15 895	16 928	17 922	19 155	20 631
Social benefit fund	0	0	0	0	0	0	0	0	0	0
Health Insurance	1 459	1 547	6 844	11 718	18 133	19 493	21 074	22 397	24 346	27 110
Teachers' pensions	156	197	425	594	817	897	1 115	1 233	1 348	1 437
Government employees pensions	0	0	0	0	0	0	0	0	0	0
2210 On a payroll basis	..	9 409	23 557	30 856	44 806	47 846	51 190	54 063	58 712	63 780
2220 On an income tax basis	..	0	0	0	0	0	0	0	0	0
2300 Self-employed or non-employed	2 306	4 772	8 258	10 021	12 023	12 566	13 391	14 488	14 691	15 609
2310 On a payroll basis	0	0	0	0	0	0	0	0	0	0
2320 On an income tax basis	2 306	4 772	8 258	10 021	12 023	12 566	13 391	14 488	14 691	15 609
2400 Unallocable between 2100, 2200 and 2300	0	0	0	0	0	0	0	0	0	0
2410 On a payroll basis	..	..	..	..	..	..	..	..	..	..
2420 On an income tax basis	..	..	..	..	..	..	..	..	..	..
3000 Taxes on payroll and workforce	**309**	**258**	**619**	**714**	**1 042**	**1 122**	**1 293**	**1 376**	**1 492**	**1 597**
Workshop tax on workforce (local)	309	258	619	714	1 042	1 122	1 293	1 376	1 492	1 597
Vocational training promotion fund	0	0	0	0	0	0	0	0	0	0
4000 Taxes on property	**13 088**	**16 846**	**33 109**	**33 516**	**40 305**	**48 625**	**49 820**	**54 406**	**58 811**	**59 732**

	1997	2000	2007	2010	2014	2015	2016	2017	2018	2019
4100 Recurrent taxes on immovable property	2 986	3 385	9 196	9 270	11 654	12 486	13 095	14 319	15 589	17 750
Property tax (local)	577	728	3 755	4 817	8 780	9 294	9 930	10 662	11 532	12 677
City planning tax on urban real estate (local)	731	815	1 883	2 465	0	0	0	0	0	0
Community facilities tax (local)	268	341	543	650	1 138	1 351	1 450	1 513	1 626	1 681
Tax on excessive land holdings (local)	0	0	0	0	0	0	0	0	0	0
Tax on aggregate land holdings (local)	1 279	1 282	5	0	0	0	0	0	0	0
Rural dev. tax on local agg. land holdings tax	63	81	1	0	0	0	0	0	0	0
Tax on excessively increased land value	-1	0	0	0	0	0	0	0	0	0
Comprehensive real estate tax	0	0	2 414	1 029	1 307	1 399	1 294	1 652	1 873	2 671
Rural dev. tax on comprehensive real estate tax	0	0	483	208	265	267	240	302	356	505
4110 Households	0	0	0	0	0	0	0	0	0	0
4120 Others	68	138	112	101	164	175	181	190	202	216
Workshop tax on property (local)	68	138	112	101	164	175	181	190	202	216
4200 Recurrent taxes on net wealth	0	0	0	0	0	0	0	0	0	0
4210 Individual	..	..	..	..	..	..	..	..	..	..
4220 Corporate	..	..	..	..	..	..	..	..	..	..
4300 Estate, inheritance and gift taxes	1 161	989	2 842	3 076	4 625	5 044	5 350	6 785	7 359	8 329
4310 Estate and inheritance taxes	605	449	1 059	1 203	1 696	1 944	1 995	2 342	2 832	3 154
Inheritance tax	605	449	1 059	1 203	1 696	1 944	1 995	2 342	2 832	3 154
Defence tax on inheritance tax	0	0	0	0	0	0	0	0	0	0
4320 Gift taxes	556	540	1 783	1 873	2 929	3 100	3 355	4 443	4 527	5 175
Gift tax	556	540	1 783	1 873	2 929	3 100	3 355	4 443	4 527	5 175
Defence tax on gift tax	0	0	0	0	0	0	0	0	0	0
4400 Taxes on financial and capital transactions	8 774	11 935	21 071	21 170	24 026	31 095	31 375	33 302	35 863	33 653
Registration tax (local)	4 257	4 528	7 254	7 370	1 485	1 831	1 708	1 608	1 718	1 837
Registration tax	0	0	0	0	0	0	0	0	0	0
Defence tax on registration tax	0	0	0	0	0	0	0	0	0	0
Rural dev. tax on local acquisition tax	164	246	627	632	843	969	954	1 028	993	947
Rural dev. tax on local registration tax	211	66	143	144	1	1	0	0	0	0
Securities transactions tax	262	2 736	3 469	3 667	3 121	4 670	4 468	4 508	6 241	4 473
Rural dev. tax on securities transaction tax	170	823	1 729	2 010	1 459	1 861	1 637	1 775	2 217	1 635
Acquisition tax (local)	3 319	3 148	7 261	6 825	16 391	20 810	21 702	23 487	23 813	23 915
Stamp tax	390	388	588	522	726	953	906	896	881	846
4500 Non-recurrent taxes	167	537	0	0	0	0	0	0	0	0
Asset revaluation tax	167	537	..	..	..	..	..	..	..	..
4510 On net wealth	..	..	..	..	..	..	..	..	..	..
4520 Other non-recurrent taxes	..	..	..	..	..	..	..	..	..	..
4600 Other recurrent taxes on property	0	0	0	0	0	0	0	0	0	0
5000 Taxes on goods and services	**43 978**	**52 271**	**80 861**	**99 769**	**109 451**	**110 326**	**121 197**	**129 065**	**133 095**	**135 276**
5100 Taxes on production, sale, transfer, etc.	41 699	50 023	78 414	96 573	102 531	103 254	113 644	121 293	125 207	127 551
5110 General taxes	19 488	23 212	40 942	51 800	62 975	60 162	68 229	74 361	77 471	82 174
5111 Value added taxes	19 488	23 212	40 942	51 800	62 975	60 162	68 229	74 361	77 471	82 174
Value added tax	19 488	23 212	40 942	51 800	62 975	60 162	68 229	74 361	77 471	82 174
5112 Sales tax	0	0	0	0	0	0	0	0	0	0
Business tax	..	..	..	..	..	..	..	..	..	..
5113 Other	0	0	0	0	0	0	0	0	0	0
5120 Taxes on specific goods and services	22 211	26 811	37 472	44 773	39 556	43 092	45 415	46 932	47 736	45 377
5121 Excise duties	14 616	18 155	27 880	31 340	28 226	31 857	34 762	35 779	36 218	34 691
Commodity tax	0	0	0	0	0	0	0	0	0	0
Defence tax on commodity tax	0	0	0	0	0	0	0	0	0	0
Liquor tax	1 790	1 963	2 268	2 878	2 852	3 228	3 209	3 035	3 261	3 504
Defence tax on liquor tax	0	0	0	0	0	0	0	0	0	0
Education tax on liquor tax	418	516	580	724	728	808	813	745	788	844
Textile tax	0	0	0	0	0	0	0	0	0	0
Petroleum tax	0	0	0	0	0	0	0	0	0	0
Transport tax on petrol products	5 547	8 404	11 464	13 970	13 440	14 055	15 303	15 553	15 335	14 563
Education tax on transport tax	758	1 247	1 715	2 133	2 074	2 154	2 289	2 320	2 304	2 190
Electricity and gas tax	0	0	0	0	0	0	0	0	0	0
Special excise tax	3 036	2 985	5 161	5 066	5 624	8 001	8 881	9 861	10 451	9 719
Defence tax on special excise tax	0	0	0	0	0	0	0	0	0	0
Education tax on special excise tax	804	498	607	501	495	515	463	602	545	455
Rural development on special excise tax	26	37	54	24	60	61	60	60	56	58
Tobacco sales tax (local)	0	0	0	0	0	0	0	0	0	0
Tobacco consumption tax (local)	2 236	2 251	2 761	2 875	2 953	3 035	3 744	3 603	3 478	3 358
Motor fuel tax (local)	0	254	3 270	3 169	0	0	0	0	0	0
5122 Profits of fiscal monopolies	0	0	0	0	0	0	0	0	0	0
Monopoly profit	..	..	..	..	..	..	..	..	..	..

	1997	2000	2007	2010	2014	2015	2016	2017	2018	2019
5123 Customs and import duties	5 941	5 936	7 690	11 046	9 132	8 907	8 434	8 938	9 213	8 250
Customs duties	5 798	5 800	7 411	10 666	8 721	8 495	8 045	8 529	8 815	7 882
Defence tax on customs duties	0	0	0	0	0	0	0	0	0	0
Special customs duties	0	0	0	0	0	0	0	0	0	0
Tonnage tax	0	0	0	0	0	0	0	0	0	0
Education tax on imports	116	99	234	336	390	390	366	382	370	345
Rural dev. tax on customs exemptions	27	37	45	44	21	22	23	27	28	23
Previous year receipts	0	0	0	0	0	0	0	0	0	0
5124 Taxes on exports	0	0	0	0	0	0	0	0	0	0
5125 Taxes on investment goods	0	0	0	0	0	0	0	0	0	0
5126 Taxes on specific services	1 654	2 720	1 902	2 387	2 198	2 328	2 219	2 215	2 305	2 436
Telephone tax	789	1 457	0	0	0	0	0	0	0	0
Defence tax on telephone tax	0	0	0	0	0	0	0	0	0	0
Entertainment tax	0	0	0	0	0	0	0	0	0	0
Defence tax on entertainment tax	0	0	0	0	0	0	0	0	0	0
Entertainment tax (local)	0	0	0	0	0	0	0	0	0	0
Travel tax	0	0	0	0	0	0	0	0	0	0
Admission tax	0	0	0	0	0	0	0	0	0	0
Defence tax on admission tax	0	0	0	0	0	0	0	0	0	0
Education tax on banking & insurance	369	473	721	951	920	1 004	951	959	1 092	1 277
Horse race tax (local)	361	566	864	1 068	1 073	1 089	1 060	1 051	1 016	970
Rural dev. tax on horse race tax	18	84	165	215	205	235	208	205	197	189
Butchery tax (local)	47	51	52	58	0	0	0	0	0	0
Regional development tax (local)	71	89	100	95	0	0	0	0	0	0
5127 Other taxes on internat. trade and transactions	0	0	0	0	0	0	0	0	0	0
5128 Other taxes	0	0	0	0	0	0	0	0	0	0
5130 Unallocable between 5110 and 5120	0	0	0	0	0	0	0	0	0	0
5200 Taxes on use of goods and perform activities	2 279	2 248	2 447	3 196	6 920	7 072	7 553	7 772	7 888	7 725
5210 Recurrent taxes	2 279	2 248	2 447	3 196	6 920	7 072	7 553	7 772	7 888	7 725
License tax (local)	225	241	77	76	0	0	0	0	0	0
Automobile tax (local)	2 054	2 007	2 370	3 120	6 920	7 072	7 553	7 772	7 888	7 725
5211 Paid by households: motor vehicles	..	..	..	..	..	..	..	..	..	..
5212 Paid by others: motor vehicles	..	..	..	..	..	..	..	..	..	..
5213 Paid in respect of other goods	..	..	..	..	..	..	..	..	..	..
5220 Non-recurrent taxes	0	0	0	0	0	0	0	0	0	0
5300 Unallocable between 5100 and 5200	0	0	0	0	0	0	0	0	0	0
6000 Other taxes	**4 041**	**4 907**	**8 155**	**9 974**	**10 093**	**9 642**	**11 281**	**11 527**	**11 514**	**13 269**
6100 Paid solely by business	0	0	0	0	0	0	0	0	0	0
6200 Other	4 041	4 907	8 155	9 974	10 093	9 642	11 281	11 527	11 514	13 269
Unallocable tax revenue	0	0	0	0	0	0	0	0	0	0
Previous year tax	779	1 474	2 965	4 449	4 049	3 435	4 147	4 389	4 430	5 873
Previous year tax (local)	340	474	672	654	589	392	868	715	540	719
Unallocable defence tax	-8	-3	0	0	0	0	0	0	0	0
Education tax on local taxes	2 931	2 962	4 518	4 871	5 455	5 815	6 266	6 423	6 544	6 677

Note: Year ending 31st December.

Data are on cash basis.

Heading 2000: From 1997 the contributions to the three funds (civil servant pension fund, private school teachers pension fund and medical insurance fund) are classified as security social contributions. The reasons for the change are that the contributions either became mandatory or the fund started to be managed by public authorities in that year, thereby meeting the OECD definition of social security contributions.

Heading 2200: From 2007, this includes long-term care insurance.

Source: Ministry of Finance and Economy, Ministry of Home Affairs.

StatLink https://stat.link/20jo4i

Table 4.10. Lao PDR: Details of tax revenue

Billion LAK

	1997	2000	2007	2010	2014	2015	2016	2017	2018	2019
Total tax revenue	..	..	..	**7 101**	**13 120**	**14 719**	**15 393**	**15 532**	**16 565**	**17 208**
1000 Taxes on income, profits and capital gains	..	..	..	**1 613**	**2 919**	**3 347**	**3 375**	**3 582**	**3 692**	**3 856**
1100 Of individuals	..	..	..	482	1 026	1 140	1 624	1 603	1 619	1 646
1110 On income and profits	..	..	..	482	1 026	1 140	1 624	1 603	1 619	1 646
1120 On capital gains	..	..	..	0	0	0	0	0	0	0
1200 Corporate	..	..	..	1 131	1 894	2 206	1 751	1 980	2 073	2 209
1210 On profits	..	..	..	1 131	1 894	2 206	1 751	1 980	2 073	2 209
1220 On capital gains of corporates	..	..	..	0	0	0	0	0	0	0
1300 Unallocable between 1100 and 1200	..	..	..	0	0	0	0	0	0	0
2000 Social security contributions	..	..	..	..	..	..	..	..	..	..
2100 Employees	..	..	..	..	..	..	..	..	..	..
2110 On a payroll basis	..	..	..	..	..	..	..	..	..	..
2120 On an income tax basis	..	..	..	..	..	..	..	..	..	..
2200 Employers	..	..	..	..	..	..	..	..	..	..
2210 On a payroll basis	..	..	..	..	..	..	..	..	..	..
2220 On an income tax basis	..	..	..	..	..	..	..	..	..	..
2300 Self-employed or non-employed	..	..	..	..	..	..	..	..	..	..
2310 On a payroll basis	..	..	..	..	..	..	..	..	..	..
2320 On an income tax basis	..	..	..	..	..	..	..	..	..	..
2400 Unallocable between 2100, 2200 and 2300	..	..	..	..	..	..	..	..	..	..
2410 On a payroll basis	..	..	..	..	..	..	..	..	..	..
2420 On an income tax basis	..	..	..	..	..	..	..	..	..	..
3000 Taxes on payroll and workforce	..	..	..	**0**	**0**	**0**	**0**	**0**	**0**	**0**
4000 Taxes on property	..	..	..	**76**	**115**	**130**	**105**	**113**	**188**	**201**
4100 Recurrent taxes on immovable property	..	..	..	76	115	130	105	113	188	201
4110 Households	..	..	..	..	..	..	..	..	..	..
4120 Others	..	..	..	..	..	..	..	..	..	..
4200 Recurrent taxes on net wealth	..	..	..	0	0	0	0	0	0	0
4210 Individual	..	..	..	..	..	..	..	..	..	..
4220 Corporate	..	..	..	..	..	..	..	..	..	..
4300 Estate, inheritance and gift taxes	..	..	..	0	0	0	0	0	0	0
4310 Estate and inheritance taxes	..	..	..	..	..	..	..	..	..	..
4320 Gift taxes	..	..	..	..	..	..	..	..	..	..
4400 Taxes on financial and capital transactions	..	..	..	0	0	0	0	0	0	0
4500 Other non-reccurrent taxes on property	..	..	..	0	0	0	0	0	0	0
4510 On net wealth	..	..	..	..	..	..	..	..	..	..
4520 Other non-recurrent taxes	..	..	..	..	..	..	..	..	..	..
4600 Other recurrent taxes on property	..	..	..	0	0	0	0	0	0	0
5000 Taxes on goods and services	..	..	..	**5 412**	**10 087**	**11 242**	**11 913**	**11 837**	**12 684**	**13 151**
5100 Taxes on production, sale, transfer, etc	..	..	..	4 720	8 922	9 834	10 524	10 172	11 718	12 083
5110 General taxes on goods and services	..	..	..	2 033	3 862	4 988	4 688	4 934	5 201	5 413
5111 Value added taxes	..	..	..	400	3 740	4 744	4 688	4 934	5 201	5 413
5112 Sales tax	..	..	..	0	0	0	0	0	0	0
5113 Other	..	..	..	1 633	123	244	0	0	0	0
5120 Taxes on specific goods and services	..	..	..	2 687	5 059	4 846	5 836	5 238	6 516	6 670
5121 Excises	..	..	..	1 749	3 340	3 253	4 124	4 234	4 743	4 972
5122 Profits of fiscal monopolies	..	..	..	0	0	0	0	0	0	0
5123 Customs and import duties	..	..	..	855	1 409	1 382	1 655	971	1 059	967
5124 Taxes on exports	..	..	..	70	287	205	49	29	38	45
5125 Taxes on investment goods	..	..	..	0	0	0	0	0	0	0
5126 Taxes on specific services	..	..	..	12	23	6	7	4	676	686
5127 Other taxes on internat. trade and transactions	..	..	..	0	0	0	0	0	0	0
5128 Other taxes	..	..	..	0	0	0	0	0	0	0
5130 Unallocable between 5110 and 5120	..	..	..	0	0	0	0	0	0	0
5200 Taxes on use of goods and to perform activities	..	..	..	692	1 165	1 408	1 389	1 665	966	1 068
5210 Recurrent taxes	..	..	..	692	1 165	1 408	1 389	1 665	966	1 068
5211 Paid by households: motor vehicles	..	..	..	0	0	0	0	0	0	0
5212 Paid by others: motor vehicles	..	..	..	0	0	0	0	0	0	0
5213 Paid in respect of other goods	..	..	..	692	1 165	1 408	1 389	1 665	966	1 068
5220 Non-recurrent taxes	..	..	..	0	0	0	0	0	0	0
5300 Unallocable between 5100 and 5200	..	..	..	0	0	0	0	0	0	0
6000 Other taxes	..	..	..	**0**	**0**	**0**	**0**	**0**	**0**	**0**
6100 Paid solely by business	..	..	..	..	..	..	..	..	..	..
6200 Other	..	..	..	..	..	..	..	..	..	..

Note: Data are reported on a calendar year.
The data are on a cash basis.
Heading 2000: Detailed data on revenues from social security contributions were not available.
Revenues from the natural resource tax are not included in this table. Although considered to be tax revenues by Lao PDR, these revenues are considered to be non-tax revenue under with the OECD classification, as set out in the Interpretative Guides in Annex A and B.
Source: Ministry of Finance, Lao PDR.

StatLink https://stat.link/543gfp

Table 4.11. Malaysia: Details of tax revenue

Million MYR

	1997	2000	2007	2010	2014	2015	2016	2017	2018	2019
Total tax revenue	**55 493**	**50 083**	**98 569**	**113 573**	**169 513**	**170 962**	**175 325**	**183 537**	**181 065**	**188 035**
1000 Taxes on income, profits and capital gains	**27 648**	**27 339**	**65 671**	**75 058**	**120 284**	**105 751**	**103 967**	**110 260**	**123 953**	**128 307**
1100 Of individuals	6 429	7 015	11 661	17 805	24 423	26 321	27 566	28 945	32 605	38 680
1110 On income and profits	6 429	7 015	11 661	17 805	24 423	26 321	27 566	28 945	32 605	38 680
1120 On capital gains	..	..	..	..	..	..	..	..	..	..
1200 Corporate	20 552	19 923	52 615	55 156	92 223	75 275	72 127	76 226	86 556	84 534
1210 On profits	20 552	19 923	52 615	55 156	92 223	75 275	72 127	76 226	86 556	84 534
Company income tax	16 688	13 905	32 149	36 266	65 240	63 679	63 625	64 465	66 474	63 751
Petroleum income tax	3 861	6 010	20 453	18 713	26 956	11 559	8 422	11 761	20 082	20 783
Offshore business activity tax	3	8	13	15	27	37	81	0	0	0
Levy on Electricity	0	0	0	162	0	0	0	0	0	0
1220 On capital gains of corporates	..	..	..	..	..	..	..	..	..	..
1300 Unallocable between 1100 and 1200	666	402	1 395	2 097	3 639	4 155	4 274	5 089	4 792	5 093
Cooperatives income tax	143	87	189	378	169	80	90	74	171	189
Withholding income tax	0	0	1 190	1 268	2 184	2 316	2 562	3 266	3 117	3 061
Other income tax	0	0	17	21	24	30	43	51	37	43
Real property gains tax	523	247	0	303	1 210	1 729	1 492	1 697	1 467	1 800
Exit levy	0	41	0	0	0	0	0	0	0	0
Windfall levy on crude palm oil	0	0	0	0	0	0	0	0	0	0
Windfall levy on crude palm kernel oil	0	26	0	0	0	0	0	0	0	0
Levy on fresh fruit bunch	0	0	0	127	51	1	87	0	0	0
2000 Social security contributions	**..**	**990**	**1 690**	**2 008**	**2 689**	**2 838**	**3 216**	**3 561**	**4 302**	**4 490**
2100 Employees	..	218	371	439	588	..	..	..	..	..
2110 On a payroll basis	..	218	371	439	588	..	..	..	..	..
2120 On an income tax basis	..	0	0	0	0	..	..	..	..	..
2200 Employers	..	772	1 319	1 569	2 101	..	..	..	..	..
2210 On a payroll basis	..	772	1 319	1 569	2 101	..	..	..	..	..
2220 On an income tax basis	..	0	0	0	0	..	..	..	..	..
2300 Self-employed or non-employed	..	0	0	0	0	..	..	..	..	..
2310 On a payroll basis	..	..	..	..	..	..	..	..	..	..
2320 On an income tax basis	..	..	..	..	..	..	..	..	..	..
2400 Unallocable between 2100, 2200 and 2300	..	0	0	0	0	2 838	3 216	3 561	4 302	4 490
2410 On a payroll basis	..	..	..	..	..	..	..	..	..	..
2420 On an income tax basis	..	..	..	..	..	..	..	..	..	..
3000 Taxes on payroll and workforce	**0**	**0**	**0**	**0**	**0**	**0**	**0**	**0**	**0**	**0**
4000 Taxes on property	**19**	**2**	**..**	**..**	**2**	**1**	**3**	**0**	**0**	**0**
4100 Recurrent taxes on immovable property	0	0	..	..	0	0	0	..	..	..
4110 Households	..	..	..	..	..	..	..	..	..	..
4120 Others	..	..	..	..	..	..	..	..	..	..
4200 Recurrent taxes on net wealth	0	0	..	..	0	0	0	..	..	..
4210 Individual	..	..	..	..	..	..	..	..	..	..
4220 Corporate	..	..	..	..	..	..	..	..	..	..
4300 Estate, inheritance and gift taxes	19	2	..	..	2	1	3	..	..	..
4310 Estate and inheritance taxes	19	2	..	..	2	1	3	..	..	..
Estate Duty	19	2	..	..	2	1	3	..	..	..
4320 Gift taxes	0	0	..	..	0	0	0	..	..	..
4400 Taxes on financial and capital transactions	0	0	..	..	0	0	0	..	..	..
4500 Other non-reccurrent taxes on property	0	0	..	..	0	0	0	..	..	..
4510 On net wealth	..	..	..	..	..	..	..	..	..	..
4520 Other non-recurrent taxes	..	..	..	..	..	..	..	..	..	..
4600 Other recurrent taxes on property	0	0	..	..	0	0	0	..	..	..
5000 Taxes on goods and services	**25 061**	**19 910**	**27 483**	**32 268**	**40 030**	**56 353**	**62 415**	**63 952**	**46 729**	**48 823**
5100 Taxes on production, sale, transfer, etc	23 195	17 990	25 772	30 218	37 411	53 669	59 649	61 148	43 810	45 843
5110 General taxes on goods and services	6 167	5 968	6 642	8 171	10 939	32 235	41 309	44 337	24 207	15 385
5111 Value added taxes	0	0	0	0	0	27 012	41 206	44 290	20 236	0
5112 Sales tax	6 167	5 968	6 642	8 171	10 939	5 223	103	47	3 971	15 385
Sales tax on local goods	4 160	3 894	4 178	4 886	6 130	3 207	..	46	1 095	6 445
Sales tax on imported goods	2 008	2 074	2 464	3 285	4 809	2 016	..	2	2 876	8 940
5113 Other	0	0	0	0	0	0	0	0	0	0
5120 Taxes on specific goods and services	15 266	10 245	16 897	19 624	23 930	18 862	15 854	14 266	16 986	27 038
5121 Excises	6 053	3 803	8 990	11 770	12 925	11 890	11 705	10 112	10 779	10 511
Excise duties on domestic goods	6 053	3 803	7 910	9 350	8 456	7 999	7 721	5 519	4 918	5 131
Malt beer (domestic)	..	..	..	..	..	..	..	..	1 696	1 861
Cigarettes (domestic)	..	..	..	..	..	..	..	..	234	66
Passenger vehicles (domestic)	..	..	..	..	..	..	..	..	2 483	2 443
Other products (domestic)	..	..	..	..	..	..	..	..	505	760
Excise duties on imported goods	0	0	1 081	2 420	4 468	3 891	3 984	4 593	5 861	5 380
Cigarettes (imported)	..	..	..	..	..	..	..	..	2 681	2 522
Motor vehicles (imported)	..	..	..	..	..	..	..	..	2 803	2 466

	1997	2000	2007	2010	2014	2015	2016	2017	2018	2019
Other products (imported)	..	..	..	..	..	..	..	..	378	392
5122 Profits of fiscal monopolies	0	0	0	0	0	0	0	0	0	0
5123 Customs and import duties	6 524	3 599	2 424	1 966	2 670	2 732	2 905	2 784	2 897	2 733
Import duty on vehicles	..	..	..	..	..	..	..	..	562	479
Import duty on motors, machines and spare parts	..	..	..	..	..	..	..	..	681	675
Import duty on alcoholic beverages	..	..	..	..	..	..	..	..	100	99
Import duty on steel and metal products	..	..	..	..	..	..	..	..	305	298
Import duty on other products	..	..	..	..	..	..	..	..	1 248	1 182
5124 Taxes on exports	1 053	1 032	2 322	1 810	1 893	1 039	980	1 355	1 725	1 126
Export duty on petroleom	..	..	..	..	..	..	..	..	1 513	1 091
Export duty on other products	..	..	..	..	..	..	..	..	212	35
5125 Taxes on investment goods	0	0	0	0	0	0	0	0	0	0
5126 Taxes on specific services	1 475	1 701	3 013	3 926	6 278	3 038	103	15	1 473	12 499
Service tax	1 475	1 701	3 013	3 926	6 278	3 038	103	15	1 473	12 283
Other taxes on specific services	0	0	0	0	0	0	0	0	0	216
5127 Other taxes on internat. trade and transactions	160	110	147	151	165	163	160	0	113	169
5128 Other taxes	0	0	0	0	0	0	0	0	0	0
5130 Unallocable between 5110 and 5120	1 761	1 777	2 233	2 423	2 542	2 572	2 486	2 545	2 617	3 420
5200 Taxes on use of goods and to perform activities	1 866	1 920	1 711	2 050	2 619	2 684	2 766	2 805	2 919	2 979
5210 Recurrent taxes	1 863	1 918	1 709	2 047	2 617	2 681	2 763	2 805	2 919	2 979
5211 Paid by households: motor vehicles	1 852	1 909	1 688	1 992	2 532	2 630	2 714	2 805	2 919	2 979
Motor vehicle licences	1 852	1 909	1 688	1 992	2 532	2 630	2 714	2 805	2 919	2 979
5212 Paid by others: motor vehicles	11	9	20	18	3	3	3	0	0	0
Commercial vehicle licences	11	9	19	17	3	3	3	..	..	..
Tour vehicle licences	0	0	1	1	0	0	0	..	..	..
5213 Paid in respect of other goods	0	0	0	38	81	48	46	0	0	0
Petroleum Permits	0	0	0	1	4	2	2	..	..	..
Bank Licences Fees	0	0	0	37	78	46	44	..	..	..
5220 Non-recurrent taxes	3	2	3	2	2	3	3	0	0	0
Environment Pollution Licences	2	2	3	2	2	3	3	..	..	..
Film rental tax	1	0	0	0	0	0	0	..	..	..
5300 Unallocable between 5100 and 5200	0	0	0	0	0	0	0	0	0	0
6000 Other taxes	**2 764**	**1 841**	**3 725**	**4 240**	**6 508**	**6 018**	**5 724**	**5 764**	**6 081**	**6 416**
6100 Paid solely by business	0	0	0	0	0	0	0	0	0	0
6200 Other	2 764	1 841	3 725	4 240	6 508	6 018	5 724	5 764	6 081	6 416
Share transfer tax	0	0	0	0	0	0	0	0	0	0
Stamp duties	2 714	1 799	3 404	4 192	6 458	5 974	5 688	5 665	5 924	6 213
Other direct taxes	50	42	321	48	51	45	37	99	157	203

Note: Year ending 31st December.

The data are on a cash basis.

Heading 2000: Starting from 2015, Social Security Contribution data is given as a lump sum. Data for 2019 are estimated.

Heading 5111: Starting from 2015, VAT (GST, Goods and Services Tax) is sourced from the IMF's Government Finance Statistics dataset. GST was abolished by the government in 2018 and replaced by sales tax and service tax.

Heading 5126: Tourism tax has been added in this edition and classified under other taxes on specific services.

Source: Ministry of Finance of Malaysia; Social Security Organisation of Malaysia (PERKESO).

StatLink https://stat.link/fynd60

Table 4.12. Maldives: Details of tax revenue

Million MVR

	1997	2000	2007	2010	2014	2015	2016	2017	2018	2019
Total tax revenue	**..**	**..**	**2 855**	**2 962**	**10 779**	**12 232**	**13 265**	**14 720**	**15 818**	**16 512**
1000 Taxes on income, profits and capital gains	**..**	**..**	**169**	**203**	**2 954**	**3 186**	**3 240**	**3 327**	**3 275**	**3 513**
1100 Of individuals	..	..	0	0	0	0	0	0	0	0
1110 On income and profits	..	..	0	0	0	0	0	0	0	0
1120 On capital gains	..	..	0	0	0	0	0	0	0	0
1200 Corporate	..	..	169	203	2 954	3 186	3 240	3 327	3 275	3 513
1210 On profits	..	..	169	203	2 954	3 186	3 240	3 327	3 275	3 513
Business profit tax	..	..	0	0	2 471	2 674	2 216	2 107	2 078	2 210
Bank profit tax	..	..	169	203	482	513	492	650	564	614
Withholding tax	..	..	0	0	0	0	532	570	633	688
1220 On capital gains of corporates	..	..	0	0	0	0	0	0	0	0
1300 Unallocable between 1100 and 1200	..	..	0	0	0	0	0	0	0	0
2000 Social security contributions	**..**	**..**	**0**	**0**	**0**	**0**	**0**	**0**	**0**	**0**
2100 Employees	..	..	..	..	..	..	..	..	..	..
2110 On a payroll basis	..	..	..	..	..	..	..	..	..	..
2120 On an income tax basis	..	..	..	..	..	..	..	..	..	..
2200 Employers	..	..	..	..	..	..	..	..	..	..
2210 On a payroll basis	..	..	..	..	..	..	..	..	..	..
2220 On an income tax basis	..	..	..	..	..	..	..	..	..	..
2300 Self-employed or non-employed	..	..	..	..	..	..	..	..	..	..
2310 On a payroll basis	..	..	..	..	..	..	..	..	..	..
2320 On an income tax basis	..	..	..	..	..	..	..	..	..	..
2400 Unallocable between 2100, 2200 and 2300	..	..	..	..	..	..	..	..	..	..
2410 On a payroll basis	..	..	..	..	..	..	..	..	..	..
2420 On an income tax basis	..	..	..	..	..	..	..	..	..	..
3000 Taxes on payroll and workforce	**..**	**..**	**0**	**0**	**0**	**0**	**0**	**0**	**0**	**0**
4000 Taxes on property	**..**	**..**	**12**	**13**	**30**	**33**	**24**	**96**	**40**	**31**
4100 Recurrent taxes on immovable property	..	..	0	0	0	0	0	0	0	0
4110 Households	..	..	..	..	..	..	..	..	..	..
4120 Others	..	..	..	..	..	..	..	..	..	..
4200 Recurrent taxes on net wealth	..	..	0	0	0	0	0	0	0	0
4210 Individual	..	..	..	..	..	..	..	..	..	..
4220 Corporate	..	..	..	..	..	..	..	..	..	..
4300 Estate, inheritance and gift taxes	..	..	0	0	0	0	0	0	0	0
4310 Estate and inheritance taxes	..	..	..	..	..	..	..	..	..	..
4320 Gift taxes	..	..	..	..	..	..	..	..	..	..
4400 Taxes on financial and capital transactions	..	..	12	13	30	33	24	96	40	31
4500 Other non-reccurrent taxes on property	..	..	0	0	0	0	0	0	0	0
4510 On net wealth	..	..	..	..	..	..	..	..	..	..
4520 Other non-recurrent taxes	..	..	..	..	..	..	..	..	..	..
4600 Other recurrent taxes on property	..	..	0	0	0	0	0	0	0	0
5000 Taxes on goods and services	**..**	**..**	**2 674**	**2 745**	**7 795**	**9 013**	**10 001**	**11 297**	**12 504**	**12 968**
5100 Taxes on production, sale, transfer, etc	..	..	2 634	2 689	7 727	8 935	9 911	11 198	12 395	12 845
5110 General taxes on goods and services	..	..	0	0	4 515	6 054	6 249	6 882	7 689	7 748
5111 Value added taxes	..	..	0	0	4 515	6 054	6 249	6 882	7 689	7 748
Tourism Goods and Services Tax	..	..	0	0	3 002	4 150	3 921	4 199	4 783	4 903
Goods and Services Tax	..	..	0	0	1 513	1 904	2 328	2 683	2 906	2 845
5112 Sales tax	..	..	0	0	0	0	0	0	0	0
5113 Other	..	..	0	0	0	0	0	0	0	0
5120 Taxes on specific goods and services	..	..	2 634	2 689	3 212	2 880	3 663	4 316	4 706	5 097
5121 Excises	..	..	0	0	0	0	0	0	0	0
5122 Profits of fiscal monopolies	..	..	0	0	0	0	0	0	0	0
5123 Customs and import duties	..	..	2 087	2 056	1 975	2 346	2 487	2 799	3 149	3 412
5124 Taxes on exports	..	..	0	0	0	0	15	114	102	103
Remittance tax	..	..	0	0	0	0	15	114	102	103
5125 Taxes on investment goods	..	..	0	0	0	0	0	0	0	0
5126 Taxes on specific services	..	..	547	633	1 237	534	1 161	1 402	1 455	1 582
Green tax	..	..	0	0	0	37	623	696	811	851
Airport service charge	..	..	0	36	432	497	538	706	645	731
Tourism tax	..	..	547	597	805	1	0	0	0	0
5127 Other taxes on internat. trade and transactions	..	..	0	0	0	0	0	0	0	0
5128 Other taxes	..	..	0	0	0	0	0	0	0	0
5130 Unallocable between 5110 and 5120	..	..	0	0	0	0	0	0	0	0
5200 Taxes on use of goods and to perform activities	..	..	40	57	69	78	90	99	108	123
5210 Recurrent taxes	..	..	39	55	66	75	87	97	106	121
5211 Paid by households: motor vehicles	..	..	0	0	0	0	0	0	0	0
5212 Paid by others: motor vehicles	..	..	37	47	52	62	76	84	92	107
5213 Paid in respect of other goods	..	..	2	8	14	12	11	13	14	13
5220 Non-recurrent taxes	..	..	1	2	3	3	3	2	2	2

	1997	2000	2007	2010	2014	2015	2016	2017	2018	2019
5300 Unallocable between 5100 and 5200	..	..	0	0	0	0	0	0	0	0
6000 Other taxes	**..**	**..**	**0**	**0**	**0**	**0**	**0**	**0**	**0**	**0**
6100 Paid solely by business	..	..	0	0	0	0	0	0	0	0
6200 Other	..	..	0	0	0	0	0	0	0	0

Note: Data are reported on a calendar year.
The data are on a cash basis.
Source: Ministry of Finance, Maldives.

StatLink https://stat.link/wsb2jl

Table 4.13. Mongolia: Details of tax revenue

Billion MNT

	1997	2000	2007	2010	2014	2015	2016	2017	2018	2019
Total tax revenue	..	..	**1 406**	**2 470**	**4 481**	**4 421**	**4 567**	**6 005**	**7 788**	**9 033**
1000 Taxes on income, profits and capital gains	..	..	**649**	**975**	**1 101**	**1 171**	**1 043**	**1 613**	**2 091**	**2 556**
1100 Of individuals	..	..	75	161	480	482	523	651	814	895
1110 On income and profits	..	..	75	161	480	482	523	651	814	895
1120 On capital gains	..	..	0	0	0	0	0	0	0	0
1200 Corporate	..	..	574	814	621	689	520	962	1 277	1 661
1210 On profits	..	..	574	814	621	689	520	962	1 277	1 661
Corporate tax income revenue	..	..	220	391	621	689	520	962	1 277	1 661
Windfall profit tax	..	..	354	423	0	0	0	0	0	0
1220 On capital gains of corporates	..	..	0	0	0	0	0	0	0	0
1300 Unallocable between 1100 and 1200	..	..	0	0	0	0	0	0	0	0
2000 Social security contributions	..	..	**161**	**323**	**871**	**972**	**1 058**	**1 259**	**1 569**	**1 787**
2100 Employees	..	..	8	170	423	438	465	535	541	701
2110 On a payroll basis	..	..	..	..	..	..	..	..	..	..
2120 On an income tax basis	..	..	..	..	..	..	..	..	..	..
2200 Employers	..	..	147	129	440	447	494	578	640	776
2210 On a payroll basis	..	..	..	..	..	..	..	..	..	..
2220 On an income tax basis	..	..	..	..	..	..	..	..	..	..
2300 Self-employed or non-employed	..	..	0	0	0	0	0	0	0	0
2310 On a payroll basis	..	..	..	..	..	..	..	..	..	..
2320 On an income tax basis	..	..	..	..	..	..	..	..	..	..
2400 Unallocable between 2100, 2200 and 2300	..	..	6	24	8	87	99	146	388	310
2410 On a payroll basis	..	..	..	..	..	..	..	..	..	..
2420 On an income tax basis	..	..	..	..	..	..	..	..	..	..
3000 Taxes on payroll and workforce	..	..	**0**	**0**	**0**	**0**	**0**	**0**	**0**	**0**
4000 Taxes on property	..	..	**28**	**47**	**115**	**117**	**125**	**157**	**169**	**222**
4100 Recurrent taxes on immovable property	..	..	20	33	66	60	54	62	67	110
4110 Households	..	..	..	..	..	..	..	..	..	..
4120 Others	..	..	..	..	..	..	..	..	..	..
4200 Recurrent taxes on net wealth	..	..	8	14	50	58	72	94	102	112
4210 Individual	..	..	0	0	0	0	0	0	0	0
4220 Corporate	..	..	8	14	50	58	72	94	102	112
4300 Estate, inheritance and gift taxes	..	..	0	0	0	0	0	0	0	0
4310 Estate and inheritance taxes	..	..	..	..	..	..	..	..	..	..
4320 Gift taxes	..	..	..	..	..	..	..	..	..	..
4400 Taxes on financial and capital transactions	..	..	0	0	0	0	0	0	0	0
4500 Other non-reccurrent taxes on property	..	..	0	0	0	0	0	0	0	0
4510 On net wealth	..	..	..	..	..	..	..	..	..	..
4520 Other non-recurrent taxes	..	..	..	..	..	..	..	..	..	..
4600 Other recurrent taxes on property	..	..	0	0	0	0	0	0	0	0
5000 Taxes on goods and services	..	..	**568**	**1 125**	**2 393**	**2 161**	**2 341**	**2 976**	**3 960**	**4 469**
5100 Taxes on production, sale, transfer, etc	..	..	508	1 048	2 206	1 990	2 129	2 686	3 671	4 182
5110 General taxes on goods and services	..	..	265	579	1 372	1 050	1 141	1 619	2 196	2 486
5111 Value added taxes	..	..	265	579	1 372	1 050	1 141	1 619	2 196	2 486
Domestic VAT	..	..	108	208	551	485	558	734	898	1 088
Import VAT	..	..	199	423	917	672	684	1 032	1 412	1 633
VAT refunds	..	..	-42	-51	-95	-107	-102	-148	-114	-235
5112 Sales tax	..	..	0	0	0	0	0	0	0	0
5113 Other	..	..	0	0	0	0	0	0	0	0
5120 Taxes on specific goods and services	..	..	243	469	835	941	989	1 067	1 475	1 696
5121 Excises	..	..	140	276	466	604	641	532	768	880
Alcoholic drinks (excluding beer)	..	..	48	93	261	210	222	247	269	310
Beer	..	..	7	17	36	28	27	27	29	32
Tobacco	..	..	10	11	46	32	33	33	29	29
Vehicles	..	..	39	55	90	44	27	89	214	232
Fuel and gasoline	..	..	36	100	34	291	332	137	227	277
5122 Profits of fiscal monopolies	..	..	0	0	0	0	0	0	0	0
5123 Customs and import duties	..	..	96	193	355	321	328	512	682	790
5124 Taxes on exports	..	..	6	0	0	0	0	0	0	0
5125 Taxes on investment goods	..	..	0	0	0	0	0	0	0	0
5126 Taxes on specific services	..	..	0	0	13	16	19	23	25	26
5127 Other taxes on internat. trade and transactions	..	..	0	0	0	0	0	0	0	0
5128 Other taxes	..	..	0	0	0	0	0	0	0	0
5130 Unallocable between 5110 and 5120	..	..	0	0	0	0	0	0	0	0
5200 Taxes on use of goods and to perform activities	..	..	60	77	187	171	212	290	289	286
5210 Recurrent taxes	..	..	60	74	109	157	192	253	247	237
5211 Paid by households: motor vehicles	..	..	6	10	28	29	32	36	38	41
5212 Paid by others: motor vehicles	..	..	0	0	0	0	0	0	0	0
5213 Paid in respect of other goods	..	..	54	63	80	128	160	218	208	196

	1997	2000	2007	2010	2014	2015	2016	2017	2018	2019
5220 Non-recurrent taxes	..	..	0	3	78	14	20	37	42	49
5300 Unallocable between 5100 and 5200	..	..	0	0	0	0	0	0	0	0
6000 Other taxes	**..**	**..**	**0**	**0**	**0**	**0**	**0**	**0**	**0**	**0**
6100 Paid solely by business	..	..	..	..	..	..	..	..	..	..
6200 Other	..	..	..	..	..	..	..	..	..	..

Note: Year ending December 31st.
The data are on a cash basis.
Source: Ministry of Finance of Mongolia.

StatLink https://stat.link/nflosx

Table 4.14. Nauru: Details of tax revenue

Thousand AUD

	1997	2000	2007	2010	2014	2015	2016	2017	2018	2019
Total tax revenue	..	..	..	..	**9 552**	**24 106**	**21 459**	**42 087**	**56 565**	**80 022**
1000 Taxes on income, profits and capital gains	..	..	..	..	**0**	**12 593**	**12 590**	**27 320**	**39 731**	**62 927**
1100 Of individuals	..	..	..	..	0	0	0	0	0	0
1110 On income and profits	..	..	..	..	0	0	0	0	0	0
1120 On capital gains	..	..	..	..	0	0	0	0	0	0
1200 Corporate	..	..	..	..	0	0	0	0	0	0
1210 On profits	..	..	..	..	0	0	0	0	0	0
1220 On capital gains of corporates	..	..	..	..	0	0	0	0	0	0
1300 Unallocable between 1100 and 1200	..	..	..	..	0	12 593	12 590	27 320	39 731	62 927
Employment Services Tax	..	..	..	..	0	12 593	10 131	8 657	17 531	19 935
Business Tax	..	..	..	..	0	0	2 459	18 663	22 200	42 992
2000 Social security contributions	..	..	..	..	**0**	**0**	**0**	**0**	**0**	**0**
2100 Employees	..	..	..	..	..	..	..	..	..	..
2110 On a payroll basis	..	..	..	..	..	..	..	..	..	..
2120 On an income tax basis	..	..	..	..	..	..	..	..	..	..
2200 Employers	..	..	..	..	..	..	..	..	..	..
2210 On a payroll basis	..	..	..	..	..	..	..	..	..	..
2220 On an income tax basis	..	..	..	..	..	..	..	..	..	..
2300 Self-employed or non-employed	..	..	..	..	..	..	..	..	..	..
2310 On a payroll basis	..	..	..	..	..	..	..	..	..	..
2320 On an income tax basis	..	..	..	..	..	..	..	..	..	..
2400 Unallocable between 2100, 2200 and 2300	..	..	..	..	..	..	..	..	..	..
2410 On a payroll basis	..	..	..	..	..	..	..	..	..	..
2420 On an income tax basis	..	..	..	..	..	..	..	..	..	..
3000 Taxes on payroll and workforce	..	..	..	..	**0**	**0**	**0**	**0**	**0**	**0**
4000 Taxes on property	..	..	..	..	**0**	**0**	**0**	**0**	**0**	**0**
4100 Recurrent taxes on immovable property	..	..	..	..	..	..	..	..	..	..
4110 Households	..	..	..	..	..	..	..	..	..	..
4120 Others	..	..	..	..	..	..	..	..	..	..
4200 Recurrent taxes on net wealth	..	..	..	..	..	..	..	..	..	..
4210 Individual	..	..	..	..	..	..	..	..	..	..
4220 Corporate	..	..	..	..	..	..	..	..	..	..
4300 Estate, inheritance and gift taxes	..	..	..	..	..	..	..	..	..	..
4310 Estate and inheritance taxes	..	..	..	..	..	..	..	..	..	..
4320 Gift taxes	..	..	..	..	..	..	..	..	..	..
4400 Taxes on financial and capital transactions	..	..	..	..	..	..	..	..	..	..
4500 Other non-reccurrent taxes on property	..	..	..	..	..	..	..	..	..	..
4510 On net wealth	..	..	..	..	..	..	..	..	..	..
4520 Other non-recurrent taxes	..	..	..	..	..	..	..	..	..	..
4600 Other recurrent taxes on property	..	..	..	..	..	..	..	..	..	..
5000 Taxes on goods and services	..	..	..	..	**9 552**	**11 513**	**8 869**	**14 767**	**16 834**	**17 094**
5100 Taxes on production, sale, transfer, etc	..	..	..	..	8 747	10 747	8 200	14 011	15 750	15 953
5110 General taxes on goods and services	..	..	..	..	0	0	0	0	0	0
5111 Value added taxes	..	..	..	..	0	0	0	0	0	0
5112 Sales tax	..	..	..	..	0	0	0	0	0	0
5113 Other	..	..	..	..	0	0	0	0	0	0
5120 Taxes on specific goods and services	..	..	..	..	8 747	10 747	8 200	14 011	15 750	15 953
5121 Excises	..	..	..	..	0	0	0	0	0	0
5122 Profits of fiscal monopolies	..	..	..	..	0	0	0	0	0	0
5123 Customs and import duties	..	..	..	..	7 581	8 271	5 121	12 055	10 000	11 604
5124 Taxes on exports	..	..	..	..	0	0	0	0	0	0
5125 Taxes on investment goods	..	..	..	..	0	0	0	0	0	0
5126 Taxes on specific services	..	..	..	..	1 166	2 476	3 079	1 955	5 750	4 349
DCA Departure tax	..	..	..	..	286	579	615	259	1 747	811
DCA Pax levy	..	..	..	..	278	991	689	289	1 846	949
Telecom tax	..	..	..	..	602	906	1 775	1 407	2 158	2 589
5127 Other taxes on internat. trade and transactions	..	..	..	..	0	0	0	0	0	0
5128 Other taxes	..	..	..	..	0	0	0	0	0	0
5130 Unallocable between 5110 and 5120	..	..	..	..	0	0	0	0	0	0
5200 Taxes on use of goods and to perform activities	..	..	..	..	805	766	670	757	1 084	1 142
5210 Recurrent taxes	..	..	..	..	213	228	286	334	455	700
5211 Paid by households: motor vehicles	..	..	..	..	0	0	0	0	0	0
5212 Paid by others: motor vehicles	..	..	..	..	0	0	0	0	32	44
5213 Paid in respect of other goods	..	..	..	..	213	228	286	334	423	656
5220 Non-recurrent taxes	..	..	..	..	592	538	384	423	629	442
5300 Unallocable between 5100 and 5200	..	..	..	..	0	0	0	0	0	0
6000 Other taxes	..	..	..	..	**0**	**0**	**0**	**0**	**0**	**0**
6100 Paid solely by business	..	..	..	..	..	..	..	..	..	..
6200 Other	..	..	..	..	..	..	..	..	..	..

Note: Data are on a fiscal year basis beginning 1st July. For example, the data for 2019 represent the period from July 2019 to July 2020.
Source: Nauru Revenue Office.

StatLink https://stat.link/n9ltqb

Table 4.15. New Zealand: Details of tax revenue

Million NZD

	1997	2000	2007	2010	2014	2015	2016	2017	2018	2019
Total tax revenue	**35 560**	**39 765**	**64 046**	**62 310**	**76 609**	**81 499**	**86 576**	**92 635**	**99 842**	**99 611**
1000 Taxes on income, profits and capital gains	**21 260**	**23 861**	**40 308**	**33 494**	**41 818**	**44 723**	**48 109**	**51 489**	**56 173**	**54 754**
1100 Of individuals	15 669	17 126	26 965	23 519	28 726	30 297	31 844	35 004	37 467	39 464
1110 On income and profits	15 669	17 126	26 965	23 519	28 726	30 297	31 844	35 004	37 467	39 464
1120 On capital gains	0	0	0	0	0	0	0	0	0	0
1200 Corporate	3 926	4 914	9 069	7 609	10 250	11 407	13 461	13 584	15 559	12 366
1210 On profits	3 926	4 914	9 069	7 609	10 250	11 407	13 461	13 584	15 559	12 366
1220 On capital gains	0	0	0	0	0	0	0	0	0	0
1300 Unallocable between 1100 and 1200	1 665	1 821	4 274	2 366	2 842	3 019	2 804	2 901	3 147	2 924
NRWT	662	760	1 506	467	470	733	594	619	651	570
Property speculation	0	0	0	0	0	0	0	0	0	0
Absentee income tax	0	0	0	0	0	0	0	0	0	0
Interest	961	990	2 699	1 704	1 829	1 660	1 468	1 530	1 659	1 528
Dividends	42	71	69	195	543	626	742	752	837	826
Other	0	0	0	0	0	0	0	0	0	0
2000 Social security contributions	**0**	**0**	**0**	**0**	**0**	**0**	**0**	**0**	**0**	**0**
2100 Employees	0	0	0	0	0	0	0	0	0	0
2110 On a payroll basis	..	..	..	..	..	..	..	..	..	..
2120 On an income tax basis	..	..	..	..	..	..	..	..	..	..
2200 Employers	0	0	0	0	0	0	0	0	0	0
2210 On a payroll basis	..	..	..	..	..	..	..	..	..	..
2220 On an income tax basis	..	..	..	..	..	..	..	..	..	..
2300 Self-employed or non-employed	0	0	0	0	0	0	0	0	0	0
2310 On a payroll basis	..	..	..	..	..	..	..	..	..	..
2320 On an income tax basis	..	..	..	..	..	..	..	..	..	..
2400 Unallocable between 2100, 2200 and 2300	0	0	0	0	0	0	0	0	0	0
2410 On a payroll basis	..	..	..	..	..	..	..	..	..	..
2420 On an income tax basis	..	..	..	..	..	..	..	..	..	..
3000 Taxes on payroll and workforce	**0**	**0**	**0**	**0**	**0**	**0**	**0**	**0**	**0**	**0**
4000 Taxes on property	**1 918**	**2 112**	**3 417**	**4 119**	**4 793**	**5 046**	**5 257**	**5 533**	**5 822**	**6 155**
4100 Recurrent taxes on immovable property	1 732	2 049	3 322	4 031	4 693	4 962	5 178	5 426	5 717	6 054
Local govt rates and services	1 732	2 049	3 322	4 031	4 693	4 962	5 178	5 426	5 717	6 054
Land tax	0	0	0	0	0	0	0	0	0	0
4110 Households	..	..	..	..	..	..	..	..	..	..
4120 Others	..	..	..	..	..	..	..	..	..	..
4200 Recurrent taxes on net wealth	0	0	0	0	0	0	0	0	0	0
4210 Individual	..	..	..	..	..	..	..	..	..	..
4220 Corporate	..	..	..	..	..	..	..	..	..	..
4300 Estate, inheritance and gift taxes	0	2	3	2	0	0	0	0	0	0
4310 Estate and inheritance taxes	..	0	0	0	..	..	..	..	..	..
4320 Gift taxes	..	2	3	2	..	..	..	..	..	..
4400 Taxes on financial and capital transactions	186	61	92	86	100	84	79	107	105	101
Instrument duty	173	51	85	82	100	84	79	107	105	101
Cheque duty	13	10	7	4	0	0	0	0	0	0
4500 Non-recurrent taxes	0	0	0	0	0	0	0	0	0	..
4510 On net wealth	..	..	..	..	..	..	..	..	..	..
4520 Other non-recurrent taxes	..	..	..	..	..	..	..	..	..	..
4600 Other recurrent taxes on property	0	0	0	0	0	0	0	0	0	0
5000 Taxes on goods and services	**12 382**	**13 792**	**20 290**	**24 692**	**29 996**	**31 728**	**33 203**	**35 612**	**37 845**	**38 700**
5100 Taxes on production, sale, transfer, etc.	11 603	12 887	18 832	23 107	28 011	29 584	30 925	33 220	35 271	36 033
5110 General taxes	8 696	9 885	15 046	19 143	23 306	24 587	25 847	27 951	29 521	30 259
5111 Value added taxes	8 696	9 885	15 046	19 143	23 306	24 587	25 847	27 951	29 521	30 259
5112 Sales tax	0	0	0	0	0	0	0	0	0	0
Motor vehicles	..	..	..	..	..	..	..	..	..	..
Other sales tax	..	..	..	..	..	..	..	..	..	..
5113 Other	0	0	0	0	0	0	0	0	0	0
5120 Taxes on specific goods and services	2 907	3 002	3 786	3 964	4 705	4 997	5 078	5 269	5 750	5 774

	1997	2000	2007	2010	2014	2015	2016	2017	2018	2019
5121 Excise duties	2 018	2 148	1 627	1 782	2 050	2 280	2 231	2 214	2 622	2 497
On alcoholic beverages	439	436	573	622	651	672	684	699	722	710
Beer	218	201	290	207	253	262	265	265	274	269
Wine	106	100	163	181	216	216	218	227	225	221
Spirits	115	135	120	234	182	194	201	207	223	220
Tobacco	681	764	159	220	310	362	352	399	483	485
Motor vehicles	0	0	0	0	0	0	0	0	0	0
Refined sugar	0	0	0	0	0	0	0	0	0	0
CA petroleum fuels	786	810	819	872	1 018	1 185	1 137	1 057	1 201	1 075
NRF fuel excise	0	0	0	0	0	0	0	0	0	0
Local petroleum fuels	25	27	30	32	35	33	34	33	190	204
CA mileage tax	0	0	0	0	0	0	0	0	0	0
NRF mileage tax	0	0	0	0	0	0	0	0	0	0
Road user charges	0	0	0	0	0	0	0	0	0	0
Energy resources levy	87	111	46	36	36	28	24	26	26	23
5122 Profits of fiscal monopolies	0	0	0	0	0	0	0	0	0	0
5123 Customs and import duties	750	648	1 857	1 916	2 391	2 442	2 550	2 738	2 814	3 001
5124 Taxes on exports	0	0	0	0	0	0	0	0	0	0
5125 Taxes on investment goods	0	0	0	0	0	0	0	0	0	0
5126 Taxes on specific services	139	206	302	266	264	275	297	317	314	276
Lottery (national)	103	167	290	253	249	260	281	301	299	266
Lottery (overseas)	0	0	0	0	0	0	0	0	0	0
Racing	36	39	12	13	15	15	16	16	15	10
Film hire tax	0	0	0	0	0	0	0	0	0	0
Domestic air travel tax	0	0	0	0	0	0	0	0	0	0
5127 Other taxes on internat. trade and transactions	0	0	0	0	0	0	0	0	0	0
Foreign fishing vessels tax	..	..	..	..	..	..	..	..	..	..
Foreign travel tax	..	..	..	..	..	..	..	..	..	..
International departure tax	..	..	..	..	..	..	..	..	..	..
5128 Other taxes	0	0	0	0	0	0	0	0	0	0
5130 Unallocable between 5110 and 5120	0	0	0	0	0	0	0	0	0	0
5200 Taxes on use of goods and perform activities	779	905	1 458	1 585	1 985	2 144	2 278	2 392	2 574	2 667
5210 Recurrent taxes	779	905	1 458	1 585	1 985	2 144	2 278	2 392	2 574	2 667
Motor vehicle registration	158	181	226	172	181	214	223	227	227	226
Heavy traffic fees	466	532	851	1 016	1 283	1 381	1 469	1 551	1 673	1 716
Accident compensation levies	0	0	0	0	0	0	0	0	0	0
5211 Paid by households: motor vehicles	0	0	0	0	0	0	0	0	0	0
5212 Paid by others: motor vehicles	0	0	0	0	0	0	0	0	0	0
5213 Paid in respect of other goods	155	192	381	397	521	549	586	614	674	725
Local authority fees and charges	155	192	381	397	521	549	586	614	674	725
5220 Non-recurrent taxes	0	0	0	0	0	0	0	0	0	0
5300 Unallocable between 5100 and 5200	0	0	0	0	0	0	0	0	0	0
6000 Other taxes	**0**	**0**	**31**	**5**	**2**	**2**	**7**	**1**	**2**	**2**
6100 Paid solely by business	..	..	0	0	0	0	0	0	0	0
6200 Other	..	..	31	5	2	2	7	1	2	2

Note: The figures follow a financial year ending on 30 June of the following year.

From 1993, data are on accrual basis.

Heading 1000: Tax credits to exporters under the export incentives schemes are non-wastable, but that part of the excess of tax liability paid out to taxpayers is not identifiable.

Heading 1100: The figures up to 1969 include revenues collected by a social security income tax. The base of this tax was the same as the ordinary income tax base and the two have now been incorporated into a single income tax.

Heading 5121: From October 1986 incorporates that portion of the selective impost on wine, spirits, tobacco and motor vehicles which was formerly collected and reported as sales tax. The revenue collected on those imported goods which are subject to the equivalent of the domestic excise has been classified as excise duty. In this respect, there is a discontinuity between the excises recorded before and after October 1986.

Heading 5210: The other local authority licence fees include some small items which could be regarded as non-tax revenues.

Heading for non-wastable tax credits 1110 comprises four Family assistance tax credits. The total in item 1100 is net of the tax expenditure component but not net of the transfer component.

Source: Local Authorities Statistics, Department of Statistics, Wellington.

StatLink https://stat.link/td0mvz

Table 4.16. Papua New Guinea: Details of tax revenue

Million PGK

	1997	2000	2007	2010	2014	2015	2016	2017	2018	2019
Total tax revenue	..	**1 305**	**5 875**	**6 573**	**10 279**	**9 142**	**8 606**	**8 986**	**9 983**	**10 518**
1000 Taxes on income, profits and capital gains	..	**936**	**4 287**	**4 562**	**6 889**	**5 956**	**5 286**	**5 474**	**6 119**	**6 055**
1100 Of individuals	..	552	1 001	1 553	3 200	3 037	2 844	3 094	3 102	3 212
1110 On income and profits	..	552	1 001	1 553	3 200	3 037	2 844	3 094	3 102	3 212
1120 On capital gains	..	..	..	..	..	..	..	..	..	..
1200 Corporate	..	384	3 285	3 009	3 689	2 919	2 441	2 380	3 017	2 843
1210 On profits	..	384	3 285	3 009	3 689	2 919	2 441	2 380	3 017	2 843
Corporate Income Tax	..	262	724	1 201	2 629	2 375	2 094	1 950	1 933	1 697
Mining and Petroleum Tax	..	0	2 334	1 476	794	169	92	114	775	760
Royalty Tax and Management fee	..	4	5	10	37	18	44	43	44	43
Dividend witholding tax	..	54	204	279	186	195	133	182	155	215
Interest witholding tax	..	64	19	42	43	162	79	91	111	128
1220 On capital gains of corporates	..	..	..	..	..	..	..	..	..	..
1300 Unallocable between 1100 and 1200	..	0	0	0	0	0	0	0	0	0
2000 Social security contributions	..	**0**	**0**	**0**	**0**	**0**	**0**	**0**	**0**	**0**
2100 Employees	..	..	..	..	..	..	..	..	..	..
2110 On a payroll basis	..	..	..	..	..	..	..	..	..	..
2120 On an income tax basis	..	..	..	..	..	..	..	..	..	..
2200 Employers	..	..	..	..	..	..	..	..	..	..
2210 On a payroll basis	..	..	..	..	..	..	..	..	..	..
2220 On an income tax basis	..	..	..	..	..	..	..	..	..	..
2300 Self-employed or non-employed	..	..	..	..	..	..	..	..	..	..
2310 On a payroll basis	..	..	..	..	..	..	..	..	..	..
2320 On an income tax basis	..	..	..	..	..	..	..	..	..	..
2400 Unallocable between 2100, 2200 and 2300	..	..	..	..	..	..	..	..	..	..
2410 On a payroll basis	..	..	..	..	..	..	..	..	..	..
2420 On an income tax basis	..	..	..	..	..	..	..	..	..	..
3000 Taxes on payroll and workforce	..	**1**	**2**	**2**	**16**	**0**	**14**	**11**	**9**	**2**
4000 Taxes on property	..	**44**	**85**	**65**	**137**	**51**	**79**	**42**	**100**	**47**
4100 Recurrent taxes on immovable property	..	0	0	0	0	0	0	0	0	0
4110 Households	..	..	..	..	..	..	..	..	..	..
4120 Others	..	..	..	..	..	..	..	..	..	..
4200 Recurrent taxes on net wealth	..	0	0	0	0	0	0	0	0	0
4210 Individual	..	..	..	..	..	..	..	..	..	..
4220 Corporate	..	..	..	..	..	..	..	..	..	..
4300 Estate, inheritance and gift taxes	..	0	0	0	0	0	0	0	0	0
4310 Estate and inheritance taxes	..	..	..	..	..	..	..	..	..	..
4320 Gift taxes	..	..	..	..	..	..	..	..	..	..
4400 Taxes on financial and capital transactions	..	44	85	65	137	51	79	42	100	47
4500 Other non-reccurrent taxes on property	..	0	0	0	0	0	0	0	0	0
4510 On net wealth	..	..	..	..	..	..	..	..	..	..
4520 Other non-recurrent taxes	..	..	..	..	..	..	..	..	..	..
4600 Other recurrent taxes on property	..	0	0	0	0	0	0	0	0	0
5000 Taxes on goods and services	..	**325**	**1 501**	**1 944**	**3 237**	**3 134**	**3 227**	**3 459**	**3 755**	**4 414**
5100 Taxes on production, sale, transfer, etc	..	325	1 501	1 944	3 237	3 134	3 227	3 459	3 755	4 414
5110 General taxes on goods and services	..	325	654	874	1 636	1 637	1 646	1 617	1 642	1 990
5111 Value added taxes	..	321	648	865	1 623	1 571	1 638	1 581	1 622	1 973
Goods and services tax (inland Collection)	..	177	468	629	1 180	1 068	1 103	1 131	1 120	1 368
GST transfers to provinces	..	144	180	236	443	503	535	450	502	605
5112 Sales tax	..	0	0	0	0	0	0	0	0	0
5113 Other	..	4	6	9	13	66	8	36	20	17
5120 Taxes on specific goods and services	..	..	846	1 070	1 601	1 497	1 581	1 842	2 113	2 424
5121 Excises	..	..	455	611	889	802	876	1 105	1 168	1 361
5122 Profits of fiscal monopolies	..	0	0	0	0	0	0	0	0	0
5123 Customs and import duties	..	..	136	189	273	243	243	246	325	409
5124 Taxes on exports	..	..	155	174	275	316	294	297	392	398
5125 Taxes on investment goods	..	0	0	0	0	0	0	0	0	0
5126 Taxes on specific services	..	61	100	97	164	136	168	193	228	256
Gaming taxes	..	58	97	93	158	126	164	179	205	227
Departure tax	..	3	3	4	6	9	4	14	23	29
5127 Other taxes on internat. trade and transactions	..	0	0	0	0	0	0	0	0	0
5128 Other taxes	..	0	0	0	0	0	0	0	0	0
5130 Unallocable between 5110 and 5120	..	0	0	0	0	0	0	0	0	0
5200 Taxes on use of goods and to perform activities	..	0	0	0	0	0	0	0	0	0
5210 Recurrent taxes	..	..	..	..	..	..	..	..	..	..
5211 Paid by households: motor vehicles	..	..	..	..	..	..	..	..	..	..
5212 Paid by others: motor vehicles	..	..	..	..	..	..	..	..	..	..
5213 Paid in respect of other goods	..	..	..	..	..	..	..	..	..	..
5220 Non-recurrent taxes	..	..	..	..	..	..	..	..	..	..

	1997	2000	2007	2010	2014	2015	2016	2017	2018	2019
5300 Unallocable between 5100 and 5200	..	0	0	0	0	0	0	0	0	0
6000 Other taxes	**..**	**0**	**0**	**0**	**0**	**0**	**0**	**0**	**0**	**0**
6100 Paid solely by business	..	..	..	..	..	..	..	..	..	..
6200 Other	..	..	..	..	..	..	..	..	..	..

Note: Year ending 31st December.
The data are on a cash basis.
Figures exclude tax revenues collected by sub-national governments as the data are not available.
Total tax revenues are not available for 2000 and 2001 as the data are incomplete, and do not include customs revenues for these two years.
Source: Ministry of Treasury and Finance of Papua New Guinea.

StatLink https://stat.link/bfvw8d

Table 4.17. Philippines: Details of tax revenue

Million PHP

	1997	2000	2007	2010	2014	2015	2016	2017	2018	2019
Total tax revenue	**447 976**	**564 343**	**1 121 594**	**1 330 768**	**2 111 568**	**2 265 139**	**2 460 823**	**2 779 896**	**3 173 744**	**3 520 186**
1000 Taxes on income, profits and capital gains	**164 170**	**217 798**	**453 338**	**521 707**	**840 680**	**912 229**	**994 543**	**1 106 711**	**1 124 589**	**1 257 675**
1100 Of individuals	59 749	83 006	141 673	167 605	283 873	309 439	344 081	391 049	386 748	499 450
1110 On income and profits	53 370	78 229	135 504	158 325	267 703	292 548	325 446	367 166	359 901	473 098
1120 On capital gains	6 379	4 777	6 170	9 280	16 170	16 891	18 635	23 883	26 847	26 352
1200 Corporate	95 449	116 980	282 504	326 967	523 183	569 485	619 067	683 929	700 990	716 763
1210 On profits	94 427	114 871	280 090	323 116	513 978	561 465	609 301	676 868	690 641	706 547
1220 On capital gains of corporates	1 022	2 110	2 414	3 851	9 205	8 020	9 766	7 061	10 348	10 215
1300 Unallocable between 1100 and 1200	8 973	17 812	29 160	27 135	33 624	33 305	31 395	31 732	36 851	41 462
2000 Social security contributions	**36 500**	**74 200**	**131 830**	**168 430**	**284 360**	**319 106**	**343 545**	**372 421**	**433 580**	**498 167**
2100 Employees	..	..	..	..	..	..	..	..	..	..
2110 On a payroll basis	..	..	..	..	..	..	..	..	..	..
2120 On an income tax basis	..	..	..	..	..	..	..	..	..	..
2200 Employers	2 800	19 900	26 520	34 300	80 130	97 598	101 003	111 496	128 526	148 400
2210 On a payroll basis	..	..	..	..	..	..	..	..	..	..
2220 On an income tax basis	..	..	..	..	..	..	..	..	..	..
2300 Self-employed or non-employed	..	..	..	..	..	..	..	..	..	..
2310 On a payroll basis	..	..	..	..	..	..	..	..	..	..
2320 On an income tax basis	..	..	..	..	..	..	..	..	..	..
2400 Unallocable between 2100, 2200 and 2300	33 700	54 300	105 310	134 130	204 230	221 508	242 542	260 925	305 054	349 767
2410 On a payroll basis	..	..	..	..	..	..	..	..	..	..
2420 On an income tax basis	..	..	..	..	..	..	..	..	..	..
3000 Taxes on payroll and workforce	**0**	**0**	**0**	**0**	**0**	**0**	**0**	**0**	**0**	**0**
4000 Taxes on property	**4 178**	**17 401**	**32 354**	**39 070**	**60 026**	**63 982**	**66 265**	**78 269**	**81 373**	**87 458**
4100 Recurrent taxes on immovable property	0	14 947	27 387	31 876	45 458	48 991	50 829	61 891	64 474	70 143
Real property tax (local government)	..	14 947	27 387	31 876	45 458	48 991	50 829	61 891	64 474	70 143
4110 Households	..	..	..	..	..	..	..	..	..	..
4120 Others	..	..	..	..	..	..	..	..	..	..
4200 Recurrent taxes on net wealth	0	0	0	0	0	0	0	0	0	0
4210 Individual	..	..	..	..	..	..	..	..	..	..
4220 Corporate	..	..	..	..	..	..	..	..	..	..
4300 Estate, inheritance and gift taxes	881	480	962	1 981	5 450	5 636	6 638	7 467	7 155	7 219
4310 Estate and inheritance taxes	677	302	650	1 451	3 489	3 341	4 723	5 001	3 654	3 299
4320 Gift taxes	204	178	312	531	1 960	2 294	1 915	2 466	3 501	3 920
4400 Taxes on financial and capital transactions	3 297	1 974	4 005	5 213	9 118	9 356	8 798	8 910	9 744	10 095
Stock transactions (RA 7717)	3 297	1 974	4 005	5 213	9 118	9 356	8 798	8 910	9 744	10 095
4500 Other non-reccurrent taxes on property	0	0	0	0	0	0	0	0	0	0
4510 On net wealth	..	..	..	..	..	..	..	..	..	..
4520 Other non-recurrent taxes	..	..	..	..	..	..	..	..	..	..
4600 Other recurrent taxes on property	0	0	0	0	0	0	0	0	0	0
5000 Taxes on goods and services	**225 025**	**237 243**	**456 497**	**549 890**	**844 442**	**884 132**	**962 763**	**1 118 976**	**1 365 047**	**1 496 800**
5100 Taxes on production, sale, transfer, etc	222 627	234 202	448 164	540 595	832 656	872 832	949 396	1 103 612	1 349 435	1 481 145
5110 General taxes on goods and services	47 273	53 879	145 013	173 284	278 794	295 502	331 414	365 235	358 169	406 084
5111 Value added taxes	47 273	53 879	145 013	173 284	278 794	295 502	331 414	365 235	358 169	406 084
5112 Sales tax	0	0	0	0	0	0	0	0	0	0
5113 Other	0	0	0	0	0	0	0	0	0	0
5120 Taxes on specific goods and services	175 354	180 323	303 151	367 312	553 862	577 330	617 982	738 376	991 266	1 075 061
5121 Excises	63 048	61 677	54 998	67 203	135 315	158 319	163 505	209 493	290 612	317 267
Alcohol products	13 412	12 997	18 786	21 781	37 525	42 214	50 272	61 050	68 809	76 999
Tobacco products	16 027	17 427	23 206	31 730	82 725	99 505	95 055	125 910	136 005	147 633
Petroleum products	29 272	28 297	10 036	9 832	9 419	11 888	13 111	15 512	39 002	42 709
Automobiles	0	0	0	0	2 636	2 452	3 128	4 308	5 814	5 523
Mineral products	77	243	942	1 306	2 814	2 079	1 758	2 251	4 918	5 453
Others	4 259	2 712	2 028	2 555	196	182	181	462	36 064	38 952
5122 Profits of fiscal monopolies	0	0	0	0	0	0	0	0	0	0
5123 Customs and import duties	94 800	95 006	209 439	259 241	369 277	367 534	396 365	458 184	593 111	630 310
5124 Taxes on exports	0	0	0	0	0	0	0	0	0	0
5125 Taxes on investment goods	0	0	0	0	0	0	0	0	0	0
5126 Taxes on specific services	17 506	23 639	38 714	40 868	49 270	51 477	58 111	70 700	107 543	127 484
Banks and financial institutions	9 696	9 538	19 434	22 857	26 677	26 915	29 602	33 471	33 087	50 876
Travel tax (CHED/NCAA)	386	1 043	1 581	1 512	1 827	1 770	1 694	2 894	3 084	3 487
Immigration tax (BID)	18	47	42	59	72	72	87	115	165	241
Other	7 406	13 011	17 657	16 440	20 694	22 720	26 728	34 220	71 207	72 880
5127 Other taxes on internat. trade and transactions	0	0	0	0	0	0	0	0	0	0
5128 Other taxes	0	0	0	0	0	0	0	0	0	0
5130 Unallocable between 5110 and 5120	0	0	0	0	0	0	0	0	0	0
5200 Taxes on use of goods and to perform activities	2 398	3 041	8 333	9 295	11 786	11 300	13 367	15 364	15 612	15 655
5210 Recurrent taxes	2 398	3 041	8 333	9 295	11 786	11 300	13 367	15 364	15 612	15 655
LTO-Motor Vehicle Users' Tax	2 398	3 041	8 333	9 295	11 786	11 300	13 367	15 364	15 612	15 655

	1997	2000	2007	2010	2014	2015	2016	2017	2018	2019
5211 Paid by households: motor vehicles	..	..	..	..	..	..	..	..	..	..
5212 Paid by others: motor vehicles	..	..	..	..	..	..	..	..	..	..
5213 Paid in respect of other goods	..	..	..	..	..	..	..	..	..	..
5220 Non-recurrent taxes	0	0	0	0	0	0	0	0	0	0
5300 Unallocable between 5100 and 5200	0	0	0	0	0	0	0	0	0	0
6000 Other taxes	**18 103**	**17 702**	**47 575**	**51 671**	**82 060**	**85 690**	**93 706**	**103 520**	**169 155**	**180 086**
6100 Paid solely by business	0	0	0	0	0	0	0	0	0	0
6200 Other	18 103	17 702	47 575	51 671	82 060	85 690	93 706	103 520	169 155	180 086
Documentary Stamp Tax	16 477	16 170	35 147	42 629	69 036	72 073	80 151	85 916	139 168	145 970
DENR-Forest charges	116	175	164	239	133	128	136	164	192	250
Miscellaneous taxes	1 510	1 356	8 944	4 391	6 051	6 219	5 888	9 086	19 708	22 684
Other taxes (local government)	0	0	3 319	4 412	6 840	7 270	7 531	8 354	10 086	11 181

Note: Year ending 31st December.
The data are on a cash basis.
Heading 5123: This category includes VAT on imports as well as excises levied on imports.
Source: Department of Finance of the Philippines.

StatLink https://stat.link/8ulidc

Table 4.18. Samoa: Details of tax revenue

Million WST

	1997	2000	2007	2010	2014	2015	2016	2017	2018	2019
Total tax revenue	..	..	**330**	**341**	**440**	**495**	**514**	**523**	**572**	**556**
1000 Taxes on income, profits and capital gains	..	..	**78**	**84**	**107**	**114**	**117**	**116**	**132**	**122**
1100 Of individuals	..	..	42	46	59	64	69	68	68	70
1110 On income and profits	..	..	42	46	59	64	69	68	68	70
1120 On capital gains	..	..	0	0	0	0	0	0	0	0
1200 Corporate	..	..	36	38	48	51	48	48	64	52
1210 On profits	..	..	36	38	48	51	48	48	64	52
1220 On capital gains of corporates	..	..	0	0	0	0	0	0	0	0
1300 Unallocable between 1100 and 1200	..	..	0	0	0	0	0	0	0	0
2000 Social security contributions	..	..	**0**	**0**	**0**	**0**	**0**	**0**	**0**	**0**
2100 Employees	..	..	..	..	..	..	..	..	..	..
2110 On a payroll basis	..	..	..	..	..	..	..	..	..	..
2120 On an income tax basis	..	..	..	..	..	..	..	..	..	..
2200 Employers	..	..	..	..	..	..	..	..	..	..
2210 On a payroll basis	..	..	..	..	..	..	..	..	..	..
2220 On an income tax basis	..	..	..	..	..	..	..	..	..	..
2300 Self-employed or non-employed	..	..	..	..	..	..	..	..	..	..
2310 On a payroll basis	..	..	..	..	..	..	..	..	..	..
2320 On an income tax basis	..	..	..	..	..	..	..	..	..	..
2400 Unallocable between 2100, 2200 and 2300	..	..	..	..	..	..	..	..	..	..
2410 On a payroll basis	..	..	..	..	..	..	..	..	..	..
2420 On an income tax basis	..	..	..	..	..	..	..	..	..	..
3000 Taxes on payroll and workforce	..	..	**0**	**0**	**0**	**0**	**0**	**0**	**0**	**0**
4000 Taxes on property	..	..	**2**	**0**	**0**	**0**	**0**	**0**	**0**	**0**
4100 Recurrent taxes on immovable property	..	..	0	..	..	..	..	..	..	..
4110 Households	..	..	..	..	..	..	..	..	..	..
4120 Others	..	..	..	..	..	..	..	..	..	..
4200 Recurrent taxes on net wealth	..	..	0	..	..	..	..	..	..	..
4210 Individual	..	..	..	..	..	..	..	..	..	..
4220 Corporate	..	..	..	..	..	..	..	..	..	..
4300 Estate, inheritance and gift taxes	..	..	0	..	..	..	..	..	..	..
4310 Estate and inheritance taxes	..	..	..	..	..	..	..	..	..	..
4320 Gift taxes	..	..	..	..	..	..	..	..	..	..
4400 Taxes on financial and capital transactions	..	..	2	..	..	..	..	..	..	..
4500 Other non-reccurrent taxes on property	..	..	0	..	..	..	..	..	..	..
4510 On net wealth	..	..	..	..	..	..	..	..	..	..
4520 Other non-recurrent taxes	..	..	..	..	..	..	..	..	..	..
4600 Other recurrent taxes on property	..	..	0	..	..	..	..	..	..	..
5000 Taxes on goods and services	..	..	**251**	**257**	**332**	**380**	**397**	**408**	**440**	**434**
5100 Taxes on production, sale, transfer, etc	..	..	251	257	332	380	397	408	440	434
5110 General taxes on goods and services	..	..	126	119	177	200	198	209	229	232
5111 Value added taxes	..	..	126	119	177	200	198	209	229	232
VAGST on Imports	..	..	100	..	..	..	..	..	..	..
VAGST on sales of goods and services	..	..	26	..	..	..	..	..	..	..
5112 Sales tax	..	..	0	0	0	0	0	0	0	0
5113 Other	..	..	0	0	0	0	0	0	0	0
5120 Taxes on specific goods and services	..	..	125	137	155	181	199	199	211	202
5121 Excises	..	..	78	95	99	120	134	127	133	133
Petroleum Levy	..	..	3	..	..	..	..	..	..	..
Import Excise	..	..	29	..	..	..	..	..	..	..
Domestic Excise	..	..	47	..	..	..	..	..	..	..
5122 Profits of fiscal monopolies	..	..	0	0	0	0	0	0	0	0
5123 Customs and import duties	..	..	43	38	50	54	55	59	63	55
5124 Taxes on exports	..	..	0	0	0	0	0	0	0	0
5125 Taxes on investment goods	..	..	0	0	0	0	0	0	0	0
5126 Taxes on specific services	..	..	4	4	6	6	10	13	15	14
5127 Other taxes on internat. trade and transactions	..	..	0	0	0	0	0	0	0	0
5128 Other taxes	..	..	0	0	0	0	0	0	0	0
5130 Unallocable between 5110 and 5120	..	..	0	0	0	0	0	0	0	0
5200 Taxes on use of goods and to perform activities	..	..	0	0	0	0	0	0	0	0
5210 Recurrent taxes	..	..	..	..	..	..	..	..	..	..
5211 Paid by households: motor vehicles	..	..	..	..	..	..	..	..	..	..
5212 Paid by others: motor vehicles	..	..	..	..	..	..	..	..	..	..
5213 Paid in respect of other goods	..	..	..	..	..	..	..	..	..	..
5220 Non-recurrent taxes	..	..	..	..	..	..	..	..	..	..
5300 Unallocable between 5100 and 5200	..	..	0	0	0	0	0	0	0	0
6000 Other taxes	..	..	**0**	**0**	**0**	**0**	**0**	**0**	**0**	**0**
6100 Paid solely by business	..	..	..	..	..	..	..	..	..	..
6200 Other	..	..	..	..	..	..	..	..	..	..

Note: Data are reported on a fiscal year basis beginning 1st July. For example, the data for 2019 represent the period from July 2019 to June 2020.

The data are on a cash basis.

Figures exclude tax revenues collected by sub-national governments as the data are not available.

The data from 2009 were provided on the basis of the IMF's GFSM 2014 classification. Prior to this year, data were provided on a different basis. The differences between the two sets of data are indicated below for the relevant tax revenue categories.

Heading 1000: Income tax revenues from 2009 onwards are net of income tax refunds. Prior to 2009, the income tax revenue figures are gross of refunds

Heading 5111: VAGST revenues from 2009 onwards net of aid, loan payments by Treasury and VAGST paid by Government departments.

Heading 5123: Import duty from 2009 onwards is net of aid and loan payments by Treasury.

Heading 5126: Data from 2009 include revenues from fisheries' licences. Fisheries' licences revenues are usually classified as non-tax revenues according to the OECD classification set out in Annex A of the Interpretative Guide, but could not be distinguished from other revenues from taxes on specific services.

Source: Bureau of Statistics of Samoa.

StatLink https://stat.link/edxcho

Table 4.19. Singapore: Details of tax revenue

Million SGD

	1997	2000	2007	2010	2014	2015	2016	2017	2018	2019
Total tax revenue	..	**25 627**	**36 630**	**41 848**	**54 110**	**55 647**	**58 699**	**66 363**	**66 203**	**67 645**
1000 Taxes on income, profits and capital gains	..	**13 538**	**16 621**	**18 687**	**23 940**	**24 890**	**26 378**	**32 065**	**30 818**	**32 535**
1100 Of individuals	..	3 543	4 537	6 470	8 927	9 235	10 526	10 724	11 706	12 368
1110 On income and profits	..	3 543	4 537	6 470	8 927	9 235	10 526	10 724	11 706	12 368
1120 On capital gains	..	0	0	0	0	0	0	0	0	0
1200 Corporate	..	9 509	10 934	11 260	13 887	14 253	14 378	19 810	17 523	18 530
1210 On profits	..	9 509	10 934	11 260	13 887	14 253	14 378	19 810	17 523	18 530
From corporate profits	..	8 316	9 250	10 687	13 372	13 815	13 602	14 944	16 032	16 732
Statutory board contributions	..	1 192	1 683	573	516	438	776	4 866	1 491	1 798
1220 On capital gains	..	0	0	0	0	0	0	0	0	0
1300 Unallocable between 1100 and 1200	..	486	1 150	957	1 126	1 402	1 474	1 532	1 590	1 637
Withholding taxes	..	486	1 150	957	1 126	1 402	1 474	1 532	1 590	1 637
2000 Social security contributions	..	**0**	**0**	**0**	**0**	**0**	**0**	**0**	**0**	**0**
2100 Employees	..	..	..	..	..	..	..	..	..	..
2110 On a payroll basis	..	..	..	..	..	..	..	..	..	..
2120 On an income tax basis	..	..	..	..	..	..	..	..	..	..
2200 Employers	..	..	..	..	..	..	..	..	..	..
2210 On a payroll basis	..	..	..	..	..	..	..	..	..	..
2220 On an income tax basis	..	..	..	..	..	..	..	..	..	..
2300 Self-employed or non-employed	..	..	..	..	..	..	..	..	..	..
2310 On a payroll basis	..	..	..	..	..	..	..	..	..	..
2320 On an income tax basis	..	..	..	..	..	..	..	..	..	..
2400 Unallocable between 2100, 2200 and 2300	..	..	..	..	..	..	..	..	..	..
2410 On a payroll basis	..	..	..	..	..	..	..	..	..	..
2420 On an income tax basis	..	..	..	..	..	..	..	..	..	..
3000 Taxes on payroll and workforce	..	**0**	**0**	**0**	**0**	**0**	**0**	**0**	**0**	**0**
4000 Taxes on property	..	**2 863**	**6 259**	**6 080**	**7 124**	**7 224**	**7 638**	**9 345**	**9 256**	**8 961**
4100 Recurrent taxes on immovable property	..	1 535	2 428	2 798	4 340	4 456	4 359	4 440	4 649	4 761
4110 Households	..	..	..	..	..	..	..	..	..	..
4120 Others	..	..	..	..	..	..	..	..	..	..
4200 Recurrent taxes on net wealth	..	0	0	0	0	0	0	0	0	0
4210 Individual	..	..	..	..	..	..	..	..	..	..
4220 Corporate	..	..	..	..	..	..	..	..	..	..
4300 Estate, inheritance and gift taxes	..	71	154	5	1	-1	0	0	0	0
4310 Estate and inheritance taxes	..	71	154	5	1	-1	0	0	0	0
4320 Gift taxes	..	0	0	0	0	0	0	0	0	0
4400 Taxes on financial and capital transactions	..	1 257	3 677	3 277	2 784	2 769	3 278	4 905	4 607	4 199
4500 Non-recurrent taxes	..	0	0	0	0	0	0	0	0	0
4510 On net wealth	..	..	..	..	..	..	..	..	..	..
4520 Other non-recurrent taxes	..	..	..	..	..	..	..	..	..	..
4600 Other recurrent taxes on property	..	0	0	0	0	0	0	0	0	0
5000 Taxes on goods and services	..	**7 967**	**12 053**	**14 376**	**16 949**	**17 657**	**18 638**	**18 933**	**19 499**	**19 466**
5100 Taxes on production, sale, transfer, etc	..	5 462	9 864	12 525	15 346	15 897	16 490	16 781	16 876	17 047
5110 General taxes	..	2 121	6 165	8 198	10 215	10 345	11 078	10 960	11 137	11 164
5111 Value added taxes	..	2 121	6 165	8 198	10 215	10 345	11 078	10 960	11 137	11 164
5112 Sales tax	..	0	0	0	0	0	0	0	0	0
5113 Other	..	0	0	0	0	0	0	0	0	0
5120 Taxes on specific goods and services	..	3 341	3 699	4 327	5 131	5 552	5 412	5 821	5 739	5 883
5121 Excises	..	1 847	1 985	2 048	2 540	2 833	2 730	3 133	3 075	3 264
Liquors	..	..	414	470	634	638	640	663	678	678
Tobacco	..	..	700	889	1 228	1 205	986	1 174	1 122	1 160
Petroleum Products	..	..	386	419	419	584	596	827	784	986
Motor Vehicles	..	..	483	267	251	399	502	463	486	435
Compressed Natural Gas Unit Duty	..	..	0	0	3	2	1	1	0	0
Others	..	..	3	5	6	5	5	5	6	5
5122 Profits of fiscal monopolies	..	0	0	0	0	0	0	0	0	0
5123 Customs and import duties	..	0	0	0	0	0	0	0	0	0
5124 Taxes on exports	..	0	0	0	0	0	0	0	0	0
5125 Taxes on investment goods	..	0	0	0	0	0	0	0	0	0
5126 Taxes on specific services	..	1 494	1 714	2 279	2 591	2 719	2 682	2 688	2 664	2 620
Betting duty	..	1 494	1 714	2 279	2 591	2 719	2 682	2 688	2 664	2 620
5127 Other taxes on internat. trade and transactions	..	0	0	0	0	0	0	0	0	0
5128 Other taxes	..	0	0	0	0	0	0	0	0	0
5130 Unallocable between 5110 and 5120	..	0	0	0	0	0	0	0	0	0
5200 Taxes on use of goods and perform activities	..	2 506	2 189	1 851	1 603	1 760	2 148	2 153	2 623	2 419
5210 Recurrent taxes	..	..	..	..	..	..	..	..	..	..
5211 Paid by households: motor vehicles	..	..	..	..	..	..	..	..	..	..
5212 Paid by others: motor vehicles	..	..	..	..	..	..	..	..	..	..
5213 Paid in respect of other goods	..	..	..	..	..	..	..	..	..	..

	1997	2000	2007	2010	2014	2015	2016	2017	2018	2019
5220 Non-recurrent taxes	..	..	..	..	..	..	..	..	..	..
5300 Unallocable between 5100 and 5200	..	0	0	0	0	0	0	0	0	0
6000 Other taxes	**..**	**1 259**	**1 698**	**2 706**	**6 097**	**5 876**	**6 045**	**6 019**	**6 629**	**6 683**
6100 Paid solely by business	..	0	0	0	0	0	0	0	0	0
6200 Other	..	1 259	1 698	2 706	6 097	5 876	6 045	6 019	6 629	6 683

Note: Data are on a fiscal year basis ending 31st March. For example, the data for 2019 represent 1 April 2019 to 31 March 2020.
The data are on a cash basis.
Heading 2000: there are no social security contributions in Singapore.
Heading 4100: recurrent taxes on immovable property includes tax levied on all private properties, as well as properties owned by statutory boards.
Heading 5121: comprises excises, customs and import duties.
Source: Ministry of Finance of Singapore.

StatLink https://stat.link/iulf6z

Table 4.20. Solomon Islands: Details of tax revenue

Million SBD

	1997	2000	2007	2010	2014	2015	2016	2017	2018	2019
Total tax revenue	..	..	**819**	**1 376**	**2 269**	**2 392**	**2 367**	**2 632**	**3 013**	**2 623**
1000 Taxes on income, profits and capital gains	..	..	**189**	**418**	**622**	**719**	**690**	**780**	**794**	**757**
1100 Of individuals	..	..	141	280	404	437	411	491	505	509
1110 On income and profits	..	..	141	280	404	437	411	491	505	509
1120 On capital gains	..	..	0	0	0	0	0	0	0	0
1200 Corporate	..	..	48	137	218	283	278	289	288	248
1210 On profits	..	..	48	137	218	283	278	289	288	248
Dividend Withholding Tax (WHT)	..	..	14	41	74	118	106	114	86	43
Non-resident WHT	..	..	16	43	63	71	68	66	59	71
Resident WHT	..	..	19	53	81	94	105	110	143	134
1220 On capital gains of corporates	..	..	..	..	..	..	..	..	..	..
1300 Unallocable between 1100 and 1200	..	..	0	0	0	0	0	0	0	0
2000 Social security contributions	..	..	**0**	**0**	**0**	**0**	**0**	**0**	**0**	**0**
2100 Employees	..	..	..	..	..	..	..	..	..	..
2110 On a payroll basis	..	..	..	..	..	..	..	..	..	..
2120 On an income tax basis	..	..	..	..	..	..	..	..	..	..
2200 Employers	..	..	..	..	..	..	..	..	..	..
2210 On a payroll basis	..	..	..	..	..	..	..	..	..	..
2220 On an income tax basis	..	..	..	..	..	..	..	..	..	..
2300 Self-employed or non-employed	..	..	..	..	..	..	..	..	..	..
2310 On a payroll basis	..	..	..	..	..	..	..	..	..	..
2320 On an income tax basis	..	..	..	..	..	..	..	..	..	..
2400 Unallocable between 2100, 2200 and 2300	..	..	..	..	..	..	..	..	..	..
2410 On a payroll basis	..	..	..	..	..	..	..	..	..	..
2420 On an income tax basis	..	..	..	..	..	..	..	..	..	..
3000 Taxes on payroll and workforce	..	..	**0**	**0**	**0**	**0**	**0**	**0**	**0**	**0**
4000 Taxes on property	..	..	**9**	**8**	**14**	**19**	**17**	**14**	**16**	**15**
4100 Recurrent taxes on immovable property	..	..	0	0	0	0	0	0	0	0
4110 Households	..	..	..	..	..	..	..	..	..	..
4120 Others	..	..	..	..	..	..	..	..	..	..
4200 Recurrent taxes on net wealth	..	..	0	0	0	0	0	0	0	0
4210 Individual	..	..	..	..	..	..	..	..	..	..
4220 Corporate	..	..	..	..	..	..	..	..	..	..
4300 Estate, inheritance and gift taxes	..	..	0	0	0	0	0	0	0	0
4310 Estate and inheritance taxes	..	..	..	..	..	..	..	..	..	..
4320 Gift taxes	..	..	..	..	..	..	..	..	..	..
4400 Taxes on financial and capital transactions	..	..	9	8	14	19	17	14	16	15
4500 Other non-reccurrent taxes on property	..	..	0	0	0	0	0	0	0	0
4510 On net wealth	..	..	..	..	..	..	..	..	..	..
4520 Other non-recurrent taxes	..	..	..	..	..	..	..	..	..	..
4600 Other recurrent taxes on property	..	..	0	0	0	0	0	0	0	0
5000 Taxes on goods and services	..	..	**621**	**951**	**1 633**	**1 654**	**1 660**	**1 838**	**2 204**	**1 852**
5100 Taxes on production, sale, transfer, etc	..	..	616	944	1 619	1 638	1 643	1 821	2 188	1 834
5110 General taxes on goods and services	..	..	621	458	747	721	682	773	867	750
5111 Value added taxes	..	..	0	0	0	0	0	0	0	0
5112 Sales tax	..	..	283	458	747	721	682	773	867	750
5113 Other	..	..	0	0	0	0	0	0	0	0
5120 Taxes on specific goods and services	..	..	333	486	872	917	961	1 047	1 321	1 084
5121 Excises	..	..	53	106	158	144	163	173	233	198
Tobacco	..	..	29	59	96	89	95	109	139	122
Beer	..	..	23	34	59	49	61	63	93	55
Spirits	..	..	0	12	4	6	7	2	0	18
Other	..	..	0	0	0	0	0	0	0	4
5122 Profits of fiscal monopolies	..	..	0	0	0	0	0	0	0	0
5123 Customs and import duties	..	..	99	136	217	214	215	243	295	261
5124 Taxes on exports	..	..	182	245	496	560	582	631	794	624
Export duty on minerals	..	..	0	2	6	1	2	1	1	2
Export duty on shells	..	..	0	1	1	1	0	0	1	0
Export duty on fish	..	..	7	2	1	1	1	2	1	2
Export duty on timber/log	..	..	174	240	487	469	579	627	790	618
Export duty on other products	..	..	0	0	2	88	1	1	1	2
5125 Taxes on investment goods	..	..	0	0	0	0	0	0	0	0
5126 Taxes on specific services	..	..	0	0	0	0	0	0	0	0
5127 Other taxes on internat. trade and transactions	..	..	0	0	0	0	0	0	0	0
5128 Other taxes	..	..	0	0	0	0	0	0	0	0
5130 Unallocable between 5110 and 5120	..	..	0	0	0	0	0	0	0	0
5200 Taxes on use of goods and to perform activities	..	..	5	7	14	16	17	17	16	18
5210 Recurrent taxes	..	..	5	7	14	16	17	17	16	18
5211 Paid by households: motor vehicles	..	..	0	0	0	0	0	0	0	0

	1997	2000	2007	2010	2014	2015	2016	2017	2018	2019
5212 Paid by others: motor vehicles	..	..	0	0	0	0	0	0	0	0
5213 Paid in respect of other goods	..	..	5	7	14	16	17	17	16	18
5220 Non-recurrent taxes	..	..	0	0	0	0	0	0	0	0
5300 Unallocable between 5100 and 5200	..	..	0	0	0	0	0	0	0	0
6000 Other taxes	**..**	**..**	**0**	**0**	**0**	**0**	**0**	**0**	**0**	**0**
6100 Paid solely by business	..	..	..	..	..	..	..	..	..	..
6200 Other	..	..	..	..	..	..	..	..	..	..

Note: Year ending 31st December.

The data are on a cash basis.

Figures exclude tax revenues collected by sub-national governments as the data are not available.

Some revenues (e.g. customs fees, penalties) amounting to about 0.9 million in 2019 are considered as non-tax revenues according to the OECD classification, described in the interpretative guide in Annex A. The national classification of Solomon Islands classifies these revenues as tax revenues.

Source: Solomon Islands Ministry of Finance and Treasury.

StatLink https://stat.link/sqodvf

Table 4.21. Thailand: Details of tax revenue

Million THB

	1997	2000	2007	2010	2014	2015	2016	2017	2018	2019
Total tax revenue	..	**740 147**	**1 553 133**	**1 870 452**	**2 410 488**	**2 568 138**	**2 595 796**	**2 673 414**	**2 857 840**	**2 897 782**
1000 Taxes on income, profits and capital gains	..	**235 421**	**614 883**	**682 860**	**881 591**	**895 205**	**894 058**	**893 754**	**975 030**	**1 031 929**
1100 Of individuals	..	87 420	177 205	187 687	237 147	268 290	283 003	275 928	281 123	298 444
1110 On income and profits	..	..	..	..	..	..	..	..	..	..
1120 On capital gains	..	..	..	..	..	..	..	..	..	..
1200 Corporate	..	148 001	437 678	495 173	644 444	626 915	611 055	617 826	693 907	733 486
1210 On profits	..	..	..	..	..	..	..	..	..	..
1220 On capital gains of corporates	..	..	..	..	..	..	..	..	..	..
1300 Unallocable between 1100 and 1200	..	0	0	0	0	0	0	0	0	0
2000 Social security contributions	..	**27 073**	**79 809**	**132 394**	**128 174**	**144 803**	**145 693**	**153 488**	**162 127**	**172 134**
2100 Employees	..	12 704	37 717	0	58 031	66 027	68 574	70 993	75 249	79 418
2110 On a payroll basis	..	..	..	..	..	..	..	..	..	..
2120 On an income tax basis	..	..	..	..	..	..	..	..	..	..
2200 Employers	..	14 369	40 567	127 844	63 615	70 103	72 714	74 681	78 656	83 320
2210 On a payroll basis	..	..	..	..	..	..	..	..	..	..
2220 On an income tax basis	..	..	..	..	..	..	..	..	..	..
2300 Self-employed or non-employed	..	0	1 525	4 549	6 528	8 674	4 405	7 814	8 222	9 396
2310 On a payroll basis	..	..	..	..	..	..	..	..	..	..
2320 On an income tax basis	..	..	..	..	..	..	..	..	..	..
2400 Unallocable between 2100, 2200 and 2300	..	0	0	0	0	0	0	0	0	0
2410 On a payroll basis	..	..	..	..	..	..	..	..	..	..
2420 On an income tax basis	..	..	..	..	..	..	..	..	..	..
3000 Taxes on payroll and workforce	..	**0**	**0**	**0**	**0**	**0**	**0**	**0**	**0**	**0**
4000 Taxes on property	..	**16 283**	**18 317**	**24 666**	**62 627**	**68 157**	**60 364**	**73 946**	**78 533**	**78 277**
4100 Recurrent taxes on immovable property	..	9 094	18 317	24 592	32 396	33 530	33 751	37 955	38 166	37 098
4110 Households	..	..	..	..	..	..	..	..	..	..
4120 Others	..	..	..	..	..	..	..	..	..	..
4200 Recurrent taxes on net wealth	..	0	0	74	0	0	0	0	0	0
4210 Individual	..	..	..	..	..	..	..	..	..	..
4220 Corporate	..	..	..	..	..	..	..	..	..	..
4300 Estate, inheritance and gift taxes	..	0	0	0	0	0	0	65	218	449
4310 Estate and inheritance taxes	..	..	..	..	..	..	..	..	..	..
4320 Gift taxes	..	..	..	..	..	..	..	..	..	..
4400 Taxes on financial and capital transactions	..	7 189	0	0	30 231	34 627	26 613	35 927	40 149	40 731
4500 Other non-reccurrent taxes on property	..	0	0	0	0	0	0	0	0	0
4510 On net wealth	..	..	..	..	..	..	..	..	..	..
4520 Other non-recurrent taxes	..	..	..	..	..	..	..	..	..	..
4600 Other recurrent taxes on property	..	0	0	0	0	0	0	0	0	0
5000 Taxes on goods and services	..	**457 826**	**829 490**	**1 016 829**	**1 322 691**	**1 442 296**	**1 477 287**	**1 533 483**	**1 621 189**	**1 596 431**
5100 Taxes on production, sale, transfer, etc	..	444 986	808 624	990 052	1 182 176	1 262 437	1 312 202	1 386 480	1 456 652	1 447 646
5110 General taxes on goods and services	..	171 113	319 655	388 856	527 902	535 121	558 192	584 342	633 623	596 676
5111 Value added taxes	..	169 425	319 655	388 856	527 902	535 121	558 192	584 342	633 623	596 676
5112 Sales tax	..	1 688	0	0	0	0	0	0	0	0
5113 Other	..	0	0	0	0	0	0	0	0	0
5120 Taxes on specific goods and services	..	273 873	488 969	601 197	654 274	727 316	754 010	802 138	823 029	850 969
5121 Excises	..	180 884	351 498	478 257	480 479	559 388	589 363	642 966	662 141	683 725
5122 Profits of fiscal monopolies	..	5 310	8 210	4 879	9 869	8 106	5 148	7 116	174	928
5123 Customs and import duties	..	84 902	87 440	92 675	105 270	100 156	97 400	90 485	93 665	97 837
5124 Taxes on exports	..	2 329	4 164	168	267	202	103	81	143	209
5125 Taxes on investment goods	..	0	0	0	0	0	0	0	0	0
5126 Taxes on specific services	..	448	37 657	25 218	58 388	59 463	61 996	61 490	66 905	68 270
5127 Other taxes on internat. trade and transactions	..	0	0	0	0	0	0	0	0	0
5128 Other taxes	..	0	0	0	0	0	0	0	0	0
5130 Unallocable between 5110 and 5120	..	0	0	0	0	0	0	0	0	0
5200 Taxes on use of goods and to perform activities	..	12 840	20 866	26 777	140 515	179 860	165 084	147 003	164 537	148 785
5210 Recurrent taxes	..	..	..	..	..	..	..	..	..	..
5211 Paid by households: motor vehicles	..	..	..	..	..	..	..	..	..	..
5212 Paid by others: motor vehicles	..	..	..	..	..	..	..	..	..	..
5213 Paid in respect of other goods	..	..	..	..	..	..	..	..	..	..
5220 Non-recurrent taxes	..	..	..	..	..	..	..	..	..	..
5300 Unallocable between 5100 and 5200	..	0	0	0	0	0	0	0	0	0
6000 Other taxes	..	**3 544**	**10 634**	**13 703**	**15 405**	**17 677**	**18 394**	**18 743**	**20 962**	**19 010**
6100 Paid solely by business	..	..	..	..	..	..	..	..	..	..
6200 Other	..	..	..	..	..	..	..	..	..	..

Note: Data are on a fiscal year basis ending 30th September. For example, the data for 2019 represents 1 October 2018 to 30 September 2019.

The data are on a cash basis.

Tax revenues submitted by the Ministry of Finance for 2000 - 2012 are based on data gathered by the IMF.

Source: Ministry of Finance in Thailand.

StatLink https://stat.link/gvd8ur

Table 4.22. Tokelau: Details of tax revenue

Thousand NZD

	1997	2000	2007	2010	2014	2015	2016	2017	2018	2019
Total tax revenue	..	..	**1 198**	**1 694**	**2 107**	**2 151**	**2 176**	**2 518**	**2 843**	**3 040**
1000 Taxes on income, profits and capital gains	..	..	**573**	**866**	**1 014**	**1 100**	**1 188**	**1 404**	**1 346**	**1 631**
1100 Of individuals	..	..	573	866	1 014	1 100	1 188	1 404	1 346	1 631
1110 On income and profits	..	..	..	..	..	..	..	..	..	..
1120 On capital gains	..	..	..	..	..	..	..	..	..	..
1200 Corporate	..	..	0	0	0	0	0	0	0	0
1210 On profits	..	..	..	..	..	..	..	..	..	..
1220 On capital gains of corporates	..	..	..	..	..	..	..	..	..	..
1300 Unallocable between 1100 and 1200	..	..	0	0	0	0	0	0	0	0
2000 Social security contributions	..	..	**0**	**0**	**0**	**0**	**0**	**0**	**0**	**0**
2100 Employees	..	..	..	..	..	..	..	..	..	..
2110 On a payroll basis	..	..	..	..	..	..	..	..	..	..
2120 On an income tax basis	..	..	..	..	..	..	..	..	..	..
2200 Employers	..	..	..	..	..	..	..	..	..	..
2210 On a payroll basis	..	..	..	..	..	..	..	..	..	..
2220 On an income tax basis	..	..	..	..	..	..	..	..	..	..
2300 Self-employed or non-employed	..	..	..	..	..	..	..	..	..	..
2310 On a payroll basis	..	..	..	..	..	..	..	..	..	..
2320 On an income tax basis	..	..	..	..	..	..	..	..	..	..
2400 Unallocable between 2100, 2200 and 2300	..	..	..	..	..	..	..	..	..	..
2410 On a payroll basis	..	..	..	..	..	..	..	..	..	..
2420 On an income tax basis	..	..	..	..	..	..	..	..	..	..
3000 Taxes on payroll and workforce	..	..	**0**	**0**	**0**	**0**	**0**	**0**	**0**	**0**
4000 Taxes on property	..	..	**0**	**0**	**0**	**0**	**0**	**0**	**0**	**0**
4100 Recurrent taxes on immovable property	..	..	..	..	..	..	..	..	..	..
4110 Households	..	..	..	..	..	..	..	..	..	..
4120 Others	..	..	..	..	..	..	..	..	..	..
4200 Recurrent taxes on net wealth	..	..	..	..	..	..	..	..	..	..
4210 Individual	..	..	..	..	..	..	..	..	..	..
4220 Corporate	..	..	..	..	..	..	..	..	..	..
4300 Estate, inheritance and gift taxes	..	..	..	..	..	..	..	..	..	..
4310 Estate and inheritance taxes	..	..	..	..	..	..	..	..	..	..
4320 Gift taxes	..	..	..	..	..	..	..	..	..	..
4400 Taxes on financial and capital transactions	..	..	..	..	..	..	..	..	..	..
4500 Other non-reccurrent taxes on property	..	..	..	..	..	..	..	..	..	..
4510 On net wealth	..	..	..	..	..	..	..	..	..	..
4520 Other non-recurrent taxes	..	..	..	..	..	..	..	..	..	..
4600 Other recurrent taxes on property	..	..	..	..	..	..	..	..	..	..
5000 Taxes on goods and services	..	..	**625**	**828**	**1 093**	**1 051**	**988**	**1 114**	**1 497**	**1 409**
5100 Taxes on production, sale, transfer, etc	..	..	625	828	1 093	1 051	988	1 114	1 497	1 409
5110 General taxes on goods and services	..	..	0	0	0	0	0	0	0	0
5111 Value added taxes	..	..	..	..	..	..	..	..	..	..
5112 Sales tax	..	..	..	..	..	..	..	..	..	..
5113 Other	..	..	..	..	..	..	..	..	..	..
5120 Taxes on specific goods and services	..	..	625	828	1 093	1 051	988	1 114	1 497	1 409
5121 Excises	..	..	624	827	1 091	1 050	984	1 104	1 489	1 406
Duty On Tobacco	..	..	258	379	600	558	539	702	966	948
Duty On Liqour	..	..	178	222	288	288	251	200	266	240
Duty On General Goods : resale	..	..	188	226	203	204	194	202	257	218
5122 Profits of fiscal monopolies	..	..	0	0	0	0	0	0	0	0
5123 Customs and import duties	..	..	0	0	0	0	0	0	0	0
5124 Taxes on exports	..	..	0	0	0	0	0	0	0	0
5125 Taxes on investment goods	..	..	0	0	0	0	0	0	0	0
5126 Taxes on specific services	..	..	1	1	2	1	4	10	8	3
5127 Other taxes on internat. trade and transactions	..	..	0	0	0	0	0	0	0	0
5128 Other taxes	..	..	0	0	0	0	0	0	0	0
5130 Unallocable between 5110 and 5120	..	..	0	0	0	0	0	0	0	0
5200 Taxes on use of goods and to perform activities	..	..	0	0	0	0	0	0	0	0
5210 Recurrent taxes	..	..	..	..	..	..	..	..	..	..
5211 Paid by households: motor vehicles	..	..	..	..	..	..	..	..	..	..
5212 Paid by others: motor vehicles	..	..	..	..	..	..	..	..	..	..
5213 Paid in respect of other goods	..	..	..	..	..	..	..	..	..	..
5220 Non-recurrent taxes	..	..	..	..	..	..	..	..	..	..
5300 Unallocable between 5100 and 5200	..	..	0	0	0	0	0	0	0	0
6000 Other taxes	..	..	**0**	**0**	**0**	**0**	**0**	**0**	**0**	**0**
6100 Paid solely by business	..	..	..	..	..	..	..	..	..	..
6200 Other	..	..	..	..	..	..	..	..	..	..

Note: Data are reported on a fiscal year basis beginning 1st July. For example, the data for 2019 represent the period from July 2019 to June 2020.
The data are on a cash basis.

Source: National Statistics Office of Tokelau.

StatLink https://stat.link/keb49d

Table 4.23. Vanuatu: Details of tax revenue

Million VUV

	1997	2000	2007	2010	2014	2015	2016	2017	2018	2019
Total tax revenue	..	**6 098**	**10 267**	**11 089**	**13 737**	**13 477**	**13 324**	**16 249**	**17 976**	**18 254**
1000 Taxes on income, profits and capital gains	..	**0**	**0**	**0**	**0**	**0**	**0**	**0**	**0**	**0**
1100 Of individuals	..	..	..	..	..	..	..	..	..	..
1110 On income and profits	..	..	..	..	..	..	..	..	..	..
1120 On capital gains	..	..	..	..	..	..	..	..	..	..
1200 Corporate	..	..	..	..	..	..	..	..	..	..
1210 On profits	..	..	..	..	..	..	..	..	..	..
1220 On capital gains of corporates	..	..	..	..	..	..	..	..	..	..
1300 Unallocable between 1100 and 1200	..	..	..	..	..	..	..	..	..	..
2000 Social security contributions	..	**0**	**0**	**0**	**0**	**0**	**0**	**0**	**0**	**0**
2100 Employees	..	..	..	..	..	..	..	..	..	..
2110 On a payroll basis	..	..	..	..	..	..	..	..	..	..
2120 On an income tax basis	..	..	..	..	..	..	..	..	..	..
2200 Employers	..	..	..	..	..	..	..	..	..	..
2210 On a payroll basis	..	..	..	..	..	..	..	..	..	..
2220 On an income tax basis	..	..	..	..	..	..	..	..	..	..
2300 Self-employed or non-employed	..	..	..	..	..	..	..	..	..	..
2310 On a payroll basis	..	..	..	..	..	..	..	..	..	..
2320 On an income tax basis	..	..	..	..	..	..	..	..	..	..
2400 Unallocable between 2100, 2200 and 2300	..	..	..	..	..	..	..	..	..	..
2410 On a payroll basis	..	..	..	..	..	..	..	..	..	..
2420 On an income tax basis	..	..	..	..	..	..	..	..	..	..
3000 Taxes on payroll and workforce	..	**0**	**0**	**0**	**0**	**0**	**0**	**0**	**0**	**0**
4000 Taxes on property	..	**196**	**449**	**485**	**430**	**402**	**383**	**488**	**566**	**648**
4100 Recurrent taxes on immovable property	..	..	..	..	..	..	..	..	..	..
4110 Households	..	..	..	..	..	..	..	..	..	..
4120 Others	..	..	..	..	..	..	..	..	..	..
4200 Recurrent taxes on net wealth	..	..	..	..	..	..	..	..	..	..
4210 Individual	..	..	..	..	..	..	..	..	..	..
4220 Corporate	..	..	..	..	..	..	..	..	..	..
4300 Estate, inheritance and gift taxes	..	..	..	..	..	..	..	..	..	..
4310 Estate and inheritance taxes	..	..	..	..	..	..	..	..	..	..
4320 Gift taxes	..	..	..	..	..	..	..	..	..	..
4400 Taxes on financial and capital transactions	..	..	..	..	..	..	..	..	..	..
4500 Other non-reccurrent taxes on property	..	..	..	..	..	..	..	..	..	..
4510 On net wealth	..	..	..	..	..	..	..	..	..	..
4520 Other non-recurrent taxes	..	..	..	..	..	..	..	..	..	..
4600 Other recurrent taxes on property	..	..	..	..	..	..	..	..	..	..
5000 Taxes on goods and services	..	**5 902**	**9 818**	**10 603**	**13 307**	**13 075**	**12 941**	**15 761**	**17 410**	**17 606**
5100 Taxes on production, sale, transfer, etc	..	5 902	9 818	8 829	10 427	10 898	10 708	13 024	14 713	14 598
5110 General taxes on goods and services	..	3 441	5 858	4 301	5 794	5 769	5 549	6 912	8 235	8 134
5111 Value added taxes	..	3 441	5 858	4 301	5 794	5 769	5 549	6 912	8 235	8 134
5112 Sales tax	..	0	0	0	0	0	0	0	0	0
5113 Other	..	0	0	0	0	0	0	0	0	0
5120 Taxes on specific goods and services	..	2 461	3 960	4 528	4 633	5 130	5 159	6 112	6 478	6 464
5121 Excises	..	76	554	1 882	1 976	2 180	2 219	2 578	2 784	2 830
5122 Profits of fiscal monopolies	..	0	0	0	0	0	0	0	0	0
5123 Customs and import duties	..	2 385	3 406	2 646	2 657	2 950	2 940	3 534	3 694	3 635
5124 Taxes on exports	..	0	0	0	0	0	0	0	0	0
5125 Taxes on investment goods	..	0	0	0	0	0	0	0	0	0
5126 Taxes on specific services	..	0	0	0	0	0	0	0	0	0
5127 Other taxes on internat. trade and transactions	..	0	0	0	0	0	0	0	0	0
5128 Other taxes	..	0	0	0	0	0	0	0	0	0
5130 Unallocable between 5110 and 5120	..	0	0	0	0	0	0	0	0	0
5200 Taxes on use of goods and to perform activities	..	0	0	0	0	0	0	0	0	0
5210 Recurrent taxes	..	..	..	..	..	..	..	..	..	..
5211 Paid by households: motor vehicles	..	..	..	..	..	..	..	..	..	..
5212 Paid by others: motor vehicles	..	..	..	..	..	..	..	..	..	..
5213 Paid in respect of other goods	..	..	..	..	..	..	..	..	..	..
5220 Non-recurrent taxes	..	..	..	..	..	..	..	..	..	..
5300 Unallocable between 5100 and 5200	..	0	0	1 774	2 880	2 177	2 233	2 737	2 697	3 008
6000 Other taxes	..	**0**	**0**	**0**	**0**	**0**	**0**	**0**	**0**	**0**
6100 Paid solely by business	..	..	..	..	..	..	..	..	..	..
6200 Other	..	..	..	..	..	..	..	..	..	..

Note: Year ending December 31st.
Source: Department of Finance and Treasury of Vanuatu.

StatLink https://stat.link/cpzwt9

Table 4.24. Viet Nam: Details of tax revenue

Billion VND

	1997	2000	2007	2010	2014	2015	2016	2017	2018	2019
Total tax revenue	..	..	**248 381**	**465 916**	**677 559**	**725 441**	**779 065**	**868 099**	**954 021**	**1 053 479**
1000 Taxes on income, profits and capital gains	..	..	**111 967**	**174 931**	**255 651**	**256 753**	**254 916**	**295 983**	**345 256**	**380 037**
1100 Of individuals	..	..	7 415	26 276	47 844	56 723	65 239	78 783	94 364	109 401
1110 On income and profits	..	..	7 415	26 276	47 844	56 723	65 239	78 783	94 364	109 401
1120 On capital gains	..	..	0	0	0	0	0	0	0	0
1200 Corporate	..	..	104 552	148 655	207 807	200 030	189 677	217 200	250 892	270 636
1210 On profits	..	..	104 552	148 655	207 807	200 030	189 677	217 200	250 892	270 636
1220 On capital gains of corporates	..	..	0	0	0	0	0	0	0	0
1300 Unallocable between 1100 and 1200	..	..	0	0	0	0	0	0	0	0
2000 Social security contributions	..	..	..	..	..	..	..	..	..	..
2100 Employees	..	..	..	..	..	..	..	..	..	..
2110 On a payroll basis	..	..	..	..	..	..	..	..	..	..
2120 On an income tax basis	..	..	..	..	..	..	..	..	..	..
2200 Employers	..	..	..	..	..	..	..	..	..	..
2210 On a payroll basis	..	..	..	..	..	..	..	..	..	..
2220 On an income tax basis	..	..	..	..	..	..	..	..	..	..
2300 Self-employed or non-employed	..	..	..	..	..	..	..	..	..	..
2310 On a payroll basis	..	..	..	..	..	..	..	..	..	..
2320 On an income tax basis	..	..	..	..	..	..	..	..	..	..
2400 Unallocable between 2100, 2200 and 2300	..	..	..	..	..	..	..	..	..	..
2410 On a payroll basis	..	..	..	..	..	..	..	..	..	..
2420 On an income tax basis	..	..	..	..	..	..	..	..	..	..
3000 Taxes on payroll and workforce	..	..	**0**	**0**	**0**	**0**	**0**	**0**	**0**	**0**
4000 Taxes on property	..	..	**824**	**1 452**	**1 524**	**1 537**	**1 479**	**1 726**	**1 901**	**2 058**
4100 Recurrent taxes on immovable property	..	..	824	1 452	1 524	1 537	1 479	1 726	1 901	2 058
4110 Households	..	..	711	1 396	1 463	1 479	1 419	1 687	1 874	2 039
4120 Others	..	..	113	56	61	58	60	39	27	19
4200 Recurrent taxes on net wealth	..	..	0	0	0	0	0	0	0	0
4210 Individual	..	..	..	..	..	..	..	..	..	..
4220 Corporate	..	..	..	..	..	..	..	..	..	..
4300 Estate, inheritance and gift taxes	..	..	0	0	0	0	0	0	0	0
4310 Estate and inheritance taxes	..	..	..	..	..	..	..	..	..	..
4320 Gift taxes	..	..	..	..	..	..	..	..	..	..
4400 Taxes on financial and capital transactions	..	..	0	0	0	0	0	0	0	0
4500 Other non-reccurrent taxes on property	..	..	0	0	0	0	0	0	0	0
4510 On net wealth	..	..	..	..	..	..	..	..	..	..
4520 Other non-recurrent taxes	..	..	..	..	..	..	..	..	..	..
4600 Other recurrent taxes on property	..	..	0	0	0	0	0	0	0	0
5000 Taxes on goods and services	..	..	**135 590**	**289 533**	**420 384**	**467 151**	**522 670**	**570 390**	**606 864**	**671 384**
5100 Taxes on production, sale, transfer, etc	..	..	129 954	276 922	404 294	444 746	495 359	542 777	574 455	631 188
5110 General taxes on goods and services	..	..	69 822	155 022	241 129	251 758	269 627	314 508	344 063	362 674
5111 Value added taxes	..	..	69 822	155 022	241 129	251 758	269 627	314 508	344 063	362 674
Domestic VAT	..	..	47 860	98 739	163 727	181 770	192 562	212 518	228 840	247 108
VAT on imports	..	..	21 962	56 283	77 402	69 988	77 065	101 990	115 223	115 566
5112 Sales tax	..	..	0	0	0	0	0	0	0	0
5113 Other	..	..	0	0	0	0	0	0	0	0
5120 Taxes on specific goods and services	..	..	60 132	121 900	163 164	192 988	225 732	228 269	230 392	268 513
5121 Excises	..	..	60 132	121 900	163 164	192 988	225 732	228 269	230 392	268 513
Domestic excises	..	..	17 365	37 311	55 474	66 653	85 853	86 585	96 025	106 753
Environmental protection tax	..	..	4 458	10 521	12 087	27 020	43 632	44 666	47 050	63 075
Excise tax on imports	..	..	38 309	74 068	95 603	99 315	96 247	97 018	87 317	98 685
5122 Profits of fiscal monopolies	..	..	0	0	0	0	0	0	0	0
5123 Customs and import duties	..	..	0	0	0	0	0	0	0	0
5124 Taxes on exports	..	..	0	0	0	0	0	0	0	0
5125 Taxes on investment goods	..	..	0	0	0	0	0	0	0	0
5126 Taxes on specific services	..	..	0	0	0	0	0	0	0	0
5127 Other taxes on internat. trade and transactions	..	..	0	0	0	0	0	0	0	0
5128 Other taxes	..	..	0	0	0	0	0	0	0	0
5130 Unallocable between 5110 and 5120	..	..	0	0	0	0	0	0	0	0
5200 Taxes on use of goods and to perform activities	..	..	5 636	12 611	16 090	22 405	27 311	27 613	32 409	40 196
5210 Recurrent taxes	..	..	0	0	0	0	0	0	0	0
5211 Paid by households: motor vehicles	..	..	..	..	..	..	..	..	..	..
5212 Paid by others: motor vehicles	..	..	..	..	..	..	..	..	..	..
5213 Paid in respect of other goods	..	..	..	..	..	..	..	..	..	..
5220 Non-recurrent taxes	..	..	5 636	12 611	16 090	22 405	27 311	27 613	32 409	40 196
5300 Unallocable between 5100 and 5200	..	..	0	0	0	0	0	0	0	0
6000 Other taxes	..	..	**0**	**0**	**0**	**0**	**0**	**0**	**0**	**0**
6100 Paid solely by business	..	..	..	..	..	..	..	..	..	..
6200 Other	..	..	..	..	..	..	..	..	..	..

Note: Year ending 31st December.

The data are on a cash basis.

Heading 2000: Detailed data on revenues from social security contributions are not available.

Heading 4110: This heading shows the revenues from the land and housing tax. A distinction between the amounts paid by households and the amounts paid by other taxpayers could not be made.

Source: General Statistics Office Viet Nam.

StatLink https://stat.link/jzua8b

5 Comparative and country tables, non-tax revenues, 2007-2019

Non-tax revenue tables, 2007-2019

In all of the following tables a ("..") indicates not available. The main series in this volume cover the years 2007 to 2019.

Complete series for the comparative tables are available on line at OECD (2021), "Revenue Statistics in Asia and the Pacific: Comparative tables", OECD Tax statistics (database). Full time series for the country tables can be accessed at https://stats.oecd.org/ within the theme Public Sector, Taxation and Market Regulation/Taxation/Revenue Statistics in Asia and the Pacific.

Table 5.1. Total non-tax revenue as percentage of GDP in selected economies, 2007-19

	2007	2010	2012	2013	2014	2015	2016	2017	2018	2019
Bhutan	26.6	22.1	16.6	20.6	14.8	17.7	15.0	16.4	13.2	19.2
Cook Islands	5.6	13.5	8.4	14.3	16.2	13.9	16.4	14.3	12.9	15.3
Fiji	..	2.9	3.0	2.9	2.9	2.9	3.2	3.5	3.6	3.4
Kazakhstan	1.5	1.0	1.8	1.0	1.5	1.3	1.2	1.1	1.7	1.5
Lao PDR	..	9.5	10.2	7.3	9.6	7.7	4.5	5.1	5.4	4.8
Maldives	14.9	10.2	6.3	5.1	7.0	6.7	7.2	6.8	6.8	6.2
Mongolia	9.5	6.5	6.9	7.2	7.8	6.3	5.1	4.3	4.6	4.4
Nauru	..	..	..	..	28.7	65.4	64.0	71.0	92.7	85.2
Papua New Guinea	4.0	4.7	3.1	2.4	3.1	3.2	3.2	3.3	3.7	2.8
Philippines	..	..	..	..	1.8	2.1	1.8	1.7	1.9	2.0
Samoa[1]	7.1	9.0	4.8	7.0	4.8	4.7	4.7	5.7	6.4	11.0
Singapore	5.8	3.5	3.5	3.5	3.9	4.4	4.4	5.3	4.3	7.2
Thailand	2.7	3.3	2.9	2.9	3.1	3.6	3.7	3.6	3.8	3.8
Tokelau[2]	149.3	154.6	192.6	246.6	173.4	230.4	236.5	210.0	236.4	220.1
Vanuatu	1.4	8.3	5.2	4.2	5.8	14.8	9.6	14.2	19.8	24.4
Viet Nam	7.1	5.7	4.9	5.1	5.1	6.5	7.2	8.4	8.6	8.2

.. Not available

Note: Figures include non-tax revenue data collected by sub-national governments for Kazakhstan, Mongolia and the Philippines. They exclude non-tax revenue collected by sub-national governments as the data are not available for the remaining economies.

1. The data prior to 2009 are reported on a different basis (for more information see Table 5.11).
2. Tokelau receives significant revenues from foreign vessels for access to Tokelau fishing waters. In the 2008 SNA, these revenues are recorded as part of GNI, but they do not add to GDP.

StatLink https://stat.link/gvtpj8

Table 5.2. Non-tax revenue of main headings as percentage of GDP in selected economies, 2019

	Grants	Property income	Sales of goods and services	Fines, penalties and forfeits	Miscellaneous and unidentified revenue
Bhutan	9.2	7.2	2.7	0.0	0.0
Cook Islands	10.0	3.3	0.5	0.0	1.4
Fiji	0.4	1.6	1.4	0.0	0.0
Kazakhstan	0.0	1.2	0.2	0.1	0.0
Lao PDR	1.6	1.7	1.2	0.0	0.3
Maldives	0.0	1.2	4.5	0.3	0.3
Mongolia	0.2	2.1	0.4	0.4	1.1
Nauru	0.0	45.8	28.0	0.0	11.4
Papua New Guinea	2.1	0.6	0.0	0.0	0.0
Philippines	0.0	0.9	0.5	0.0	0.6
Samoa[1]	7.6	0.5	2.9	0.0	0.0
Singapore	0.0	6.2	0.9	0.1	0.1
Thailand	0.0	2.0	1.2	0.1	0.4
Tokelau[2]	98.3	112.7	9.1	0.0	0.0
Vanuatu	10.4	..	..	..	14.0
Viet Nam	0.1	0.6	4.4	0.0	3.1

.. Not available

Note: Figures include non-tax revenue data collected by sub-national governments for Kazakhstan, Mongolia and the Philippines. They exclude non-tax revenue collected by sub-national governments as the data are not available for the remaining economies.

1. The data prior to 2009 are reported on a different basis (for more information see Table 5.11).
2. Tokelau receives significant revenues from foreign vessels for access to Tokelau fishing waters. In the 2008 SNA, these revenues are recorded as part of GNI, but they do not add to GDP.

StatLink https://stat.link/1e04l7

Table 5.3. Non-tax revenue of main headings as percentage of total non-tax revenues in selected economies, 2019

	Grants	Property income	Sales of goods and services	Fines, penalties and forfeits	Miscellaneous and unidentified revenue
Bhutan	48.1	37.6	14.1	0.2	0.0
Cook Islands	65.4	21.7	3.5	0.3	9.2
Fiji	11.4	45.6	41.5	0.4	1.1
Kazakhstan	0.0	78.1	13.4	8.4	0.0
Lao PDR	33.2	36.1	24.9	0.4	5.4
Maldives	0.0	18.9	71.9	4.2	4.9
Mongolia	5.4	48.8	9.7	9.7	26.3
Nauru	0.0	53.8	32.8	0.0	13.4
Papua New Guinea	75.8	22.6	1.6	0.1	0.0
Philippines	0.1	44.9	24.9	0.0	30.1
Samoa	68.6	4.9	26.3	0.3	0.0
Singapore	0.0	85.7	12.4	0.9	1.0
Thailand	0.3	52.6	32.5	3.1	11.6
Tokelau	44.7	51.2	4.1	0.0	0.0
Vanuatu	42.6	0	0	0	57.4
Viet Nam	1.3	7.4	53.3	0.0	38.0

.. Not available

Note: Figures include non-tax revenue data collected by sub-national governments for Kazakhstan, Mongolia and the Philippines. They exclude non-tax revenue collected by sub-national governments as the data are not available for the remaining economies.

StatLink https://stat.link/m0xhyz

Table 5.4. Total non-tax revenue in selected economies in millions of US dollars at market exchange rates

	2007	2010	2012	2013	2014	2015	2016	2017	2018	2019
Bhutan	306.2	364.0	326.3	411.9	295.5	380.7	337.7	416.9	335.4	492.0
Cook Islands	12.9	33.1	24.6	43.2	54.9	42.5	53.1	51.3	49.0	53.2
Fiji	..	89.8	118.6	121.0	142.9	134.7	158.0	187.6	199.0	188.3
Kazakhstan	1 619.2	1 451.3	3 843.4	2 408.6	3 211.3	2 460.0	1 651.2	1 760.1	3 108.5	2 705.3
Lao PDR	..	711.3	1 035.2	872.5	1 269.5	1 100.0	709.9	878.2	974.8	912.1
Maldives	277.6	264.2	183.0	168.7	258.0	274.8	316.4	322.0	359.6	359.8
Mongolia	403.6	470.4	851.1	902.0	948.6	740.4	566.0	494.6	602.5	610.3
Nauru	..	..	..	..	29.5	51.1	65.1	78.9	110.8	98.3
Papua New Guinea	381.7	671.6	657.6	513.0	718.5	703.0	658.8	753.3	890.9	691.9
Philippines	..	..	..	..	5 380.0	6 356.5	5 795.3	5 688.2	6 446.1	7 460.7
Samoa	46.0	61.8	36.8	54.7	39.8	40.4	38.2	47.1	53.5	91.1
Singapore	10 656.9	8 539.4	10 253.3	10 872.5	12 519.6	13 526.3	14 340.4	18 536.4	16 462.7	26 837.8
Thailand	6 825.1	11 147.6	11 078.6	12 271.0	12 659.8	14 140.3	14 942.5	16 003.4	19 019.7	20 313.7
Tokelau	9.2	10.7	16.5	23.2	17.8	22.9	24.4	22.4	25.7	22.9
Vanuatu	7.6	56.4	40.3	33.7	47.6	114.4	76.3	125.0	184.1	225.5
Viet Nam	5 464.9	6 405.8	7 664.2	8 689.4	9 441.0	12 444.6	14 411.2	18 514.4	20 749.2	21 422.8

.. Not available

Note: This table is derived by dividing the total non-tax revenue figures for each country (in millions of national currency) by the exchange rate figures shown in Table 3.20.

StatLink https://stat.link/p41ltn

Table 5.5. Bhutan: Details of non-tax revenue

Million NU

	1997	2000	2007	2010	2014	2015	2016	2017	2018	2019
Total non-tax revenue	**3 558**	**6 437**	**13 532**	**16 981**	**18 163**	**24 270**	**22 838**	**26 864**	**22 737**	**34 168**
Grants	1 816	3 711	5 935	10 498	9 955	14 890	12 987	14 847	10 516	16 426
Property income	1 187	2 193	5 054	5 627	7 288	8 295	8 748	10 763	10 838	12 850
Rents and royalties	170	286	573	711	1 564	1 565	1 938	3 855	4 640	4 346
Interest and dividends	1 017	1 907	4 481	4 915	5 724	6 729	6 810	6 907	6 198	8 505
Druk Holding and Investments (DHI) dividends	0	0	368	1 470	1 812	3 781	4 037	4 020	3 349	4 551
DGPC dividends	856	1 201	1 749	1 519	1 877	0	0	0	0	0
Other dividends	65	95	363	8	4	5	5	41	57	55
Net surplus transfers from the Royal Monetary Authority (RMA)	50	562	341	187	0	789	874	1 001	1 550	3 011
Interest receipt from corporations	..	..	..	1 731	2 031	2 155	1 895	1 846	1 242	887
Other property income	0	0	0	0	0	0	0	0	0	0
Sales of goods and services	552	531	2 520	838	805	993	1 026	1 148	1 186	4 823
Fines, penalties and forfeits	0	0	0	0	0	92	77	107	197	69
Miscellaneous and unidentified revenue	3	2	23	19	115	0	0	0	0	0
Total tax and non-tax revenue	4 767	8 288	18 145	27 797	34 881	42 788	42 487	49 268	44 483	52 565

.. Not available

Note: Data are reported on a fiscal year basis beginning 1st July. For example, the data for 2019 represent the period from July 2019 to June 2020.
The data are on a cash basis.

Source: Ministry of Finance, Bhutan.

StatLink https://stat.link/ohv21d

Table 5.6. Cook Islands: Details of non-tax revenue

Thousand NZD

	1997	2000	2007	2010	2014	2015	2016	2017	2018	2019
Total non-tax revenue	**..**	**..**	**17 586**	**45 942**	**66 251**	**60 999**	**76 336**	**72 214**	**70 821**	**80 832**
Grants	..	..	5 034	22 411	44 449	35 902	47 172	47 449	33 060	52 827
Green Climate Fund (GCF)	..	..	0	0	0	0	0	0	1 823	7 704
OIDGF Aid Fund	..	..	177	306	22 619	0	7 730	0	0	0
NZODA Revenue	..	..	4 097	20 123	8 645	20 889	26 081	25 021	21 876	32 496
AusAid Revenue	..	..	0	0	0	498	84	2 250	66	0
UNESCO Revenue	..	..	65	0	87	84	110	1 371	0	0
UNDP Revenue	..	..	223	619	1 122	1 559	206	2 302	2 183	6 887
EU Revenue	..	..	22	179	955	603	6 826	6 587	945	0
Global Environment Facility (GEF)	..	..	0	0	0	0	0	0	3 140	3 614
Other	..	..	451	1 183	11 021	12 269	6 135	9 918	3 027	2 126
Property income	..	..	9 768	9 327	15 613	11 307	21 366	18 680	28 321	17 550
Rents and royalties	..	..	595	3 528	10 887	7 714	18 057	12 797	20 522	13 262
Fishing Licences	..	..	595	3 528	8 064	7 714	14 197	7 651	15 164	5 219
Fisheries Catch Revenue	..	..	0	0	1 777	0	2 312	255	0	0
Fisheries - US Treaties	..	..	0	0	1 046	0	1 548	4 890	5 358	8 043
Interest and dividends	..	..	9 173	5 800	4 725	3 593	3 309	5 883	7 799	4 288
Dividend Income	..	..	2 350	2 672	0	0	0	0	0	0
Interest Income (Crown Accounts)	..	..	3 795	3 100	1 820	1 673	2 140	2 372	2 483	2 968
Interest Inc from SOE Advances	..	..	69	28	976	1 102	787	791	760	360
Other dividends	..	..	2 958	0	1 929	818	382	2 720	4 556	960
Other property income	..	..	0	0	0	0	0	0	0	0
Sales of goods and services	..	..	2 157	2 843	3 347	3 497	2 401	3 682	3 176	2 794
Immigration Fees	..	..	495	496	656	715	886	935	1 064	965
Financial Supervisory Comm	..	..	325	605	899	917	324	262	279	319
Numismatic Revenue	..	..	386	457	501	600	354	511	537	172
Drivers Licence Fees	..	..	403	718	125	292	87	214	289	256
Censorship Fees	..	..	0	12	5	2	2	3	2	1
Upper Air Space Fees	..	..	354	442	985	545	545	545	577	922
Other fees	..	..	193	112	175	426	203	1 212	428	159
Fines, penalties and forfeits	..	..	81	72	1 249	23	553	248	2 302	246
Miscellaneous and unidentified revenue	..	..	545	11 289	1 594	10 271	4 844	2 155	3 962	7 415
Total tax and non-tax revenue	..	..	95 916	137 104	156 823	178 444	202 346	214 752	234 243	222 238

.. Not available

Note: Data are reported on a fiscal year basis beginning 1st July. For example, the data for 2019 represent the period from July 2019 to June 2020.
The data are on a cash basis.
Figures exclude non-tax revenues collected by sub-national governments as the data are not available.
Other grants include revenue from Japan, China, India as well as other sources.

Source: Ministry of Finance and Economic Management of the Cook Islands.

StatLink https://stat.link/59yeuw

Table 5.7. Fiji: Details of non-tax revenue

Million FJD

	1997	2000	2007	2010	2014	2015	2016	2017	2018	2019
Total non-tax revenue	..	..	..	**172**	**270**	**282**	**331**	**388**	**415**	**407**
Grants	..	..	..	9	26	18	26	20	57	46
Property income	..	..	..	54	102	109	143	174	178	186
Rents and royalties	..	..	..	1	36	40	49	63	81	74
Interest and dividends	..	..	..	52	66	70	94	111	97	112
Other property income	..	..	..	0	0	0	0	0	0	0
Sales of goods and services	..	..	..	99	125	136	136	178	169	169
Fines, penalties and forfeits	..	..	..	3	4	3	3	3	2	2
Miscellaneous and unidentified revenue	..	..	..	8	13	16	22	13	9	5
Total tax and non-tax revenue	..	..	..	1 476	2 350	2 601	2 719	3 067	3 155	3 044

.. Not available

Note: Year ending 31st December.

The data are on a cash basis.

Figures exclude non-tax revenues collected by sub-national governments as the data are not available.

Source: Ministry of Economy, Fiji.

StatLink https://stat.link/5trk9w

Table 5.8. Kazakhstan: Details of non-tax revenue

Million KZT

	1997	2000	2007	2010	2014	2015	2016	2017	2018	2019
Total non-tax revenue	..	**8 577**	**198 439**	**213 863**	**575 447**	**545 447**	**564 930**	**573 780**	**1 071 522**	**1 035 462**
Grants	..	0	0	0	0	0	0	0	0	0
Property income	..	52	91 107	121 760	419 640	351 753	305 424	342 509	872 985	809 180
Rents and royalties	..	0	55 466	103 118	396 228	303 211	278 626	309 080	837 280	727 203
Interest and dividends	..	52	31 871	16 289	18 288	46 163	24 014	30 784	33 709	79 558
Other property income	..	0	3 770	2 352	5 124	2 379	2 785	2 645	1 996	2 419
Sales of goods and services	..	8 525	42 383	59 965	79 083	122 511	183 868	129 057	123 938	138 926
Fines, penalties and forfeits	..	0	7 083	32 138	75 915	68 087	69 673	102 234	74 572	87 333
Miscellaneous and unidentified revenue	..	0	57 866	0	810	3 096	5 965	-21	26	21
Total tax and non-tax revenue	..	526 354	3 547 757	5 396 242	8 940 516	6 898 410	7 570 983	9 264 458	11 555 937	12 630 402

.. Not available

Note: Year ending 31st December.

Data are on a cash basis.

The share of the Republic of Kazakhstan under production sharing contracts of oil companies, the bonuses of oil and non-oil sector companies, the levy for the use of the radio-frequency spectrum, the payment to compensate for historic costs as well as certain other items are classified as non-tax revenues according to the OECD Interpretative Guide, but are considered as tax revenues in Kazakhstan.

Source: Ministry of Finance of the Republic of Kazakhstan.

StatLink https://stat.link/0u2kvn

Table 5.9. Lao PDR: Details of non-tax revenue

Million LAK

	1997	2000	2007	2010	2014	2015	2016	2017	2018	2019
Total non-tax revenue	..	..	..	**5 877**	**10 220**	**8 980**	**5 770**	**7 244**	**8 194**	**7 923**
Grants	..	..	..	3 931	5 947	4 618	1 749	2 197	2 929	2 632
Property income	..	..	..	1 417	2 457	2 696	2 019	3 089	3 156	2 858
Rents and royalties	..	..	..	701	1 487	1 545	971	1 316	1 097	1 180
Timber royalties	..	..	..	48	254	546	127	335	38	22
Hydro-power royalties	..	..	..	140	372	378	369	371	418	538
Natural resource taxes	..	..	..	513	861	620	474	610	641	620
Interest and dividends	..	..	..	716	970	1 152	1 048	1 773	2 058	1 678
Other property income	..	..	..	0	0	0	0	0	0	0
Sales of goods and services	..	..	..	486	1 211	1 533	1 800	1 744	1 869	1 971
Fines, penalties and forfeits	..	..	..	37	94	124	180	83	49	35
Miscellaneous and unidentified revenue	..	..	..	5	512	9	23	131	191	427
Total tax and non-tax revenue	..	..	..	12 978	23 340	23 699	21 163	22 777	24 758	25 132

.. Not available

Note: Data are reported on a calendar year.

The data are on a cash basis.

Grants: Data are taken from the IMF WEO April 2021.

Source: Ministry of Finance, Lao PDR.

StatLink https://stat.link/ebdurc

Table 5.10. Maldives: Details of non-tax revenue

Million MVR

	1997	2000	2007	2010	2014	2015	2016	2017	2018	2019
Total non-tax revenue	..	..	**3 553**	**3 381**	**3 976**	**4 234**	**4 875**	**4 962**	**5 541**	**5 544**
Grants	..	..	0	0	0	0	0	0	0	0
Property income	..	..	1 102	1 244	929	627	758	1 008	1 152	1 048
Rents and royalties	..	..	141	93	114	104	94	102	104	115
Interest and dividends	..	..	961	1 151	815	523	664	907	1 048	933
Other property income	..	..	0	0	0	0	0	0	0	0
Sales of goods and services	..	..	2 306	1 737	2 740	3 260	3 718	3 610	3 904	3 987
Fines, penalties and forfeits	..	..	58	114	257	269	327	244	278	235
Miscellaneous and unidentified revenue	..	..	87	287	50	78	72	100	208	274
Total tax and non-tax revenue	..	..	6 408	6 343	14 756	16 467	18 141	19 682	21 359	22 056

.. Not available

Note: Data are reported on a calendar year.

The data are on a cash basis.

Source: Ministry of Finance, Maldives.

StatLink https://stat.link/4av7y6

Table 5.11. Mongolia: Details of non-tax revenue

Billion MNT

	1997	2000	2007	2010	2014	2015	2016	2017	2018	2019
Total non-tax revenue	..	..	**472**	**639**	**1 724**	**1 459**	**1 214**	**1 207**	**1 486**	**1 626**
Grants	..	..	22	39	0	53	77	62	89	88
Property income	..	..	249	320	960	824	470	482	670	793
Rents and royalties	..	..	107	265	916	813	466	446	593	766
Interest and dividends	..	..	142	55	44	12	4	36	77	27
Other property income	..	..	0	0	0	0	0	0	0	0
Sales of goods and services	..	..	25	33	70	98	118	150	170	158
Fines, penalties and forfeits	..	..	34	36	210	178	193	75	113	159
Miscellaneous and unidentified revenue	..	..	142	211	484	305	355	438	445	427
Total tax and non-tax revenue	..	..	1 878	3 109	6 205	5 879	5 781	7 211	9 275	10 659

.. Not available

Note: Year ending December 31st.

Data are on a cash basis.

Source: Ministry of Finance, Mongolia.

StatLink https://stat.link/4r2hxp

Table 5.12. Nauru: Details of non-tax revenue

Thousand AUD

	1997	2000	2007	2010	2014	2015	2016	2017	2018	2019
Total non-tax revenue	..	..	..	..	**32 765**	**67 975**	**87 640**	**102 890**	**148 267**	**141 378**
Grants	..	..	..	..	21	20	32	31	33	15
Property income	..	..	..	..	17 998	38 618	48 042	48 170	73 684	76 021
Rents and royalties	..	..	..	..	17 557	38 160	46 910	47 111	72 492	73 771
Fishing days, licences and support vessels	..	..	..	..	16 762	37 477	46 897	46 363	71 374	73 279
DCA Air navigation and rental fees	..	..	..	..	795	683	13	748	1 118	492
Interest and dividends	..	..	..	..	441	458	1 132	1 059	1 192	2 250
Other property income	..	..	..	..	0	0	0	0	0	0
Sales of goods and services	..	..	..	..	14 746	28 043	33 591	49 802	57 661	46 399
Visa Fees RPB	..	..	..	..	12 804	24 978	27 844	28 357	20 282	21 113
DJBC Operations	..	..	..	..	0	729	3 740	2 657	5 450	3 370
Other sales of goods and services	..	..	..	..	1 942	2 335	2 007	18 788	31 929	21 916
Fines, penalties and forfeits	..	..	..	..	0	0	0	0	0	0
Miscellaneous and unidentified revenue	..	..	..	..	0	1 295	5 975	4 887	16 889	18 943
Total tax and non-tax revenue	..	..	..	..	42 317	92 081	109 099	144 977	204 832	221 399

.. Not available

Note: Data are on a fiscal year basis beginning 1st July. For example, the data for 2019 represent the period from July 2019 to July 2020.

Source: Nauru Revenue Office; Grant data are taken from the IMF World Economic Outlook April 2021.

StatLink https://stat.link/zgmw3u

Table 5.13. Papua New Guinea: Details of non-tax revenue

Million PGK

	1997	2000	2007	2010	2014	2015	2016	2017	2018	2019
Total non-tax revenue	..	..	**1 132**	**1 826**	**1 768**	**1 946**	**2 064**	**2 402**	**2 934**	**2 344**
Grants	..	..	721	1 391	868	820	1 430	1 440	1 836	1 776
Property income	..	..	291	341	666	911	529	842	1 064	529
Rents and royalties	..	..	0	0	0	0	0	0	30	28
Interest and dividends	..	..	291	341	666	911	529	842	1 034	501
Dividends	..	..	65	40	152	455	228	279	380	120
Mining and Petroleum Dividends	..	..	226	299	514	456	301	562	654	381
SWF Receipts	..	..	0	0	0	0	0	0	0	0
Interests and fees from lending	..	..	1	1	0	0	0	0	0	0
Other property income	..	..	0	0	0	0	0	0	0	0
Sales of goods and services	..	..	0	0	0	0	0	0	32	37
Fines, penalties and forfeits	..	..	0	0	0	0	0	0	3	2
Miscellaneous and unidentified revenue	..	..	120	95	235	215	105	121	0	0
Total tax and non-tax revenue	..	..	7 007	8 399	12 047	11 088	10 670	11 388	12 917	12 862

.. Not available

Note: Year ending 31st December.

The data are on a cash basis.

Figures exclude non-tax revenues collected by sub-national governments as the data are not available.

Source: Ministry of Treasury and Finance of Papua New Guinea.

StatLink https://stat.link/4s98dv

Table 5.14. Philippines: Details of non-tax revenue

Million PHP

	1997	2000	2007	2010	2014	2015	2016	2017	2018	2019
Total non-tax revenue	..	..	..	..	**238 844**	**289 238**	**275 231**	**286 706**	**339 462**	**386 432**
Grants	..	..	..	..	233	164	78	39	51	259
Property income	..	..	..	..	107 253	125 070	118 984	120 400	137 641	173 600
Rents and royalties	..	..	..	..	2 683	1 307	1 086	1 126	1 187	1 405
Interest and dividends	..	..	..	..	873	1 288	1 772	2 202	2 131	3 377
Other property income	..	..	..	..	103 697	122 475	116 126	117 072	134 323	168 818
Sales of goods and services	..	..	..	..	60 232	66 857	72 722	76 860	91 228	96 142
Fines, penalties and forfeits	..	..	..	..	0	0	0	0	0	0
Miscellaneous and unidentified revenue	..	..	..	..	71 126	97 147	83 447	89 407	110 542	116 431
Total tax and non-tax revenue	..	..	..	..	2 350 412	2 554 377	2 736 054	3 066 602	3 513 206	3 906 617

.. Not available

Note: Year ending 31st December.

The data are on a cash basis.

Source: Department of Finance of the Philippines.

StatLink https://stat.link/tf8z36

Table 5.15. Samoa: Details of non-tax revenue

Million WST

	1997	2000	2007	2010	2014	2015	2016	2017	2018	2019
Total non-tax revenue	..	..	**125**	**157**	**92**	**98**	**100**	**120**	**135**	**239**
Grants	..	..	77	105	41	45	41	61	46	164
Property income	..	..	24	8	11	7	6	7	22	12
Rents and royalties	..	..	24	1	1	1	1	2	3	2
Interest and dividends	..	..	0	7	11	6	6	6	18	10
Other property income	..	..	0	0	0	0	0	0	0	0
Sales of goods and services	..	..	23	31	33	37	41	40	67	63
Administrative fees	..	..	..	28	23	26	28	24	38	31
Incidental sales by nonmarket establishments	..	..	..	2	10	11	13	17	30	32
Fines, penalties and forfeits	..	..	0	1	7	8	11	11	0	1
Miscellaneous and unidentified revenue	..	..	0	11	0	0	0	0	0	0
Total tax and non-tax revenue	..	..	455	498	532	593	614	643	706	795

.. Not available

Note: Data are reported on a fiscal year basis beginning 1st July. For example, the data for 2019 represent the period from July 2019 to June 2020.

The data are on a cash basis.

Figures exclude non-tax revenues collected by sub-national governments as the data are not available.

The data from 2009 were provided on the basis of the IMF's GFSM 2014 classification. Prior to this year, data were provided on a different basis. The differences between the two sets of data are indicated below for the relevant non-tax revenue categories.

Heading Grants: Data from 2009 includes only cash grants whereas data prior to that year also includes aid-funded projects.

Heading Sales of Goods and services: Data from 2009 exclude fisheries' licences currently included in tax revenue under heading "5126 taxes on specific services" (more information can be found in Table 4.12) . Fisheries' licences revenues are usually classified as non-tax revenues according to the the OECD classification set out in Annex A of the Interpretative Guide.

Source: Bureau of Statistics of Samoa.

StatLink https://stat.link/zgf96o

Table 5.16. Singapore: Details of non-tax revenue

Million SGD

	1997	2000	2007	2010	2014	2015	2016	2017	2018	2019
Total non-tax revenue	..	**17 088**	**16 061**	**11 644**	**15 863**	**18 596**	**19 812**	**25 597**	**22 206**	**36 612**
Grants	..	0	0	0	0	0	0	0	0	0
Property income	..	11 154	13 040	8 348	10 351	10 821	10 865	17 428	16 106	31 391
Rents and royalties	..	..	..	..	..	1 400	1 319	1 284	1 436	1 408
Interest and dividends	..	..	..	..	..	9 420	9 547	16 144	14 670	29 983
Other property income	..	..	..	..	..	0	0	0	0	0
Sales of goods and services	..	4 921	2 738	2 844	4 926	6 943	8 152	7 425	5 284	4 530
Fines, penalties and forfeits	..	187	168	226	262	331	289	367	386	336
Miscellaneous and unidentified revenue	..	826	115	226	324	502	506	378	430	354
Total tax and non-tax revenue	..	42 715	52 691	53 492	69 973	74 243	78 511	91 960	88 409	104 257

.. Not available

Note: Data are on a fiscal year basis ending 31st March. For example, the data for 2019 represent 1 April 2019 to 31 March 2020.

The data are on a cash basis.

Scope of data provided is limited to the Budgetary Central Government.

Source: Ministry of Finance of Singapore.

StatLink https://stat.link/ac1t38

Table 5.17. Thailand: Details of non-tax revenue

Million THB

	1997	2000	2007	2010	2014	2015	2016	2017	2018	2019
Total non-tax revenue	..	..	**235 534**	**353 402**	**411 153**	**484 461**	**527 248**	**542 953**	**614 782**	**630 757**
Grants	..	..	1 687	2 081	5 369	1 450	2 984	2 415	2 401	1 584
Property income	..	..	155 317	191 289	287 830	306 528	281 647	300 896	311 258	331 914
Rents and royalties	..	..	41 537	46 429	101 284	88 895	80 580	75 554	78 839	83 980
Interest and dividends	..	..	113 780	144 442	186 546	217 633	201 067	225 343	232 420	247 934
Other property income	..	..	0	418	0	0	0	0	0	0
Sales of goods and services	..	..	65 093	103 797	97 574	127 522	185 322	174 056	220 257	204 826
Fines, penalties and forfeits	..	..	7 640	9 197	7 429	13 287	23 063	14 095	17 733	19 330
Miscellaneous and unidentified revenue	..	..	5 797	47 037	12 952	35 672	34 231	51 491	63 133	73 102
Total tax and non-tax revenue	..	..	1 788 667	2 223 854	2 821 641	3 052 599	3 123 043	3 216 367	3 472 622	3 528 539

.. Not available

Note: Data are on a fiscal year basis ending 30th September. For example, the data for 2019 represents 1 October 2018 to 30 September 2019.

The data are on a cash basis.

Source: Ministry of Finance in Thailand.

StatLink https://stat.link/3ciy4g

Table 5.18. Tokelau: Details of non-tax revenue

Thousand NZD

	1997	2000	2007	2010	2014	2015	2016	2017	2018	2019
Total non-tax revenue	..	..	**12 537**	**14 836**	**21 424**	**32 773**	**35 088**	**31 507**	**37 212**	**34 780**
Grants	..	..	10 508	13 115	12 354	12 000	12 000	11 010	13 500	15 538
New Zealand Budgetary Grants	..	..	10 508	13 115	12 305	12 000	12 000	11 010	13 500	15 538
External donor funding	..	..	0	0	49	0	0	0	0	0
Property income	..	..	1 478	1 051	8 363	20 001	22 340	19 726	22 335	17 810
Rents and royalties	..	..	1 257	955	8 067	19 901	21 866	18 909	21 684	17 259
Tokelau EEZ Revenues	..	..	1 257	955	8 067	19 901	21 866	18 909	21 684	17 259
Interest and dividends	..	..	221	96	296	100	474	817	651	551
Other property income	..	..	0	0	0	0	0	0	0	0
Sales of goods and services	..	..	551	670	707	772	748	771	1 377	1 432
Handicrafts & Tourism (ENDRE)	..	..	0	0	0	154	4	7	7	10
Commemorative coins	..	..	0	0	71	0	0	0	115	32
Stamp sales	..	..	0	0	0	0	0	0	0	5
Transport - Boatfares	..	..	159	117	132	123	174	243	295	215
Transport - Freights Payments	..	..	291	409	397	386	430	398	618	649
Transport - Sale of Assets	..	..	0	1	0	6	10	0	4	0
Charter fees	..	..	25	10	0	0	0	0	171	323
Postage	..	..	2	3	1	1	0	0	0	0
Registry Certificates: Birth & Death	..	..	1	1	2	2	4	5	10	4
Service Fees	..	..	19	45	22	20	37	31	73	82
Miscellaneous Revenues	..	..	1	1	0	0	0	0	3	51
Revenue - Debt Recovery (MISC)	..	..	0	0	0	0	2	0	0	0
Gains - Sale of Assets (Vehicles)	..	..	0	0	0	66	19	0	0	0
House Rental Subsidies	..	..	22	46	66	1	55	74	62	51
Tokelau Savings Bank Passbook Fees	..	..	0	0	1	2	1	0	1	1
Tokelau Higano: accommodation	..	..	31	37	15	11	12	13	18	9
Fines, penalties and forfeits	..	..	0	0	0	0	0	0	0	0
Miscellaneous and unidentified revenue	..	..	0	0	0	0	0	0	0	0
Total tax and non-tax revenue	..	..	13 735	16 530	23 531	34 924	37 264	34 025	40 055	37 820

.. Not available

Note: Data are reported on a fiscal year basis beginning 1st July. For example, the data for 2019 represent the period from July 2019 to June 2020.
The data are on a cash basis.

Source: Tokelau National Statistics Office.

StatLink https://stat.link/unt5qr

Table 5.19. Vanuatu: Details of non-tax revenue

Million VUV

	1997	2000	2007	2010	2014	2015	2016	2017	2018	2019
Total non-tax revenue	..	**388**	**774**	**5 619**	**4 615**	**12 244**	**8 340**	**13 470**	**19 984**	**26 064**
Grants	..	373	745	4 431	3 072	8 943	4 551	7 032	7 807	11 113
Property income	..	0	0	0	0	0	0	0	0	0
Rents and royalties	..	..	..	..	..	..	..	..	..	..
Interest and dividends	..	..	..	..	..	..	..	..	..	..
Other property income	..	..	..	..	..	..	..	..	..	..
Sales of goods and services	..	0	0	0	0	0	0	0	0	0
Fines, penalties and forfeits	..	0	0	0	0	0	0	0	0	0
Miscellaneous and unidentified revenue	..	15	29	1 187	1 542	3 302	3 789	6 438	12 177	14 950
Total tax and non-tax revenue	..	6 486	11 041	16 708	18 352	25 721	21 664	29 719	37 960	44 318

.. Not available

Note: Year ending December 31st.

Source: Department of Finance and Treasury of Vanuatu.

StatLink https://stat.link/rd6ic2

Table 5.20. Viet Nam: Details of non-tax revenue

Billion VND

	1997	2000	2007	2010	2014	2015	2016	2017	2018	2019
Total non-tax revenue	..	..	**87 893**	**122 514**	**200 137**	**272 776**	**322 312**	**420 566**	**477 639**	**497 595**
Grants	..	..	6 012	11 868	11 050	11 844	8 519	7 910	7 780	6 688
Property income	..	..	21 461	26 316	38 048	29 110	27 080	32 822	38 195	36 773
Rents and royalties	..	..	21 461	26 316	38 048	29 110	27 080	32 822	38 195	36 773
Interest and dividends	..	..	0	0	0	0	0	0	0	0
Other property income	..	..	0	0	0	0	0	0	0	0
Sales of goods and services	..	..	43 039	66 702	73 378	113 628	143 685	216 679	245 849	265 143
Fees and charges	..	..	7 366	11 347	17 801	27 200	19 177	36 062	37 530	40 993
Land rents	..	..	4 668	5 987	11 375	17 434	25 755	27 432	31 064	37 320
Revenue from land user right assignment	..	..	31 005	49 368	44 202	68 994	98 753	125 287	147 815	152 922
Lottery revenue	..	..	0	0	0	0	0	27 898	29 440	33 908
Fines, penalties and forfeits	..	..	0	0	0	0	0	0	0	0
Miscellaneous and unidentified revenue	..	..	17 381	17 628	77 661	118 194	143 028	163 155	185 815	188 991
Total tax and non-tax revenue	..	..	336 274	588 430	877 696	998 217	1 101 377	1 288 665	1 431 660	1 551 074

.. Not available

Note: Year ending 31st December.

The data are on a cash basis.

Source: General Statistics Office Viet Nam.

StatLink https://stat.link/ebitrh

Annex A. The OECD Classification of Taxes and Interpretative Guide

Table of Contents

A.1 the OECD Classification of Taxes

1. **1000. Taxes on income, profits and capital gains**
    - 1100. Taxes on income, profits and capital gains of individuals
        - 1110. On income and profits
        - 1120. On capital gains
    - 1200. Corporate taxes on income, profits and capital gains
        - 1210. On income and profits
        - 1220. On capital gains
    - 1300. Unallocable as between 1100 and 1200
2. **2000. Social security contributions**
    - 2100. Employees
        - 2110. On a payroll basis
        - 2120. On an income tax basis
    - 2200. Employers
        - 2210. On a payroll basis
        - 2220. On an income tax basis
    - 2300. Self-employed or non-employed
        - 2310. On a payroll basis
        - 2320. On an income tax basis
    - 2400 Unallocable as between 2100, 2200 and 2300
        - 2410. On a payroll basis
        - 2420. On an income tax basis
3. **3000. Taxes on payroll and workforce**
4. **4000. Taxes on property**
    - 4100. Recurrent taxes on immovable property
        - 4110. Households
        - 4120. Other
    - 4200 Recurrent taxes on net wealth
        - 4210. Individual
        - 4220. Corporate
    - 4300. Estate, inheritance and gift taxes
        - 4310. Estate and inheritance taxes
        - 4320. Gift taxes
    - 4400. Taxes on financial and capital transactions

4500. Other non-recurrent taxes on property

4510. On net wealth

4520. Other non-recurrent taxes

4600. Other recurrent taxes on property

5. **5000. Taxes on goods and services**

5100. Taxes on production, sale, transfer, leasing and delivery of goods and rendering of services

5110. General taxes

5111. Value added taxes

5112. Sales taxes

5113. Turnover and other general taxes on goods and services

5120. Taxes on specific goods and services

5121. Excises

5122. Profits of fiscal monopolies

5123. Customs and import duties

5124. Taxes on exports

5125. Taxes on investment goods

5126 . Taxes on specific services

5127. Other taxes on international trade and transactions

5128. Other taxes on specific goods and services

5130. Unallocable as between 5110 and 5120

5200. Taxes on use of goods, or on permission to use goods or perform activities

5210. Recurrent taxes

5211. Paid by households in respect of motor vehicles

5212. Paid by others in respect of motor vehicles

5213. Other recurrent taxes

5220. Non-recurrent taxes

5300. Unallocable as between 5100 and 5200

6. **6000. Other taxes**

6100. Paid solely by business

6200. Paid by other than business or unidentifiable

A.2 Coverage

General criteria

1. In the OECD classification the term "taxes" is confined to compulsory unrequited payments to general government. Taxes are unrequited in the sense that benefits provided by government to taxpayers are not normally in proportion to their payments.

2. The term "tax" does not include fines, penalties and compulsory loans paid to government. Borderline cases between tax and non-tax revenues in relation to certain fees and charges are discussed in §11–14.

3. General government consists of the central administration, agencies whose operations are under its effective control, state and local governments and their administrations, certain social security schemes and autonomous governmental entities, excluding public enterprises. This definition of government follows that of the 2008 *System of National Accounts* (SNA).[1] In that publication, the general government sector and its sub-sectors are defined in Chapter 4, paragraphs 4.117 to 4.165.

4. Extra-budgetary units are part of the general government system. These are general government entities with individual budgets that are not fully covered by the main or general budget. These entities operate under the authority or control of a central, state, or local government. Extra-budgetary entities may have their own revenue sources, which may be supplemented by grants (transfers) from the general budget or from other sources. Even though their budgets may be subject to approval by the legislature, similar to that of budgetary accounts, they have discretion over the volume and composition of their spending. Such entities may be established to carry out specific government functions, such as road construction, or the nonmarket production of health or education services. Budgetary arrangements vary widely across countries, and various terms are used to describe these entities, but they are often referred to as "extra-budgetary funds" or "decentralised agencies."

5. Compulsory payments to supra-national bodies and their agencies are no longer included as taxes as from 1998, with some exceptions. However, custom duties collected by EU member states on behalf of the European Union are still identified as memorandum items and included in overall tax revenue amounts in the country tables (Chapter 5) of the country in which they are collected. (See §99). In countries where the church forms part of general government church taxes are included, provided they meet the criteria set out in §1 above. As the data refer to receipts of general government, levies paid to non-government bodies, welfare agencies or social insurance schemes outside general government, trade unions or trade associations, even where such levies are compulsory, are excluded. Compulsory payments to general government earmarked for such bodies are, however, included, provided that the government is not simply acting in an agency capacity.[2] Profits from fiscal monopolies are distinguished from those of other public enterprises and are treated as taxes because they reflect the exercise of the taxing power of the state by the use of monopoly powers (see §65–67), as are profits received by the government from the purchase and sale of foreign exchange at different rates (see §74).

6. Taxes paid by governments (e.g., social security contributions and payroll taxes paid by governments in their capacity as an employer, consumption taxes on their purchases or taxes on their property) are not excluded from the data provided. However, where it is possible to identify the amounts of revenue involved,[3] they are shown in Table 5.38 of this Report.

7. The relationship between this classification and that of the System of National Accounts (SNA) is set out in Sections A.9 and A.11 below. Because of the differences between the two classifications, the data shown in national accounts are sometimes calculated or classified differently from the practice set out in this guide. These and other differences are mentioned where appropriate (e.g., in §30 below) but it is not possible to refer to all of them. There may also be some differences between this classification and that employed domestically by certain national administrations (e.g., see §12 below), so that OECD and

national statistics data may not always be consistent: any such differences, however, are likely to be very slight in terms of amounts of revenues involved.

Social security contributions

8. Compulsory social security contributions, as defined in §39, and paid to general government, are treated here as tax revenues. Being compulsory payments to general government they clearly resemble taxes. They may, however, differ from other taxes in that the receipt of social security benefits depends, in most countries, upon appropriate contributions having been made, although the size of the benefits is not necessarily related to the amount of the contributions. Better comparability between countries is obtained by treating social security contributions as taxes, but they are listed under a separate heading so that they can be distinguished in any analysis.

9. The strict dividing line between tax revenues (compulsory unrequited payments to general government) and non-tax compulsory payments (NTCPs) (payments that are either requited or made to other institutions) is clearly defined. However, within the range of different compulsory payments to governments existing across countries, it is not always straightforward in practice to decide whether specific payments are either taxes or NTCPs. For example, compulsory pension savings that are controlled by general government and that accumulate on an individual account earning a market return or a rate that compensates for inflation would at first sight be categorised as NTCPs as opposed to taxes. However, even these payments might still be 'unrequited' and therefore classify as taxes instead of NTCPs (for example if these pension savings are not paid out when the taxpayer dies before reaching the pension age and the funds are then used to provide a minimum pension to all taxpayers that are insured). These issues result in the social security revenue figures reported for most countries being based on the premise that all types of compulsory payments to general government are judged to some extent to have a re-distributional element. It should be noted that this conclusion is based on a typically broad interpretation of the term 'unrequited' in the tax definition.

10. Social security contributions which are either voluntary or not payable to general government (see §1) are not treated as taxes, though in some countries, as indicated in the country footnotes, there are difficulties in completely eliminating voluntary contributions and certain compulsory payments to the private sector from the revenue figures. Imputed social security contributions are also not treated as taxes.

Fees, user charges and licence fees

11. Apart from vehicle licence fees, which are universally regarded as taxes, it is not easy to distinguish between those fees and user charges which are to be treated as taxes and those which are not, since, whilst a fee or charge is levied in connection with a specific service or activity, the strength of the link between the fee and the service provided may vary considerably, as may the relation between the amount of the fee and the cost of providing the service. Where the recipient of a service pays a fee clearly related to the cost of providing the service, the levy may be regarded as requited and under the definition of §1 would not be considered as a tax. In the following cases, however, a levy could be considered as 'unrequited':

- *a)* where the charge greatly exceeds the cost of providing the service;
- *b)* where the payer of the levy is not the receiver of the benefit (e.g., a fee collected from slaughterhouses to finance a service which is provided to farmers);
- *c)* where government is not providing a specific service in return for the levy which it receives even though a licence may be issued to the payer (e.g., where the government grants a hunting, fishing or shooting licence which is not accompanied by the right to use a specific area of government land);

d) where benefits are received only by those paying the levy but the benefits received by each individual are not necessarily in proportion to his payments (e.g., a milk marketing levy paid by dairy farmers and used to promote the consumption of milk).

12. In marginal cases, however, the application of the criteria set out in §1 can be particularly difficult. The solution adopted — given the desirability of international uniformity and the relatively small amounts of revenue usually involved — is to follow the predominant practice among tax administrations rather than to allow each country to adopt its own view as to whether such levies are regarded as taxes or as non-tax revenue.[4]

13. A list of the main fees and charges in question and their normal[5] treatment in this publication is as follows:

Non-tax revenues:	court fees; driving licence fees; harbour fees; passport fees; radio and television licence fees where public authorities provide the service
Taxes within heading 5200	permission to perform such activities as distributing films; hunting, fishing and shooting; providing entertainment or gambling facilities; selling alcohol or tobacco; permission to own dogs or to use or own motor vehicles or guns; severance taxes

14. In practice it may not always be possible to isolate tax receipts from non-tax revenue receipts when they are recorded together. If it is estimated that the bulk of the receipts derive from non-tax revenues, the whole amount involved is treated as a non-tax revenue; otherwise, such government receipts are included and classified according to the rules provided in §32 below.

Royalties

15. The ownership of subsoil assets in the form of deposits of minerals or fossil fuels (coal, oil, or natural gas) depends upon the way in which property rights are defined by law and also on international agreements in the case of deposits below international waters. In some cases, either the ground below which the mineral deposits are located, the deposits themselves or both may belong to a local or central government unit.

16. In such cases, these general government units may grant leases to other institutional units that permit them to extract these deposits over a specified period of time in return for a payment or series of payments. These payments are often described as 'royalties' but they are essentially rent that accrues to owners of natural resources in return for putting these assets at the disposal of other units for specified periods of time. The rent may take the form of periodic payments of fixed amounts, irrespective of the rate of extraction, or, more commonly, they may be a function of the quantity, volume, or value of the asset extracted. Enterprises engaged in exploration on government land may make payments to general government units in exchange for the right to undertake test drilling or otherwise investigate the existence and location of subsoil assets. Such payments are also recorded as rents even though no extraction may take place. These payments are therefore classified as non-tax revenues.

17. The same principles apply when other institutional units are granted leases that permit them to fell timber in natural forests on land owned by general government units. These payments are also classified as non-tax revenues.

18. These rents or royalties paid to general government should not be confused with taxes on income and profits, severance taxes, business licenses, or other taxes. If the payments are levied on the profits from the extraction activity, then they should be classified as taxes on incomes, profits and gains (1000). In addition, any severance payments that are imposed on the extraction of minerals and fossil fuels from reserves owned privately or by another government should be classified as taxes. Payments related to the gross value of production should be classified as other taxes on goods and services (5128). Payments for

a license or permit to conduct extraction operations should be classified as taxes on use of goods and on permission to use goods or perform activities (5213).

Fines and penalties

19. In principle, fines and penalties charged on overdue taxes or penalties imposed for the attempted evasion of taxes should not be recorded as tax revenues. However it may not be possible to separate payments of fines or other penalties from the revenues from the taxes to which they relate. In this case the fines and penalties relating to a particular tax are recorded together with the revenues from that tax and fines and penalties paid with revenue from unidentifiable taxes are classified as other taxes in Category 6000. Fines not relating to tax offences (e.g., for parking offences), or not identifiable as relating to tax offences, are also not treated as tax revenues.

A.3 Basis of reporting

Accrual reporting

20. The data reported in this publication for recent years are predominantly recorded on an accrual basis, i.e. recorded at the time that the tax liability was created. Further information is provided in the footnotes to the country table in Chapter 5 of the Report.

21. However, data for earlier years are still predominantly recorded on a cash basis, i.e. at the time at which the payment was received by government. Thus, for example, taxes withheld by employers in one year but paid to the government in the following year and taxes due in one year but actually paid in the following year are both included in the receipts of the second year. Corrective transactions, such as refunds, repayments and drawbacks, are deducted from gross revenues of the period in which they are made.

22. Data on tax revenues are recorded without offsets for the administrative expenses connected with tax collection. Similarly, where the proceeds of tax are used to subsidise particular members of the community, the subsidy is not deducted from the yield of the tax, though the tax may be shown net of subsidies in the national records of some countries.

23. As regards fiscal monopolies (heading 5122), only the amount actually transferred to the government is included in government revenues. However, if any expenditures of fiscal monopolies are considered to be government expenditures (e.g., social expenditures undertaken by fiscal monopolies at the direction of the government) they are added back for the purpose of arriving at tax revenue figures (see §65 below).

The distinction between tax and expenditure provisions[6]

24. Because this publication is concerned only with the revenue side of government operations, no account being taken of the expenditure side, a distinction has to be made between tax and expenditure provisions. Normally there is no difficulty in making this distinction as expenditures are made outside the tax system and the tax accounts and under legislation separate from the tax legislation. In borderline cases, cash flow is used to distinguish between tax provisions and expenditure provisions. Insofar as a provision affects the flow of tax payments from the taxpayer to the government, it is regarded as a tax provision and is taken into account in the data shown in this publication. A provision which does not affect this flow is seen as an expenditure provision and is disregarded in the data recorded in this publication.

25. Tax allowances, exemptions and deductions against the tax base clearly affect the amount of tax paid to the government and are therefore considered as tax provisions. At the other extreme, those subsidies which cannot be offset against tax liability and which are clearly not connected with the

assessment process, do not reduce tax revenues as recorded in this publication. Tax credits are amounts deductible from tax payable (as distinct from deductions from the tax base). Two types of tax credits are distinguished, those (referred to here as wastable tax credits) which are limited to the amount of the tax liability and therefore cannot give rise to a payment by the authorities to the taxpayer, and those (referred to as non-wastable tax credits) which are not so limited, so that the excess of the credit over the tax liability can be paid to the taxpayer.[7] A wastable tax credit, like a tax allowance, clearly affects the amount of tax paid to the government, and is therefore considered as a tax provision. The practice followed for non-wastable tax credits[8] is to distinguish between the 'tax expenditure component',[9] which is that portion of the credit that is used to reduce or eliminate a taxpayer's liability, and the 'transfer component', which is the portion that exceeds the taxpayer's liability and is paid to that taxpayer. Reported tax revenues should be reduced by the amount of the tax expenditure component but not by the amount of the transfer component. In addition, the amounts of the tax expenditure and transfer components should be reported as memorandum items in the country tables. Countries that are unable to distinguish between the tax expenditure and transfer components should indicate whether or not the tax revenues have been reduced by the total of these components, and provide any available estimates of the amounts of the two components. Further information is given in Chapter 1 of the Report, which illustrates the effect of alternative treatments of non-wastable tax credits on tax to GDP.

Calendar and fiscal years

26. National authorities whose fiscal years do not correspond to the calendar year show data, where possible, on a calendar year basis to permit maximum comparability with the data of other countries. There remain a few countries where data refer to fiscal years. For these the GDP data used in the comparative tables also correspond to the fiscal years.

A.4 General classification criteria

The main classification criteria

27. The classification of receipts among the main headings (1000, 2000, 3000, 4000, 5000 and 6000) is generally governed by the base on which the tax is levied: 1000 income, profits and capital gains; 2000 and 3000 earnings, payroll or number of employees; 4000 property; 5000 goods and services; 6000 multiple bases, other bases or unidentifiable bases. Where a tax is calculated on more than one base, the receipts are, where possible, split among the various headings (see §32 and §81). The headings 4000 and 5000 cover not only taxes where the tax base is the property, goods or services themselves but also certain related taxes. Thus, taxes on the transfer of property are included in 4400[10] and taxes on the use of goods or on permission to perform activities in 5200. In headings 4000 and 5000 a distinction is made in certain sub-headings between recurrent and non-recurrent taxes: recurrent taxes are defined as those levied at regular intervals (usually annually) and non-recurrent taxes are levied once and for all (see also §47 to §50, §53, §54 and §79 for particular applications of this distinction).

28. Earmarking of a tax for specific purposes does not affect the classification of tax receipts. However, as explained in §39 on the classification of social security contributions, the conferment of an entitlement to social benefits is crucial to the definition of the 2000 main heading.

29. The way that a tax is levied or collected (e.g., by use of stamps) does not affect classification.

Classification of taxpayers

30. In certain sub-headings distinctions are made between different categories of taxpayers. These distinctions vary from tax to tax:

a) Between individuals and corporations in relation to income and net wealth taxes

The basic distinction is that corporation income taxes, as distinct from individual income taxes, are levied on the corporation as an entity, not on the individuals who own it, and without regard to the personal circumstances of these individuals. The same distinction applies to net wealth taxes on corporations and those on individuals. Taxes paid on the profits of partnerships and the income of institutions, such as life insurance or pension funds, are classified according to the same rule. They are classified as corporate taxes (1200) if they are charged on the partnership or institution as an entity without regard to the personal circumstances of the owners. Otherwise, they are treated as individual taxes (1100). Usually, there is different legislation for the corporation taxes and for the individual taxes.[11] The distinction made here between individuals and corporations does not follow the sector classification between households, enterprises, and so on of the System of National Accounts for income and outlay accounts. The SNA classification requires certain unincorporated businesses[12] to be excluded from the household sector and included with non-financial enterprises and financial institutions. The tax on the profits of these businesses, however, cannot always be separated from the tax on the other income of their owners, or can be separated only on an arbitrary basis. No attempt at this separation is made here and the whole of the individual income tax is shown together without regard to the nature of the income chargeable.

b) Between households and others in relation to taxes on immovable property

Here the distinction is that adopted by the SNA for the production and consumption expenditure accounts. The distinction is between households as consumers (i.e. excluding non-incorporated business) on the one hand and producers on the other hand. However, taxes on dwellings occupied by households, whether paid by owner-occupiers, tenants or landlords, are classified under households. This follows the common distinction made between taxes on domestic property versus taxes on business property. Some countries are not, however, in a position to make this distinction.

c) Between households and others in relation to motor vehicle licences

Here the distinction is between households as consumers on the one hand and producers on the other, as in the production and consumption expenditure accounts of the SNA.

d) Between business and others in relation to the residual taxes (6000)

The distinction is the same as in c) above between producers on the one hand and households as consumers on the other hand. Taxes which are included under the heading 6000 because they involve more than one tax base or because the tax base does not fall within any of the previous categories but which are identifiable as levyable only on producers and not on households are included under 'business'. The rest of the taxes which are included under the heading 6000 are shown as 'other' or non-identified.

Surcharges

31. Receipts from surcharges in respect of particular taxes are usually classified with the receipts from the relevant tax whether or not the surcharge is temporary. If, however, the surcharge has a characteristic which would render it classifiable in a different heading of the OECD list, receipts from the surcharge are classified under that heading separately from the relevant tax.

Unidentifiable tax receipts and residual sub-headings

32. .A number of cases arise where taxes cannot be identified as belonging entirely to a heading or sub-heading of the OECD classification and the following practices are applied in such cases:

a) The heading is known, but it is not known how receipts should be allocated between sub-headings: receipts are classified in the appropriate residual sub-heading (1300, 2400, 4520, 4600, 5130, 5300 or 6200).

b) It is known that the bulk of receipts from a group of taxes (usually local taxes) is derived from taxes within a particular heading or sub-heading, but some of the taxes in the group whose amount cannot be precisely ascertained may be classifiable in other headings or sub-headings: receipts are shown in the heading or sub-heading under which most of the receipts fall.

c) Neither the heading nor sub-heading of a tax (usually local) can be identified: the tax is classified in 6200 unless it is known that it is a tax on business in which case it is classified in 6100.

A.5 Commentaries on items of the list

1000 — Taxes on income, profits and capital gains

33. This heading covers taxes levied on the net income or profits (i.e. gross income minus allowable tax reliefs) of individuals and enterprises. Also covered are taxes levied on the capital gains of individuals and enterprises, and gains from gambling.

34. Included in the heading are:

a) taxes levied predominantly on income or profits, though partially on other bases. Taxes on various bases which are not predominantly income or profits are classified according to the principles laid down in §32 and §81;

b) taxes on property, which are levied on a presumed or estimated income as part of an income tax (see also §47(a), (c) and (d));

c) compulsory payments to social security fund contributions that are levied on income but do not confer an entitlement to social benefits. When such contributions do confer an entitlement to social benefits, they are included in heading 2000 (see §39);

d) receipts from integrated scheduler income tax systems are classified as a whole in this heading, even though certain of the scheduler taxes may be based upon gross income and may not take into account the personal circumstances of the taxpayer.

35. The main subdivision of this heading is between levies on individuals (1100) and those on corporate enterprises (1200). Under each subdivision a distinction is made between taxes on income and profits (1110 and 1210), and taxes on capital gains (1120 and 1220). If certain receipts cannot be identified as appropriate to either 1100 or 1200, or if in practice this distinction cannot be made (e.g., because there are no reliable data on the recipients of payments from which withholding taxes are deducted) they are classified in 1300 as not-allocable.

Treatment of credits under imputation systems

36. Under imputation systems of corporate income tax, a company's shareholders are wholly or partly relieved of their liability to income tax on dividends paid by the company out of income or profits liable to corporate income tax. In countries with such systems,[13] part of the tax on the company's profits is available to provide relief against the shareholders' own tax liability. The relief to the shareholder takes the form of a tax credit, the amount of which may be less than, equal to, or more than the shareholder's overall tax liability. If the tax credit exceeds this tax liability the excess may be payable to the shareholder. As this type of tax credit is an integral part of the imputation system of corporate income tax, any payment to the shareholders is treated as a repayment of tax and not as expenditure (compare the treatment of other tax credits described in §25).

37. As the tax credit under imputation systems (even when exceeding tax liability) is to be regarded as a tax provision, the question arises whether it should be deducted from individual income tax receipts (1110) or corporate income tax receipts (1210). In this Report, the full amount of corporate income tax paid is shown under 1210 and no imputed tax is included under 1110. Thus, the full amount of the credit reduces the amount of 1110 whether the credit results in a reduction of personal income tax liability or whether an actual refund is made because the credit exceeds the income tax liability. (Where, however, such tax credits are deducted from corporation tax in respect of dividends paid to corporations the amounts are deducted from the receipts of 1210).

1120 and 1220 — Taxes on capital gains

38. These sub-headings comprise taxes imposed on capital gains, 1120 covering those levied on the gains of individuals and 1220 those levied on the gains of corporate enterprises, where receipts from such taxes can be separately identified. In many countries this is not the case and the receipts from such taxes are then classified with those from the income tax. Heading 1120 also includes taxes on gains from gambling.

2000 — Social security contributions

39. Classified here are all compulsory payments that confer an entitlement to receive a (contingent) future social benefit. Such payments are usually earmarked to finance social benefits and are often paid to institutions of general government that provide such benefits. However, such earmarking is not part of the definition of social security contributions and is not required for a tax to be classified here. However, conferment of an entitlement is required for a tax to be classified under this heading. So, levies on income or payroll that are earmarked for social security funds but do not confer an entitlement to benefit are excluded from this heading and shown under personal income taxes (1100) or taxes on payroll and workforce (3000). Taxes on other bases, such as goods and services, which are earmarked for social security benefits are not shown here but are classified according to their respective bases because they generally confer no entitlement to social security benefits.

40. Contributions for the following types of social security benefits would, *inter alia*, be included: unemployment insurance benefits and supplements, accident, injury and sickness benefits, old-age, disability and survivors' pensions, family allowances, reimbursements for medical and hospital expenses or provision of hospital or medical services. Contributions may be levied on both employees and employers.

41. Contributions may be based on earnings or payroll ('on a payroll basis') or on net income after deductions and exemptions for personal circumstances ('on an income tax basis'), and the revenues from the two bases should be separately identified if possible. However, where contributions to a general social security scheme are on a payroll basis, but the contributions of particular groups (such as the self-employed) cannot be assessed on this basis and net income is used as a proxy for gross earnings, the receipts may still be classified as being on a payroll basis. In principle, this heading excludes voluntary contributions paid to social security schemes. When separately identifiable these are shown in the memorandum item on the financing of social security benefits. In practice, however, they cannot always be separately identified from compulsory contributions, in which case they are included in this heading.

42. Contributions to social insurance schemes which are not institutions of general government and to other types of insurance schemes, provident funds, pension funds, friendly societies or other saving schemes are not considered as social security contributions. Provident funds are arrangements under which the contributions of each employee and of the corresponding employer on his/her behalf are kept in a separate account earning interest and withdrawable under specific circumstances. Pension funds are separately organised schemes negotiated between employees and employers and carry provisions for

different contributions and benefits, sometimes more directly tied to salary levels and length of service than under social security schemes. When contributions to these schemes are compulsory or quasi-compulsory (e.g., by virtue of agreement with professional and union organisations) they are shown in the memorandum item (refer to Table 5.37 of the Report).

43. Contributions by government employees and by governments in respect of their employees, to social security schemes classified within general government are included in this heading. Contributions to separate schemes for government employees, which can be regarded as replacing general social security schemes, are also regarded as taxes.[14] Where, however, a separate scheme is not seen as replacing a general scheme and has been negotiated between the government, in its role as an employer, and its employees, it is not regarded as social security and contributions to it are not regarded as taxes, even though the scheme may have been established by legislation.

44. This heading excludes 'imputed' contributions, which correspond to social benefits paid directly by employers to their employees or former employees or to their representatives (e.g., when employers are legally obliged to pay sickness benefits for a certain period).

45. Contributions are divided into those of employees (2100), employers (2200), and self-employed or non-employed (2300), and then further sub-divided according to the basis on which they are levied. Employees are defined for this purpose as all persons engaged in activities of business units, government bodies, private non-profit institutions, or other paid employment, except the proprietors and their unpaid family members in the case of unincorporated businesses. Members of the armed forces are included, irrespective of the duration and type of their service, if they contribute to social security schemes. The contributions of employers are defined as their payments on account of their employees to social security schemes. Where employees or employers are required to continue the payment of social security contributions when the employee becomes unemployed these contributions, data permitting, are shown in 2100 and 2200 respectively. Accordingly, the sub-heading 2300 is confined to contributions paid by the self-employed and by those outside of the labour force (e.g., disabled or retired individuals).

3000 — Taxes on payroll and workforce

46. These consist of taxes payable by enterprises assessed either as a proportion of the wages or salaries paid or as a fixed amount per person employed. They do not include compulsory social security contributions paid by employers or any taxes paid by employees themselves out of their wages or salaries

4000 — Taxes on property

47. This heading covers recurrent and non-recurrent taxes on the use, ownership or transfer of property. These include taxes on immovable property or net wealth, taxes on the change of ownership of property through inheritance or gift and taxes on financial and capital transactions. The following kinds of tax are excluded from this heading:

- *a)* taxes on capital gains resulting from the sale of a property (1120 or 1220);
- *b)* taxes on the use of goods or on permission to use goods or perform activities (5200); see §76;
- *c)* taxes on immovable property levied on the basis of a presumed net income which take into account the personal circumstances of the taxpayer. They are classified as income taxes along with taxes on income and capital gains derived from property (1100);
- *d)* taxes on the use of property for residence, where the tax is payable by either proprietor or tenant and the amount payable is a function of the user's personal circumstances (pay, dependants, and so on). They are classified as taxes on income (1100);

e) taxes on building in excess of permitted maximum density, taxes on the enlargement, construction or alteration of certain buildings beyond a permitted value and taxes on building construction. They are classified as taxes on permission to perform activities (5200);

f) taxes on the use of one's own property for special trading purposes like selling alcohol, tobacco, meat or for exploitation of land resources (e.g., United States severance taxes). They are classified as taxes on permission to perform activities (5200).

4100 — Recurrent taxes on immovable property

48. This sub-heading covers taxes levied regularly in respect of the use or ownership of immovable property.

- these taxes are levied on land and buildings;
- they can be in the form of a percentage of an assessed property value based on a national rental income, sales price, or capitalised yield; or in terms of other characteristics of real property, (for example size or location) from which a presumed rent or capital value can be derived.
- such taxes can be levied on proprietors, tenants, or both. They can also be paid by one level of government to another level of government in respect of property under the jurisdiction of the latter.
- debts are not taken into account in the assessment of these taxes, and they differ from taxes on net wealth in this respect.

49. Taxes on immovable property are further sub-divided into those paid by households (4110) and those paid by other entities (4120), according to the criteria set out in §30(*b*) above.

4200 — Recurrent taxes on net wealth

50. This sub-heading covers taxes levied regularly (in most cases annually) on net wealth, i.e. taxes on a wide range of movable and immovable property, net of debt. It is sub-divided into taxes paid by individuals (4210) and taxes paid by corporate enterprises (4220) according to the criteria set out in §30(*a*) above. If separate figures exist for receipts paid by institutions, the tax payments involved are added to those paid by corporations.

4300 — Estate, inheritance and gift taxes

51. This sub-heading is divided into taxes on estates and inheritances (4310) and taxes on gifts (4320).[15] Estate taxes are charged on the amount of the total estate whereas inheritance taxes are charged on the shares of the individual recipients; in addition the latter may take into account the relationship of the individual recipients to the deceased.

4400 — Taxes on financial and capital transactions

52. This sub-heading comprises, *inter alia*, taxes on the issue, transfer, purchase and sale of securities, taxes on cheques, and taxes levied on specific legal transactions such as validation of contracts and the sale of immovable property. The heading does not include:

a) taxes on the use of goods or property or permission to perform certain activities (5200);

b) fees paid to cover court charges, charges for birth, marriage or death certificates, which are normally regarded as non-tax revenues (see §11);

c) taxes on capital gains (1000);

d) recurrent taxes on immovable property (4100);

e) recurrent taxes on net wealth (4200);

f) once-and-for-all levies on property or wealth (4500).

4500 — Other non-recurrent taxes on property16

53. This sub-heading covers once-and-for-all, as distinct from recurrent, levies on property. It is divided into taxes on net wealth (4510) and other non-recurrent taxes on property (4520). Heading 4510 would include taxes levied to meet emergency expenditures, or for redistribution purposes. Heading 4520 would cover taxes levied to take account of increases in land value due to permission given to develop or provision of additional local facilities by general government, any taxes on the revaluation of capital and once-and-for-all taxes on particular items of property.

4600 — Other recurrent taxes on property

54. These rarely exist in OECD member countries, but the heading would include taxes on goods such as cattle, jewellery, windows, and other external signs of wealth.

5000 — Taxes on goods and services

55. All taxes and duties levied on the production, extraction, sale, transfer, leasing or delivery of goods, and the rendering of services (5100), or in respect of the use of goods or permission to use goods or to perform activities (5200) are included here. The heading thus covers:

a) multi-stage cumulative taxes;
b) general sales taxes — whether levied at manufacture/production, wholesale or retail level;
c) value-added taxes;
d) excises;
e) taxes levied on the import and export of goods;
f) taxes levied in respect of the use of goods and taxes on permission to use goods, or perform certain activities;
g) taxes on the extraction, processing or production of minerals and other products.

56. Borderline cases between this heading and heading 4000 (taxes on property) and 6100 (other taxes on business) are referred to in §47, §52 and §78. Residual sub-headings (5300) and (5130) cover tax receipts which cannot be allocated between 5100 and 5200 and between 5110 and 5120, respectively; see §32.

5100 — Taxes on the production, sale, transfer, leasing and delivery of goods and rendering of services

57. This sub-heading consists of all taxes, levied on transactions in goods and services on the basis of their intrinsic characteristics (e.g., value, weight of tobacco, strength of alcohol, and so on) as distinct from taxes imposed on the use of goods, or permission to use goods or perform activities, which fall under 5200.

5110 — General taxes on goods and services

58. This sub-heading includes all taxes, other than import and export duties (5123 and 5124), levied on the production, leasing, transfer, delivery or sales of a wide range of goods and/or the rendering of a wide range of services, irrespective of whether they are domestically produced or imported and irrespective of the stage of production or distribution at which they are levied. It thus covers value-added taxes, sales taxes and multi-stage cumulative taxes. Receipts from border adjustments in respect of such taxes when

goods are imported are added to gross receipts for this category, and repayments of such taxes when goods are exported are deducted. These taxes are subdivided into 5111 value-added taxes, 5112 sales taxes, 5113 turnover and other general taxes on goods and services.

59. Borderline cases arise between this heading and taxes on specific goods (5120) when taxes are levied on a large number of goods, for example, the United Kingdom purchase tax (repealed in 1973) and the Japanese commodity tax (repealed in 1988). In conformity with national views, the former United Kingdom purchase tax is classified as a general tax (5112) and the former Japanese commodity tax as excises (5121).

5111 — Value-added taxes

60. All general consumption taxes charged on value-added are classified in this sub-heading, irrespective of the method of deduction and the stages at which the taxes are levied. In practice, all OECD countries with value-added taxes normally allow immediate deduction of taxes on purchases by all but the final consumer and impose tax at all stages. In some countries the heading may include certain taxes, such as those on financial and insurance activities, either because receipts from them cannot be identified separately from those from the value-added tax, or because they are regarded as an integral part of the value-added tax, even though similar taxes in other countries might be classified elsewhere (e.g., 5126 as taxes on services or 4400 as taxes on financial and capital transactions).

5112 — Sales taxes

61. All general taxes levied at one stage only, whether at manufacturing or production, wholesale or retail stage are classified here.

5113 — Turnover and other general taxes on goods and services

62. These are multi-stage cumulative taxes and taxes where elements of consumption taxes are combined with multistage taxes. These taxes are levied each time a transaction takes place without deduction for taxes paid on inputs. Multi-stage taxes can be combined with elements of value-added or sales taxes.

5120 — Taxes on specific goods and services

63. Excises, profits generated and transferred from fiscal monopolies, and customs and imports duties as well as taxes on exports, foreign exchange transactions, investment goods and betting stakes and special taxes on services, which do not form part of a general tax of 5110, are included in this category.

5121 — Excises

64. Excises are taxes levied as a product specific unit tax on a predefined limited range of goods. Excises are usually levied at differentiated rates on nonessential or luxury goods, alcoholic beverages, tobacco, and energy. Excises may be imposed at any stage of production or distribution and are usually assessed as a specific charge per unit based on characteristics by reference to the value, weight, strength, or quantity of the product. Included are special taxes on individual products such as sugar, sugar beets, matches, and chocolates; taxes levied at varying rates on a certain range of goods; and taxes levied on tobacco goods, alcoholic drinks, motor fuels, and hydrocarbon oils. If a tax collected principally on imported goods also applies, or would apply, under the same law to comparable domestically produced goods, then the revenue from this tax is classified as arising from excises rather than from import duties. This principle applies even if there is no comparable domestic production or no possibility of such production. Taxes on the use of utilities such as water, electricity, gas, and energy are regarded as excises rather than taxes on

specific services (5126). Excises exclude those taxes that are levied as general taxes on goods and services (5110); profits of fiscal monopolies (5122); customs and other import duties (5123); or taxes on exports (5124).

5122 — Profits of fiscal monopolies

65. This sub-heading covers that part of the profits of fiscal monopolies which is transferred to general government or which is used to finance any expenditures considered to be government expenditures (see §23). Amounts are shown when they are transferred to general government or used to make expenditures considered to be government expenditures.

66. Fiscal monopolies reflect the exercise of the taxing power of government by the use of monopoly powers. Fiscal monopolies are non-financial public enterprises exercising a monopoly in most cases over the production or distribution of tobacco, alcoholic beverages, salt, matches, playing cards and petroleum or agricultural products (i.e. on the kind of products which are likely to be, alternatively or additionally, subject to the excises of 5121), to raise the government revenues which in other countries are gathered through taxes on dealings in such commodities by private business units. The government monopoly may be at the production stage or, as in the case of government-owned and controlled liquor stores, at the distribution stage.

67. Fiscal monopolies are distinguished from public utilities such as rail transport, electricity, post offices, and other communications, which may enjoy a monopoly or quasi-monopoly position but where the primary purpose is normally to provide basic services rather than to raise revenue for government. Transfers from such other public enterprises to the government are considered as non-tax revenues. The traditional concept of fiscal monopoly is not generally extended to include state lotteries, the profits of which are usually accordingly regarded as non-tax revenues. However, they can be included as tax revenues if the prime reason for their operation is to raise revenues to finance government expenditure. Fiscal monopoly profits are distinguished from export and import monopoly profits (5127) transferred from marketing boards or other enterprises dealing with international trade.

5123 — Customs and other import duties

68. Taxes, stamp duties and surcharges restricted by law to imported products are included here. Also included are levies on imported agricultural products which are imposed in member countries of the European Union and amounts paid by certain of these countries under the Monetary Compensation Accounts (MCA) system.[16] Starting from 1998, customs duties collected by European Union member states on behalf of the European Union are no longer reported under this heading in the country tables (in Chapter 5 of the Report). Excluded here are taxes collected on imports as part of a general tax on goods and services, or an excise applicable to both imported and domestically produced goods.

5124 — Taxes on exports

69. In the 1970s, export duties were levied in Australia, Canada and Portugal as a regular measure and they have been used in Finland for counter-cyclical purposes. Some member countries of the European Union pay, as part of the MCA system, a levy on exports (see note 16 to §68). Where these amounts are identifiable, they are shown in this heading. This heading does not include repayments of general consumption taxes or excises or customs duties on exported goods, which should be deducted from the gross receipts under 5110, 5121 or 5123, as appropriate.

5125 — Taxes on investment goods

70. This sub-heading covers taxes on investment goods, such as machinery. These taxes may be imposed for a number of years or temporarily for counter-cyclical purposes. Taxes on industrial inputs which are also levied on consumers [e.g., the Swedish energy tax which is classified under (5121)] are not included here.

5126 — Taxes on specific services

71. All taxes assessed on the payment for specific services, such as taxes on insurance premiums, banking services, gambling and betting stakes (e.g., from horse races, football pools, lottery tickets), transport, entertainment, restaurant and advertising charges, fall into this category. Taxes levied on the gross income of companies providing the service (e.g., gross insurance premiums or gambling stakes received by the company) are also classified under this heading. Tax revenues from bank levies and payments to deposit insurance and financial stability schemes are provisionally included here for the 2012 edition. The detailed classification is set out in §108.

72. Excluded from this sub-heading are:

a) taxes on services forming part of a general tax on goods and services (5110);

b) taxes on electricity, gas and energy (5121 as excises);

c) taxes on individual gains from gambling (1120 as taxes on capital gains of individuals and non-corporate enterprises) and lump-sum taxes on the transfer of private lotteries or on the permission to set up lotteries (5200);[17]

d) taxes on cheques and on the issue, transfer or redemption of securities (4400 as taxes on financial and capital transactions).

5127 — Other taxes on international trade and transactions

73. This sub-heading covers revenue received by the government from the purchase and sale of foreign exchange at different rates. When the government exercises monopoly powers to extract a margin between the purchase and sales price of foreign exchange, other than to cover administrative costs, the revenue derived constitutes a compulsory levy exacted in indeterminate proportions from both purchaser and seller of foreign exchange. It is the common equivalent of an import duty and export duty levied in a single exchange rate system or of a tax on the sale or purchase of foreign exchange. Like the profits of fiscal monopolies and import or export monopolies transferred to government, it represents the exercise of monopoly powers for tax purposes and is included in tax revenues.

74. The sub-heading covers also the profits of export or import monopolies, which do not however exist in OECD countries, taxes on purchase or sale of foreign exchange, and any other taxes levied specifically on international trade or transactions.

5128 — Other taxes on specific goods and services

75. This item includes taxes on the extraction of minerals, fossil fuels and other exhaustible resources from deposits owned privately or by another government together with any other unidentifiable receipts from taxes on specific goods and services. Taxes on the extraction of exhaustible resources are usually a fixed amount per unit of quality or weight, but can be a percentage of value. The taxes are recorded when the resources are extracted. Payments from the extraction of exhaustible resources from deposits owned by the government unit receiving the payment are classified as rent.

5200 — Taxes on use of goods or on permission to use goods or perform activities

76. This sub-heading covers taxes which are levied in respect of the use of goods as distinct from taxes on the goods themselves. Unlike the latter taxes – reported under 5100 –, they are not assessed on the value of the goods but usually as fixed amounts. Taxes on permission to use goods or to perform activities are also included here, as are pollution taxes not based upon the value of particular goods. It is sometimes difficult to distinguish between compulsory user charges and licence fees which are regarded as taxes and those which are excluded as non-tax revenues. The criteria which are employed are noted in §11–12.

77. Although the sub-heading refers to the 'use' of goods, registration of ownership rather than use may be what generates liability to tax, so that the taxes of this heading may apply to the ownership of animals or goods rather than their use (e.g., race horses, dogs and motor vehicles) and may apply even to unusable goods (e.g., unusable motor vehicles or guns).

78. Borderline cases arise with:

a) taxes on the permission to perform business activities which are levied on a combined income, payroll or turnover base and, accordingly, are classified following the rules in §81;

b) taxes on the ownership or use of property of headings 4100, 4200 and 4600. The heading 4100 is confined to taxes on the ownership or tenancy of immovable property and – unlike the taxes of 5200 – they are related to the value of the property. The net wealth taxes and taxes on chattels of 4200 and 4600 respectively are confined to the ownership rather than the use of assets, apply to groups of assets rather than particular goods and again are related to the value of the assets,

5210 — Recurrent taxes on use of goods and on permission to use goods or perform activities

79. The principal characteristic of taxes classified here is that they are levied at regular intervals and that they are usually fixed amounts. The most important item in terms of revenue receipts is vehicle licence taxes. This sub-heading also covers taxes on permission to hunt, shoot, fish or to sell certain products and taxes on the ownership of dogs and on the performance of certain services, provided that they meet the criteria set out in §11–12. The sub-divisions of 5210 are user taxes on motor vehicles paid by households (5211) and those paid by others (5212). Sub-heading 5213 covers dog licences and user charges for permission to perform activities such as selling meat or liquor when the levies are on a recurring basis. It also covers recurrent general licences for hunting, shooting and fishing where the right to carry out these activities is not granted as part of a normal commercial transaction (e.g., the granting of the licence is not accompanied by the right to use a specific area which is owned by government).

5220 — Non-recurrent taxes on use of goods and on permission to use goods or perform activities

80. This section covers non-recurrent taxes levied on the use of goods or on permission to use goods or perform activities and taxes levied each time goods are used. It includes taxes levied on the emission or discharge into the environment of noxious gases, liquids or other harmful substances.

- Payments for tradable emission permits issued by governments under cap and trade schemes should be recorded here at the time the emissions occur. No revenue should be recorded for permits that governments issue free of charge. The accrual basis of recording means that there can be a timing difference between the cash being received by government for the permits and the time the emission occurs. In the national accounts, this timing gives rise to a financial liability for government during the period.

- Payments made for the collection and disposal of waste or noxious substances by public authorities should be excluded as they constitute a sale of services to enterprises.

81. Other taxes falling under heading 5200 that are not levied recurrently are also included here. Thus, once-and-for-all payments for permission to sell liquor or tobacco or to set up betting shops are included provided they meet the criteria set out in §11–12.

6000 — Other taxes

82. Taxes levied on a base, or bases, other than those described under headings 1000, 3000, 4000 and 5000, or on bases of which cannot be considered to be related to any one of these headings, are included here. Where taxes are levied on a multiple base and it is possible to estimate the receipts related to each base the separate amounts are included under the appropriate headings. If separate amounts cannot be estimated and it is known that most of the receipts are derived from one base, the whole of the receipts are classified according to that base. Otherwise, they are classified here. Other revenues included here are presumptive taxes not included elsewhere in the classification system, taxes on individuals in the form of a poll tax or capitation tax, stamp taxes not related to financial and capital transactions nor falling exclusively on a single category of transaction, expenditure taxes where personal deductions or exemptions are applied and unidentifiable tax receipts. A subdivision is made between taxes levied wholly or predominantly on business (6100) and those levied on others (6200).

A.6 Conciliation with National Accounts

83. This section of the tables provides a re-conciliation between the OECD calculation of total tax revenues and the total of all taxes and social contributions paid to general government as recorded in the country's National Accounts. Where the country is a member of the European Union (EU), the comparison is between the OECD calculation of total tax revenues and the sum of tax revenues and social contributions recorded in the combination of the general government and the institutions of the EU sectors of the National Accounts.

A.7 Memorandum item on the financing of social security benefits

84. In view of the varying relationship between taxation and social security contributions and the cases referred to in §39 to §45, a memorandum item collects together all payments earmarked for social security-type benefits, other than voluntary payments to the private sector. Data are presented as follows (refer Table 5.37 of the Report):

a) Taxes of 2000 series.

b) Taxes earmarked for social security benefits.

c) Voluntary contributions to the government.

d) Compulsory contributions to the private sector.

Guidance on the breakdown of (a) to (d) above is provided in §39 to §45.

A.8 Memorandum item on identifiable taxes paid by government

85. Identifiable taxes actually paid by government are presented in a memorandum item classified by the main headings of the OECD classification of taxes. In the vast majority of countries, only social security contributions and payroll taxes paid by government can be identified. These are, however, usually the most important taxes paid by governments (refer to Table 5.38 of the Report).

A.9 Relation of OECD classification of taxes to national accounting systems

86. A system of national accounts (SNA) seeks to provide a coherent framework for recording and presenting the main flows relating respectively to production, consumption, accumulation and external transactions of a given economic area, usually a country or a major region within a country. Government revenues are an important part of the transactions recorded in SNA. The final version of the 2008 SNA was jointly published by five international organisations: the United Nations, the International Monetary Fund, the European Union, the Organisation for Economic Co-operation and Development, and the World Bank in August 2009. The *System* is a comprehensive, consistent and flexible set of macroeconomic accounts. It is designed for use in countries with market economies, whatever their stage of economic development, and also in countries in transition to market economies. The important parts of the SNA's conceptual framework and its definitions of the various sectors of the economy have been reflected in the OECD's classification of taxes.

87. There are, however, some differences between the OECD classification of taxes and SNA concepts that are listed below. They arise because the aim of the former is to provide the maximum disaggregation of statistical data on what are generally regarded as taxes by tax administrations.

a) OECD includes compulsory social security contributions paid to general government in total tax revenues. Imputed and voluntary contributions plus those paid to private funds are not treated as taxes (§8 and §10 above);

b) there are different points of view on whether or not some levies and fees are classified as taxes (§11 and §12 above);

c) OECD excludes imputed taxes or subsidies resulting from the operation of official multiple exchange rates or from the central bank paying a rate of interest on required reserves that is different from other market rates;

d) there are differences in the treatment of non-wastable tax credits

88. As noted in §1 and §2, headings 1000 to 6000 of the OECD list of taxes cover all unrequited payments to general government, other than compulsory loans and fines. Such unrequited payments including fines, but excluding compulsory loans can be obtained from adding together the following figures in the 2008 SNA

- value-added type taxes (D.211);
- taxes and duties on imports, excluding VAT (D.212);
- export taxes (D.213);
- taxes on products, excluding VAT, import and export taxes (D.214);
- other taxes on production (D.29);
- taxes on income (D.51);
- other current taxes (D.59);
- social contributions (D.61), excluding voluntary contributions;
- capital taxes (D.91).

A.10 The OECD classification of taxes and the International Monetary Fund (GFS) system

89. The coverage and valuation of tax revenues in the GFS system and the 2008 SNA are very similar. Therefore, the differences between the OECD classification and that of the 2008 SNA (see §87 above) also apply to the GFS. In addition the International Monetary Fund subdivides the OECD 5000 heading

into section IV (Domestic Taxes on Goods and Services) and section V (Taxes on International Trade and Transactions). This reflects the fact that while the latter usually yield insignificant amounts of revenue in OECD countries, this is not the case in many non-OECD countries.

A.11 Comparison of the OECD classification of taxes with other international classifications

90. The table below describes an item by item comparison of the OECD classification of taxes and the classifications used in the following:

a) System of National Accounts (2008 SNA);

b) European System of Accounts (2010 ESA);

c) IMF Government Finance Statistics Manual (GFSM2014).

91. These comparisons represent those that would be expected to apply in the majority of cases. However in practice some flexibility should be used in their application. This is because in particular cases, countries can adopt varying approaches to the classification of revenues in National Accounts.

	OECD Classification				2008 SNA	2010 ESA	GFSM2014
1000	Taxes on income, profits and capital gains						
	1100	Individuals					
		1110	Income and profits		D51-8.61a	D51A	1111
		1120	Capital gains		D51-8.61c, d	D51C, D	1111
	1200	Corporations					
		1210	Income and profits		D51-8.61b	D51B	1112
		1220	Capital gains		D51-8.61c	D51C	1112
	1300	Unallocable as between 1100 and 1200					1113
2000	Social security contributions						
	2100	Employees			D613-8.85	D613	1211
	2200	Employers			D611-8.83	D611	1212
	2300	Self-employed, non-employed			D613-8.85	D613	1213
	2400	Unallocable as between 2100, 2200 and 2300					1214
3000	Taxes on payroll and workforce				D29-7.97a	D29C	112
4000	Taxes on property						
	4100	Recurrent taxes on immovable property					
		4110	Households		D59-8.63a	D59A	1131
		4120	Other		D29-7.97b	D29A	1131
	4200	Recurrent net wealth taxes					
		4210	Individual		D59-8.63b	D59A	1132
		4220	Corporations		D59-8.63b	D59A	1132
	4300	Estate, inheritance and gift taxes					
		4310	Estate and inheritance taxes		D91-10.207b	D91A	1133
		4320	Gift taxes		D91-10.207b	D91A	1133
	4400	Taxes on financial and capital transactions			D59-7.96d; D29-7.97e	D214B, C	114114; 1161
	4500	Other non-recurrent taxes on property			D91-10.207a	D91B	1135
	4600	Other recurrent taxes on property			D59-8.63c	D59A	1136
5000	Taxes on goods and services						
	5100	Taxes on production, sale and transfer of goods and services					
		5110	General taxes on goods and services				
			5111	Value-added taxes	D211-7.89	D211; D29G	11411
			5112	Sales taxes	D2122-7.94a; D214-7.96a	D21224; D214I	11412
			5113	Other general taxes on goods and services	D214-7.96a	D214I	11413
		5120	Taxes on specific goods and services				
			5121	Excises	D2122-7.94b; D214-7.96b	D21223; D214A, B, D	1142
			5122	Profits of fiscal monopolies	D214-7.96e	D214J	1143
			5123	Customs and other import duties	D2121-7.93	D2121; D21221, 2	1151
			5124	On exports	D213-7.95a	D214K	1152-4
			5125	On investment goods			
			5126	On specific services	D2122-7.94c; D214-7.96c	D21225; D214E, F, G, H; D29F	1144; 1156
			5127	Other taxes on international trade and transactions	D2122-7.94d D29-7.95b D29-7.97g D59-8.64d	D21226; D29D; D59E	1153; 1155-6
			5128	Other taxes on specific goods and services			1146
		5130	Unallocable between 5110 and 5120				
	5200	Taxes on use of goods and on permission to use goods or					

		perform activities					
		5210	Recurrent taxes on use of goods and on permission to use goods or perform activities				
			5211	Motor vehicle taxes households	D59-8.64c	D59D	11451
			5212	Motor vehicles taxes others	D29-7.97d	D214D; D29B	11451
			5213	Other recurrent taxes on use of goods and on permission to use goods or perform activities	D29-7.97c, d, f D59-8.64c	D29B, E, F; D59D	11452
		5220	Non-recurrent taxes on permission to use goods or perform activities				11452
	5300	Unallocable as between 5100 and 5200					
6000	Other taxes						
	6100	Payable solely by business					1161
	6200	Payable by other than business, or unidentifiable			D59-8.64a, b	D59B, C	1162

A.12 Attribution of tax revenues by sub-sectors of general government

92. The OECD classification requires a breakdown of tax revenues by sub-sectors of government. The definition of each sub-sector and the criteria to be used to attribute tax revenues between these sub-sectors are set out below. They follow the guidance of the 2008 SNA and GFSM 2014.

Sub-sectors of general government to be identified

a) Central government

93. The central government sub-sector includes all governmental departments, offices, establishments and other bodies which are agencies or instruments of the central authority whose competence extends over the whole territory, with the exception of the administration of social security funds. Central government therefore has the authority to impose taxes on all resident and non-resident units engaged in economic activities within the country.

b) State, provincial or regional government

94. This sub-sector consists of intermediate units of government exercising a competence at a level below that of central government. It includes all such units operating independently of central government in a part of a country's territory encompassing a number of smaller localities, with the exception of the administration of social security funds. In unitary countries, regional governments may be considered to have a separate existence where they have substantial autonomy to raise a significant proportion of their revenues from sources within their control and their officers are independent of external administrative control in the actual operation of the unit's activities.

95. At present, federal countries comprise the majority of cases where revenues attributed to intermediate units of government are identified separately. Spain is the only unitary country in this position. In the remaining unitary countries, regional revenues are included with those of local governments.

c) Local government

96. This sub-sector includes all other units of government exercising an independent competence in part of the territory of a country, with the exception of the administration of social security funds. It encompasses various urban and/or rural jurisdictions (e.g., local authorities, municipalities, cities, boroughs, districts).

d) Social security funds

97. Social security funds form a separate sub-sector of general government. The social security sub-sector is defined in the 2008 SNA by the following extracts from paragraphs 4.124 to 4.126 and 4.147:

"Social security schemes are social insurance schemes covering the community as a whole or large section of the community that are imposed and controlled by government units. The schemes cover a wide variety of programmes, providing benefits in cash or in kind for old age, invalidity or death, survivors, sickness and maternity, work injury, unemployment, family allowance, health care, etc. There is not necessarily a direct link between the amount of the contribution paid by an individual and the benefits he or she may receive." (Paragraph 4.124).

"When social security schemes are separately organised from the other activities of government units and hold their assets and liabilities separately from the latter and engage in financial transactions on their own account they qualify as institutional units that are described as social security funds." (Paragraph 4.125).

"The amounts raised, and paid out, in social security contributions and benefits may be deliberately varied in order to achieve objectives of government policy that have no direct connection with the concept of social security as a scheme to provide social benefits to members of the community. They may be raised or lowered in order to influence the level of aggregate demand in the economy, for example. Nevertheless, so long as they remain separately constituted funds, they must be treated as separate institutional units in the SNA. (Paragraph 4.126).

"The social security funds sub-sector (of general government) consists of the social security funds operating at all levels of government. Such funds are social insurance schemes covering the community as a whole or large section of the community that are imposed by government units." (Paragraph 4.147).

98. This definition of social security funds is followed in the OECD classification with the two following exceptions which are excluded

- Schemes imposed by government and operated by bodies outside the general government sector, as defined in §3 of this manual; and
- Schemes to which all contributions are voluntary.

Supra-national Authorities

99. This sub-sector covers the revenue-raising operations of supra-national authorities within a country. In practice, the only relevant supra-national authority in the OECD area is that of the institutions of the European Union (EU). As from 1998, supra-national authorities are no longer included in the *Revenue Statistics*, to achieve consistency with the SNA definition of general government which excludes them. For example, income taxes and social security contributions collected by European Institutions and paid by European civil servants who are resident of EU member countries should not be included. However the specific levies paid by the member states of the EU continue to be included in total tax revenues and they are shown under this heading.

Criteria to be used for the attribution of tax revenues

100. When a government collects taxes and pays them over in whole or in part to other governments, it is necessary to determine whether the revenues should be considered to be those of the collecting government which it distributes to others as grants, or those of the beneficiary governments which the collecting government receives and passes on only as their agent. The criteria to be used in the attribution of revenues are set out in §101 to §104 which replicate paragraphs 3.70 to 3.73 from the 2008 SNA.

101. In general, a tax is attributed to the government unit that

a) exercises the authority to impose the tax (either as a principal or through the delegated authority of the principal),

b) has final discretion to set and vary the rate of the tax

102. Where an amount is collected by one government for and on behalf of another government, and the latter government has the authority to impose the tax, and set and vary its rate, then the former is acting as an agent for the latter and the tax is reassigned. Any amount retained by the collecting government as a collection charge should be treated as a payment for a service. Any other amount retained by the collecting government, such as under a tax-sharing arrangement, should be treated as a current grant. If the collecting government was delegated the authority to set and vary the rate, then the amount collected should be treated as tax revenue of this government.

103. Where different governments jointly and equally set the rate of a tax and jointly and equally decide on the distribution of the proceeds, with no individual government having ultimate overriding authority, then the tax revenues are attributed to each government according to its respective share of the proceeds. If an arrangement allows one government unit to exercise ultimate overriding authority, then all of the tax revenue is attributed to that unit.

104. There may also be the circumstance where a tax is imposed under the constitutional or other authority of one government, but other governments individually set the tax rate in their jurisdictions. The proceeds of the tax generated in each respective government's jurisdiction are attributed as tax revenues of that government.

Levies paid by member states of the European Union

105. The levies paid by the member states of the EU take the form specific levies which include

a) custom duties and levies on agricultural goods (5123),

b) gross monetary compensation accounts (5123 if relating to imports and 5124 if relating to exports); and

c) Steel, coal, sugar and milk levies (5128).

106. The custom duties collected by member states on behalf of the EU are recorded

- on a gross of collection fee basis;
- using figures adjusted so that duties are shown on a 'final destination' as opposed to a 'country of first entry' basis where such adjustments can be made. These adjustments concern in particular duties collected at important (sea) ports. Although the EU duties are collected by the authorities of the country of first entry, when possible these duties should be excluded from the revenue of the collecting country and be included in the revenue of the country of final destination

107. This is the specific EU levy that most clearly conforms to the attribution criterion described in §99 above. Consequently as from 1998, these amounts are footnoted as a memorandum item to the EU member state country tables (in Chapter 5) and no longer shown under heading 5123. However the figures are included in the total tax revenue figures on the top line for all the relevant years shown in the tables.

A.13 Provisional classification of revenues from bank levies and payments to deposit insurance and financial stability schemes

108. The OECD have adopted the following interim approach to reporting revenue from bank levies plus deposit insurance and stability fees for the 2012 and subsequent editions of *OECD Revenue Statistics*. It is recommended that the amounts should be recorded under category 5126.

- Compulsory payments of stability fees, bank levies and deposit insurance should generally be treated as tax revenues where the payments are made to General Government and allocated to the governments' consolidated or general funds so that the Government is free to make immediate use of the money for the purposes that it chooses. This principle would apply regardless of whether the Government is promising to make payments to guarantee the banks' customer deposits in some future contingency.
- If the compulsory payments are made to general government and placed in funds that are earmarked to be entirely channelled back to the sector of the economy that comprises the companies that are subject to the payment, they would still generally be treated as tax revenues on the grounds that the funds would be available for the government and would reduce its budget deficit, the fee is unrequited for an individual entity and the amounts raised could be unrelated to any eventual pay out to depositors or expenditure on wider support for the financial sector.
- Payments to made to the smaller long-standing schemes for insuring 'retail' deposits, where the payment levels are consistent with the costs of insurance should be classified as fee for service.
- Any payments which involve governments realising the assets of a failed institution or receiving a priority claim on its assets in liquidation in order to fund payments of compensation to customers for their lost deposits would be treated as a fee for a service as opposed to tax revenues.
- Compulsory payments that are made to funds operated outside the government sector and non-state institutions backed by the deposit takers and all payments to voluntary schemes should not be treated as tax revenues.

Notes

1. All references to SNA are to the 2008 edition.

2. See section A.12 of this guide for a discussion of the concept of agency capacity.

3. It is usually possible to identify amounts of social security contributions and payroll taxes, but not other taxes paid by government.

4. If, however, a levy which is considered as non-tax revenue by most countries is regarded as a tax — or raises substantial revenue — in one or more countries, the amounts collected are footnoted at the end of the relevant country tables, even though the amounts are not included in total tax revenues.

5. Names, however, can frequently be misleading. For example, though a passport fee would normally be considered a non-tax revenue, if a supplementary levy on passports (as is the case in Portugal) were imposed in order to raise substantial amounts of revenue relative to the cost of providing the passport, the levy would be regarded as a tax under 5200.

6. A more detailed explanation of this distinction can be found in the special feature, 'Current issues in reporting tax revenues', in the 2001 edition of the *Revenue Statistics*.

7. Sometimes the terms 'non-refundable' and 'refundable' are used, but it may be considered illogical to talk of 'refundable' when nothing has been paid.

8. A different treatment, however, is accorded to non-wastable tax credits under imputation systems of corporate income tax (§36–38).

9. This is not strictly a true tax expenditure in the formal sense. Such tax expenditures require identification of a benchmark tax system for each country or, preferably, a common international benchmark. In practice it has not been possible to reach agreement on a common international benchmark.

10. Unless based on the profit made on a sale, in which case they would be classified as capital gains taxes under 1120 or 1220.

11. In some countries the same legislation applies to both individual and corporate enterprises for particular taxes on income. However, the receipts from such taxes are usually allocable between individuals and enterprises and can therefore be shown in the appropriate sub-heading.

12. For example, "...sufficiently self-contained and independent that they behave in the same way as corporations.......(including) keeping a complete set of accounts" (2008 SNA, section 4.44).

13. In Canada — a country also referred to as having an imputation system — the (wastable) tax credit for the shareholder is in respect of domestic corporation tax deemed to have been paid whether or not a corporation tax liability has arisen. As there is no integral connection between the corporation tax liability and the credit given against income tax under such systems, these credits for dividends are treated, along with other tax credits, on the lines described in §25.

14. This may also apply where a scheme for government employees existed prior to the introduction of a general social security scheme.

15. In the 2008 SNA these are regarded as capital transfers and not as taxes (see section A.8).

16. This is the system by which the European Union adjusts for differences between the exchange rates used to determine prices under the Common Market Agricultural Policy and actual exchange rates. Payments under the system may relate to imports or exports and where these amounts are separately identifiable they are shown under the appropriate heading (5123 or 5124). In this Report, these amounts are shown gross (i.e. without deducting any subsidies paid out under the MCA system).

17. Transfers of profits of State lotteries are regarded as non-tax revenues (see also §67).

Annex B. Interpretative Guide to non-tax revenue in Revenue Statistics in Asia and the Pacific

Table of contents

1. Coverage

The definition of non-tax revenues and the main subcategories identified in this publication generally correspond to the concepts laid out in the 2014 IMF Government Finance Statistics Manual (GFSM). Non-tax revenues refer to increases in government net worth resulting from transactions other than tax revenues. They exclude funds arising from the repayment of previous lending by governments or from borrowing, or proceeds derived from sales of fixed capital assets, stocks, land and intangible assets or private gifts.

Non-tax revenues are made up of the following elements.

2. Grants

The GFSM 2014 states "Grants are transfers receivable by government units from non-resident government units or international organisations without the receipt of any goods, services, or assets in return. Grants are normally receivable in cash, but may also take the form of the receipt of goods or services (in kind)". These transfers are un-refundable and unrequited. Grants encompass reparations and gifts given for particular projects or programmes. The term "grants" is not used to refer to transfers to or from non-governmental units and excludes inter-governmental transfers. The remission of funds collected by one government for another in an agency capacity should not be shown as receipt of a grant by the beneficiary government but as its direct receipt of revenue.

3. Property income

This category includes income to government arising from their ownership of property, enterprises, financial assets, or intangible assets when government units place them at the disposal of other units. Sales of non-financial assets such as the sales of lands are not recorded as revenue because disposal of such an asset does not increase the net worth. Similarly, repayments on loans and loan disbursements are not revenue. Property income may take the form of dividends, interest, land rents, royalties, or withdrawals from entrepreneurial income. The main components are:

- Interest and dividends: Interest is the revenue earned by the government unit from a financial asset by putting it at the disposal of another institutional unit. Dividends are the revenue earned by placing equity funds at the disposal of a corporation (resident or non-resident corporation). This category also consists of profits of state-owned enterprises except those classified as fiscal monopolies (see §62-§64 of the OECD Interpretative Guide to tax revenue in Annex A), export and import monopoly profits (see §70-§71 of the same document) or those providing public utilities such as rail transport, electricity, post offices and other communications. In this category are included revenue from public financial institutions such as the central banks' profits, profits transferred or distributed from the operation of monetary authority functions outside the central bank and the profits of state lotteries transferred to the government. Transfers from public utilities enterprises are recorded as non-tax revenue under "sales of goods and services" whereas profits for fiscal, export or import monopolies are classified as tax revenue.
- Rents or royalties: Rent is the revenue generated from natural resources, such as land, mining, or oil resources, when a government unit places these at the disposal of private or foreign entities. The rents received relate to a resource lease-giving agreement for the exploitation and extraction of a natural resource by the lessee in return for a payment. Payments for exploration rights are also treated as rent. Rents should not be confused with other payments a government may receive related to the exploitation of subsoil and similar assets, such as severance taxes, business licenses, or other taxes (e.g. value added taxes, excises, taxes on exports, etc.). They should also

not be taken to mean incomes from the rental of buildings and equipment, which are treated as sales of goods and services. Revenues from rents and royalties are in some cases difficult to establish and depend on the agreement between the government unit and the lessee. For example rents, royalties and taxes such as corporate income taxes and VAT are sometimes encompassed in a single payment to the general government. In such cases the revenue should be classified under the category to which the majority of revenue belongs (see §71 of Annex A for further explanation.)

- Other property income: This includes revenue earned by a government unit placing funds at a disposal of quasi-corporations.[1] Conceptually this source of revenue is equivalent to that of dividends from a corporation but by definition, quasi-corporations cannot distribute income in the form of dividends. This category of "other property income" also includes retained or reinvested earnings, i.e. the percentage of distributable revenue not paid out as dividends, but retained by the corporation or quasi-corporation on foreign investment; property income from investment income disbursements and unidentified property income.

4. Sales of goods and services

Revenue under the category "sales of goods and services" is generally reported on a gross basis, without deduction of costs. Since these costs can represent a significant proportion of revenues, they cannot be regarded in total as funds available for governments to finance their general activities. This contrasts with tax revenues, where the collection costs are usually a small proportion of revenue. This difference implies that it may not be meaningful to sum tax and non-tax revenues as part of a calculation of generally available funds.

The proceeds of sales of nonfinancial assets such as the sale of buildings or lands are not classified as revenues since their disposal does not increase the net worth.

Sales of goods and services consist of:

- Sales by market establishments.[2]
- Administrative fees for services (i.e. fees for drivers' licences, passports, visas, court fees, harbour fees, fees for birth, marriage or death certificates, patent registrations, radio and television licenses when public authorities provide general broadcasting services).
- Administrative fees that are sales of services associated with a regulatory function of government (such as fees for the inspection of premises before delivering a business licence) and considered to be proportional to the cost of producing the service are included in this category. If the fee in return for the service provided by the government unit is disproportionate, then the fee will be classified as a tax. Specific examples of fees that are considered taxes include fees for permission to perform activities such as hunting, fishing and shooting; and fees for business registration where this is a legal requirement for the business to operate.
- Sales by nonmarket establishments such as fees at government hospitals, tuition fees at government schools and admission fees to museums and parks.
- Leasing of buildings and equipment.

5. Fines, penalties and forfeits

The GFSM 2014 states "Fines and penalties are compulsory transfers imposed by courts of law or bodies for violations of laws or administrative rules. Out-of-court agreements are also included (...). Forfeits are amounts deposited with a general government unit pending a legal or administrative proceeding, and that will be transferred to the unit upon resolution". For example traffic fines are included here. Fines and penalties charged on overdue taxes or penalties imposed for the evasion of taxes should be recorded in this category and not as taxes. However if it is not possible to separate the amounts paid in taxes and fines, the whole amount should be classified under the tax to which the fine relates (see §14 of Annex A for further explanation).

6. Other social contributions

This category includes the actual and imputed contributions to social insurance schemes operated by governments as employers on behalf of their employees that do not create a future defined liability. This category also includes the sum of the total voluntary contributions.[3] Excluded from this category are any contributions to funds in which the contributions of each participant and of his employer on his behalf are kept in a separate account earning interest and withdrawable under specified circumstances or any contributions to a pension fund autonomous to the general government. This category is not included in this publication.

7. Miscellaneous and unidentified revenue

This category consists of unidentified non-tax revenues or those that do not fit into any of the other categories listed above. It includes revenue such as gifts and transfers from individuals, private non-profit institutions, nongovernmental foundations, corporations, or sources other than governments and international organisations. Major non-recurrent payments receivable in compensation for extensive damages or serious injuries not covered by insurance policies are also included, such as payments of compensation for damages caused by major explosions; oil spillages; or payments receivable for damage to property other than payments from an insurance settlement.

Notes

[1] Quasi-corporations are unincorporated enterprises that exercise some functions of corporations, but have not been granted separate legal personality by statute.

[2] A market establishment is an establishment that charges economically significant prices.

[3] The IMF includes these contributions as part of their total of social security contributions.

Printed by Libri Plureos GmbH in Hamburg,
Germany